The Ethics of Voting

The Ethics of Voting

Jason Brennan

PRINCETON UNIVERSITY PRESS

PRINCETON AND OXFORD

Published by Princeton University Press, 41 William Street, Princeton, New Jersey 08540
In the United Kingdom: Princeton University Press, 6 Oxford Street, Woodstock, Oxfordshire OX20 1TW

press.princeton.edu

Jacket photograph: Man and Woman at Voting Booths in a Cropfield.

Photographer: Andy Reynolds/Getty Images.

Library of Congress Cataloging-in-Publication Data

Brennan, Jason.
    The ethics of voting / Jason Brennan.
        p.   cm.—(Voting as an ethical issue—Arguments for a duty to vote—Civic virtue without politics—Wrongful voting—Deference and abstention—For the common good—Buying and selling votes—How well do voters behave?)
    Includes bibliographical references and index.
    ISBN 978-0-691-14481-8 (hardcover : alk. paper) 1. Voting—Moral and ethical aspects.
I. Title.
    JF1001.B742 2011
    172'.1—dc22   2010047879

British Library Cataloging-in-Publication Data is available

This book has been composed in Sabon

Printed on acid-free paper. ∞

Printed in the United States of America

10 9 8 7 6 5 4 3 2 1

To Lauren and Aiden

Contents

Acknowledgments

BROWN UNIVERSITY is a dynamic and exciting place to do political philosophy. I have benefited enormously from discussions with David Estlund and Charles Larmore in philosophy, and John Tomasi, Corey Brettschneider, and Sharon Krause in political science. John in particular was instrumental in my coming to Brown, so I owe him thanks for bringing and keeping me here. John and Dave have done much to mentor me and help me develop as a professional. I have also benefited from discussions and exchanges with, and criticisms from, the excellent postdoctoral research fellows we have been fortunate to host: Sahar Ahktar, Barbara Buckinx, Yvonne Chui, Mark Koyama, Hélène Landemore, Emily Nacol, Dennis Rasmussen, Andrew Volmert, and Daniel Wewers. In addition, graduate students Sean Aas, Daniel Berntson, Derek Bowman, Dana Howard, Jennifer Ikuta, Jed Silverstein, Timothy Syme, and Joshua Tropp helped to shape this book. Thanks are also due to Mark Gladis, Thomas Lewis, and Mark Suchman. For inviting me to speak on some of the issues presented in this book, I thank the undergraduates at the Janus Forum and Philosophy Undergraduate Club.

My colleagues generously held a workshop devoted to my manuscript. The commentators at the workshop—Richard Arneson, Julia Driver, and David Estlund—gave me highly valuable feedback. I have long been a fan of Dick's and Julia's work, and it was an honor to have them provide comments, criticisms, and encouragement for mine. Corey organized the conference, Dina Egge took care of the logistics, and Corey, John, and Sharon chaired sessions. Thanks go to them and also to everyone who attended.

I thank Bryan Caplan for his book *The Myth of the Rational Voter*. I have been fascinated by the logic and ethics of collective action for a long time, but if I had not read Caplan, I never would have written this book.

During the summers of 2008 and 2009, I had the opportunity to lecture on some of these ideas before large interdisciplinary groups of graduate students as part of The Social Change Workshop, sponsored by The Institute for Humane Studies, George Mason University. I thank Jonathan Fortier for inviting me to participate.

Will Wilkinson, who hosts *Free Will*, a philosophy talk show, on Bloggingheads.tv, discussed morally mandatory abstention with me shortly after my "Polluting the Polls" article was accepted for publication. I am pretty sure I would not have written this book had I never discussed the topic with Will. Thanks also to reporters at the *Guardian* and *Radio Netherlands*.

A number of other people have helped me by commenting on drafts or previous articles, asking questions at professional presentations, or simply by discussing these issues: Julia Annas, Neera Badhwar, Geoffrey Brennan, Elizabeth Busch, Sam Clark, Tom Christiano, Ross Corbett, Richard Dagger, Ryan Davis, Christopher Freiman, Michael Fuerstein, Gerry Gaus, Robert Goodin, Paul Gowder, Robert Gressis, Andrew Lister, Loren Lomasky, Aaron Maltais, Steven Maloney, Simon Cabulea May, Christian Rostbøll, Ben Saunders, David Schmidtz, Rebecca Stangl, Kyle Swan, Christine Swanton, Kevin Vallier, Matt Zwolinski, and audience members at the American Philosophical Association, the University of Arizona, the New England Political Science Association, and the Midwest Political Science Association. I also thank Rob Tempio, my editor, for his interest and encouragement. Dave Schmidtz has been a fabulous mentor over the years, and I owe him much gratitude as well. Josiah S. Carberry also offered significant (unsolicited) advice, all of which I ignored.

Finally, thanks are due to my mom and dad for showing me how to have a good work ethic and to my partner Lauren and son Aiden for bringing me so much joy.

Most of this work is new, but there are pieces drawn from previously published work.

A portion of chapter 1 was published as "Tuck on the Rationality of Voting," *Journal of Ethics and Social Philosophy* 3 (2009): 1–5.

Parts of chapters 3 and 4 are based on "Polluting the Polls: When Citizens Should Not Vote," *Australasian Journal of Philosophy* 87 (2009): 535–49.

The Ethics of Voting

Voting as an Ethical Issue

WHY VOTING MATTERS

WHEN WE VOTE, we can make government better or worse. In turn, our votes can make people's lives better or worse.

If we make bad choices at the polls, we get racist, sexist, and homophobic laws. Economic opportunities vanish or fail to materialize. We fight unjust and unnecessary wars. We spend trillions on ill-conceived stimulus plans and entitlement programs that do little to stimulate economies or alleviate poverty. We fail to spend money on programs that would work better. We get overregulation in some places, underregulation in others, and lots of regulation whose sole effect is to secure unfair economic advantages for special interests. We inflict and perpetuate injustice. We leave the poor behind. We wage drug wars that ghettoize inner cities. We throw too many people in jail. We base our immigration and trade policies on xenophobia and defunct economic theories.

Voting is morally significant. Voting changes the quality, scope, and kind of government. The way we vote can help or harm people. Electoral outcomes can be harmful or beneficial, just or unjust. They can exploit the minority for the benefit of the majority. They can do widespread harm with little benefit for anyone. So, in this book, I argue that we have moral obligations concerning how we should vote. Not just any vote is morally acceptable.

This is a book on voting ethics. In particular, it concerns the ethics of voting in political contexts. (It is not about voting for MLB All-Stars or American Idol contestants.) The purpose of this book is to determine whether a citizen should vote at all and how she should vote if she chooses to do so. The field of voting ethics asks questions such as: Should citizens choose to vote or abstain? If a person is indifferent to the outcome of an election, should she abstain? When citizens do vote, how should they vote? May voters use their religious beliefs in deciding how to vote? Must voters vote sincerely, for the candidate or position they believe best? What counts as voting for the best candidate? In particular, should voters vote solely for their own interest, or should they vote for the common good, whatever that is? Is it ever acceptable to buy, sell, or trade votes?

There are related topics from the standpoint of political philosophy, such as: What should the government do about promoting participation? Which people should have the right to vote? How should elections be structured, and how often should they be held? Should the government attempt to educate voters, and if so, how? May governments compel citizens to vote? Should ballots be secret or public? These are worthy questions, but I am not concerned with them here. This book is about the obligations of citizens, not of governments. To determine what governments should do about voting would require another book's worth of work.

What Voting Is Not

From a moral point of view, voting is not like ordering food off of a menu. When you order salad at a restaurant, you alone bear the consequences of your decision. No one else gets stuck with a salad. If you make a bad choice, at least you are hurting only yourself. For the most part, you internalize all of the costs and benefits of your decision.

Voting is not like that. If anything, when we vote, we are imposing one meal on everybody.[1] If you were appointed the Dinner Czar—who must decide what everyone will have for dinner each night—your decisions would be of obvious moral consequence. As Dinner Czar, you would externalize most of the costs and benefits of your decisions. It would be a big responsibility. You better not force diabetics to eat too much sugar, make vegans eat meat, or make Muslims eat pork. Or, if you did do these things, you better have good reasons.

Now, in voting, nobody chooses by herself. Each vote counts, but it does not count much. We decide electoral outcomes together. How *we* vote has consequences; how *you* vote does not. However, there are moral principles governing how people ought to behave when participating in collective activities. Even though individual votes almost never have a significant impact on election results in any large-scale election, I argue that this does not let individuals off the hook. Individual voters have moral obligations concerning how they vote.

Obviously, the good and bad that governments do are not entirely attributable to how we vote. Our voting behavior is just one of many factors affecting political outcomes. Despite steadfast and sure democratic oversight, a bad policy might be implemented out of bureaucratic caprice or a politician's corruption. For my purposes, what matters is that votes, on the whole, do make a difference. Political parties have policy bents—dispositions to implement certain kinds of policies rather than others. When voters vote for members of a party with a particular policy bent, this greatly increases the probability that those kinds of policies will be implemented.[2]

Other factors besides voting also determine policy outcomes. This means that we cannot solve all political problems just by getting voters to vote better. That said, better voting would tend to lead to better government.

Against the Commonsense View

Voting is the principal way that citizens influence the quality of government. No activity is more emblematic of democracy. Some call voting a civic sacrament. Many people approach democracy, and voting especially, with a quasi-religious reverence.[3]

This means that people tend to have firm opinions about when and how people should vote. They tend to think the answers to the questions of voting ethics are obvious. They treat their views on voting as sacred doctrine. They dislike having their views challenged.

There is a widely held, commonsense view on the ethics of voting. Non-philosophers tend to subscribe to what I call the folk theory of voting ethics.

The Folk Theory of Voting Ethics:

1. Each citizen has a civic duty to vote. In extenuating circumstances, one can be excused from voting, but otherwise, one should vote.[4]
2. While it is true that there can be better or worse candidates, in general any good faith vote is morally acceptable. At the very least, it is better to vote than to abstain.
3. It is inherently wrong to buy or sell one's vote.

Of course, this so-called commonsense view is not common to everyone. People disagree. Still, the typical American endorses the folk theory.

Many people endorse the folk theory, but they do so for different reasons. For some people, points 1–3 express what they take to be close-to-fundamental moral principles. For others, they are all-things-considered conclusions, perhaps dependent on certain empirical considerations. For instance, some people endorse the first point because they think political participation is right in itself. Others think we should vote because individual votes make a big difference.

Many philosophers and political theorists endorse some version of the folk theory. Many do not.[5] Some philosophers who reject the folk theory believe we have no duties whatsoever regarding voting. They think we have no duty to vote, but if we do vote, we may vote however we please. Other philosophers believe that we have a duty not merely to vote but to vote well.[6] The philosophers who endorse this second position debate what it means to vote well, but they tend to think it involves more than good faith. They tend to think citizens should keep an eye out for the public interest, should listen to and debate one another about what is best, and should vote on the basis of sound evidence.

In this book, I argue against the folk theory and also against these other popular philosophical positions. Instead, I argue for these claims:

1. Citizens typically have no duty to vote.[7] However, if citizens do vote, they must vote well, on the basis of sound evidence for what is likely to promote the common good. They must make sure their reasons for voting as they do are morally and epistemically justified. In general, they must vote for the common good rather than for narrow self-interest. Citizens who lack the motive, knowledge, rationality, or ability to vote well should abstain from voting.

2. Vote buying, selling, and trading are morally permissible provided they do not violate the duties described in point 1. When vote buying, selling, and trading are wrong, what makes them wrong is that they lead to violations of the duties described in point 1. So long as these duties are not violated, vote buying, selling, and trading are not wrong.

On my view, citizens generally have no standing obligation to vote. They can abstain if they prefer. However, they do have strict duties regarding voting: they must vote well or must abstain. Voting well tends to be difficult, but discharging one's duties regarding voting is easy, because one may abstain instead.[8]

I am not arguing that voters should vote for whatever they *believe* promotes the common good. Instead, I am arguing that voters ought to vote for what they *justifiedly* believe promotes the common good. So, on my view, if a voter votes for some candidate whom she believes will promote the common good, but this voter lacks good grounds for her beliefs, then the voter has acted wrongly. She might have good intentions, but she has acted wrongly nonetheless. Consider, in parallel, a parent who feeds her child potassium cyanide because she believes it will cure the common cold, despite the overwhelming evidence that cyanide is poison. The parent has good intentions and believes herself to be promoting the child's interests. But she is not justified in this belief and does something wrong.

My position on voting ethics has counterintuitive implications. Some citizens cannot be bothered to vote. They would rather sit home and play video games. On my view, there is nothing morally wrong about abstaining for such frivolous reasons. (Whether this shows bad character is a more complicated issue.)

On the other hand, many politically active citizens—writers, activists, community organizers, pundits, celebrities, and the like—try to make the world better and vote with the best of intentions. They vote for what they believe will promote the common good. However, despite their best intentions, on my view, many of them are blameworthy for voting. Although they are politically engaged, they are nonetheless often ignorant of or misinformed about the relevant facts or, worse, are simply irrational. Though they intend to promote the common good, they all too often lack sufficient evidence to justify the policies they advocate. When they do vote, I argue, they *pollute* democracy with their votes and make it more likely that we will have to suffer from bad governance.

The Right to Vote versus the Rightness of Voting

These claims make some people furious. Partly, this is because many people are deeply irrational and emotionally invested in their political ideologies.[9] Partly, it is because people make the same basic philosophical mistake. People tend to confuse two distinct issues:

A. The right to vote
B. The rightness of voting

I argue that some citizens should *not* vote. This does not imply that they should not *have the right* to vote. Claiming that you have a right to do something but should not do it is perfectly consistent. The right to vote and the rightness of voting are different things. I do not argue that we should disenfranchise anyone. Though I think many voters are wrong to vote, I will not argue that anyone should prevent them from voting.

People often assume that if it is morally wrong to do X, then it is morally permissible to stop people from doing X. Consider the following argument for disenfranchising bad voters:

1. It is wrong for people to vote when they are ignorant or irrational about politics.
2. If it is wrong for people to do X, then they ought to be prohibited, by law, from doing X.
3. Therefore, people who are ignorant and irrational about politics should be disenfranchised.

This argument fails because premise 2 is false. Sometimes it is wrong for you to do something, but the law and other people should allow you to do it. Sometimes it is within your rights to do something morally wrong.

In general, if you have the right to do something, this does not presuppose that it is morally right for you to do it.[10] Rights are not about what is morally permissible for the rights holder to do. Instead, they are more about what is morally permissible for other people to do to the rights holder.[11] If a citizen has a right to vote, this means at minimum that she ought to be permitted to vote—no one should stop her or deprive her of the vote—and that her vote must be counted. This does not say anything about whether her choice to vote was good or bad, praiseworthy or blameworthy.

Consider an analogy to the right of free speech. The right to free speech means, at the very least, that people should not be interfered with or punished for saying and writing certain things.[12] This does not mean that saying anything one likes is morally right. Neo-Nazi rocker Michael Regener has the right to write music spreading the hatred of Jews. It is perverse and unjust of Germany to imprison him for doing so, but it was also wrong for Regener to write those songs. I have the political right of free association to participate in neo-Nazi rallies. A society that prevented me from participating would be to that extent unjust. Still, my participating would be wrong, even though it is within my rights.

So, when I say that individuals sometimes have a duty to abstain from voting, I am not saying that they thereby lack the right to vote. If someone is going to vote wrongly, it does not automatically follow that she should be disenfranchised.

IN PRAISE OF EQUAL VOTING RIGHTS

Having the right to vote is important, even if it is not always important to exercise that right. It makes sense that people would fight for such a right.

Joel Feinberg writes that rights are a kind of moral furniture.[13] They allow you to stand up and look others in the eyes as equals. To have rights is to have a kind of dignity. According to his "Letter from Birmingham Jail," this lack of dignity is what Martin Luther King finds most appalling. People such as King or Alice Paul worked to improve the material welfare and opportunities available for blacks and women, respectively. But they also wanted respect and public acknowledgment of their equal status. We have made significant moral progress since King's time, even if there is plenty more work to be done. We could not have made this progress without protecting women's and blacks' right to vote.

Despite this, I do not regard it as self-evident that we have a natural right to political equality, nor do I hold that the symbolic value of equal voting rights is sufficient to justify them. Political equality has to be justified against inequality, and part of what justifies political equality is how well it promotes the common good as compared to other kinds of arrangements.[14]

I do not want to overstate the value of the right to vote, either. If the rest of you voted to disenfranchise me, and only me, that would certainly send me a message. On the other hand, suppose I, and only I, had a choice between having the right to vote and having $50,000. In this case, I would find it hard to choose the right to vote, and it is not because I am particularly materialistic. It is one thing to have a right denied to you or taken away. It is another to relinquish it voluntarily. Different rights have different value to different people. Because I write and philosophize for a living, the right to free speech probably means more to me than it means to the average businessman, who probably cares more about economic rights. A politically active citizen would care more about the right to vote than I do.

This book articulates standards of good voting. Many people violate these standards. If there are moral standards, should we not enforce them? If bad voting can be harmful, should we not stop it? Why not have a poll exam—a test of competence that determines whether a citizen may vote? Or why not give extra votes to educated people, as Britain did until 1949? In later chapters, I respond partly to these points. However, answering these questions goes largely beyond the scope of this book. I am concerned with how people ought to vote, not with what governments ought to do about voting.[15]

Some readers will view this book as an upper-middle class, Ivy League expression of disdain for the poor and uneducated. On the contrary, I hope readers recognize (especially in chapter 2) that this book presents an unusually egalitarian and populist conception of civic responsibility. Also, others will be tempted to read this book as a defense of technocracy—of creating powerful bureaucracies staffed by experts (such as the Federal Reserve) that lack voter oversight. Currently all major democracies are to some extent technocratic. Whether this is good or bad deserves study, but this book does not study that question and should not be interpreted as offering an answer.

HOORAY, DEMOCRACY

I support democracy. I am not antidemocratic. Some political theorists have more enthusiasm for democracy than I do and will thus regard me as antidemocratic. That is a mistake. I am a fan of democracy, if not its biggest fan.

I take a certain view of the value of institutions.[16] On my view, political institutions are like hammers. We judge them in the first instance by how functional they are, by how well they help us lead our lives together in peace and prosperity. Institutions are not, for the most part, like people—valuable as ends in themselves. Nor are they like paintings, to be judged on their beauty, by who made them, or what they symbolize. Institutions that hinder our ability to live well, regardless of what they symbolize or the good intentions of their creators, give us little reason to support them.[17]

At base, democracy is just a decision-making method.[18] In politics, democracy is a method for deciding when and how to coerce people into doing things they do not wish to do. Political democracy is a method for deciding (directly or indirectly) when, how, and in what ways a government will threaten people with violence. The symbol of democracy is not just the ballot—it is the ballot connected to a gun.

Democracy is good because liberal, constitutional democratic governments perform well compared to the feasible alternatives. People living under liberal, constitutional democratic governments tend to have higher standards of living, greater educational levels, longer life expectancy, higher exposure and access to culture and diversity, greater reported happiness and life satisfaction, more freedom of all kinds, and more wealth than people living under alternative regimes. From a humanitarian point of view, liberal constitutional democracy is a clear winner, at least compared to the alternatives we have tried.

That said, we should avoid democratic fetishism. Some political theorists love democracy so much that they wish to see it pervade nearly every aspect of life. They advocate democracy as a way of living. They want democratic neighborhood associations with weekly meetings, democracy in the workplace, democracy on TV. They want political deliberation everywhere. They see all of this as a way of giving people more control over their lives and of making them freer.

Democracy could be a way of giving people control and making them freer, if only human beings were not the way they are. Actual human beings are wired not to seek truth and justice but to seek consensus. They are shackled by social pressure. They are overly deferential to authority. They cower before uniform opinion. They are swayed not so much by reason but by a desire to belong, by emotional appeal, and by sex appeal. We evolved as social primates who depended on tight in-group cooperative behavior. Unfortunately, this leaves us with a deep bent toward tribalism and conformity. Too much and too frequent democracy threatens to rob us of our autonomy.[19]

For some people, heavy political participation is necessary for them to lead what they consider a full life. For many others, active political participation would inhibit them from leading the kind of lives they want to lead. The first kind of person is not inherently more noble or sophisticated than the second.

Some people in the first camp will see this book as antidemocratic. Perhaps they are too democratic. Democracy is not a way of life, at least, not for all of us. Democracy is a method for selecting leaders and policies. Its point is to help us lead our lives, not to be our lives. Government should set the stage, not be the play.

How Good Are Real Voters?

My goal is to outline a theory of voting ethics. That is, I want to describe how voters should vote, if they should vote at all. This is a normative, philosophical question. There is a related descriptive, social-scientific question: how do voters behave? Combining the answers to these two questions would allow us to answer a third question: do voters behave well?

To assess actual voters, you need to combine a normative theory of how voters should behave with a descriptive theory of how they in fact behave. That is, you need both A and B to get C:

A. *Normative Theory*: Voters ought to do X.
B. *Empirical Account*: Voters in fact do Y.
C. *Evaluation of Actual Voters*: Voters behave well/badly.

My main goal in this book is to provide A, a normative theory of how voters ought to behave. However, in chapter 7, I discuss B, social-scientific evidence describing how voters in fact behave. In light of this, I conclude C, that many voters in fact behave badly and that many nonvoters would behave badly were they to vote. Yet, if I am wrong in thinking voters often behave wrongly, it might not be because my normative standards (A) are wrong but because my empirical views (B) of how voters behave are wrong.

Not all voters are equal. They have equal voting power, but their contributions are not of equal quality. Some people tend to make government better; some tend to make it worse.

Some voters are well informed about what candidates are likely to do. They know what policies candidates endorse and whether the candidates are sincere. They know the track records and general trends of different political parties. Other voters are ignorant of such things. Others are misinformed rather than ignorant. So one way voters vary is in *knowledge*. Voters are on a continuum between extraordinarily well informed and completely ignorant, and on a continuum between well informed and misinformed.

Some voters form their policy preferences by studying social-scientific evidence—from economics, sociology, and history—about how institutions and policies work. They are self-critical and use reliable methods of reasoning in forming their policy preferences. They actively engage contrary points of view and work hard to overcome their own biases. Other citizens form policy preferences on the basis of what they find emotionally appealing. They believe various economic or sociological theories (about how economies, governments, institutions, and the like function) because they find these theories comforting or flattering to their ideologies, not because the evidence supports those theories. They ignore and evade evidence, demonize the other side, and form their preferences through unreliable processes. They are unjustified in their beliefs. Their policy preferences reflect biases and nonrational or irrational bents. So another way voters vary is in their degree of *rationality*. Some voters are scrupulously rational, while others are irrational. Some have patently stupid beliefs. For instance, a 2009 poll of likely voters in New Jersey showed that 8 percent of them (including 5 percent of Democrats and 14 percent of Republicans) believe that Barack Obama is the anti-Christ, while 19 percent of them (including 40 percent of self-identified left-liberals) believe George W. Bush had knowledge of the 9/11 attacks before 9/11.[20]

Some voters vote on the basis of sound moral values. They pursue ends that are worth pursuing, and which they know are worth pursuing. Others vote for morally despicable reasons. Consider, for example, that many voters in the 2008 U.S. presidential election rejected Obama on grounds that he is "a black Muslim terrorist-sympathizer." These voters were not merely misinformed and irrational—they were bigots. So another way voters vary is in their moral attitudes.

One potential problem with campaigns to increase voter participation is that they might lower the average level of voter quality. Of course, in most cases, voting does not translate directly into a set of policies. During their campaigns, politicians promise to enact certain policies, but they rarely enact all of these policies. Still, our best available social-scientific research shows that politicians generally attempt to give people what they ask for.[21] Increased political participation could mean that most voters start asking for foolish, ineffective, or immoral policies. It could mean that we are stuck with lower-quality governance than we otherwise would have. Having elections decided by irrational, stupid, immoral, or ignorant voters could mean that citizens have to live with racist and sexist laws, unnecessary wars, fewer and lower-quality opportunities, higher levels of crime and pollution, and lower levels of welfare.

Most activities—such as piloting aircraft, performing surgery, playing guitar, dancing, writing philosophy, nursing patients—require skill, training, and practice to do adequately. Some activities—such as being a professional physicist or athlete—require exceptional skill, such that most people could not do them no matter how hard they tried. Others—such as being a truck driver—are within most people's ability but still require training and expertise to do well. There is no obvious reason to think voting is an exception to these norms. It is easy to vote—just show up and check a few boxes—but it is not easy to vote *well*.

DIFFERENT WAYS TO BE INFORMED

There are different kinds of information needed to vote well. It is one thing to know which policies different politicians favor and are likely to promote. However, it is another matter to have the relevant social-scientific knowledge needed to evaluate these positions. The first kind of information is more easily acquired than the second.

To decide between two otherwise identical candidates, it is not enough to know that one favors free trade while the other favors protectionism. You would need to know the likely outcomes of such policies, for example, which policy package—free trade or protectionism—is more likely to promote well-being, prosperity, and other values.

Similarly, imagine you are choosing between two physicians who have proposed different treatments for your asthma. One physician wants to prescribe albuterol; the other, monoxidine. Knowing which medicine each favors does not give you enough information to decide between the physicians. You would need to know something about albuterol and monoxidine or to have some reliable way of checking the physicians' credentials to determine which physician is more reliable. Otherwise, you are in no position to choose.

You are unlikely to encounter a physician who would prescribe monoxidine (a blood pressure medication) for asthma. Politicians, alas, are not consistently as good as medical doctors. They are far more likely to advocate bad or counterproductive policies. Even when they sincerely believe the policies they favor will deliver the promised results—and there is no doubt that they quite often are sincere—that does not mean that they are reliable or trustworthy. Politicians make mistakes and are frequently in the grip of false, long-refuted social-scientific theories.[22] And checking their credentials is difficult.

EVERY VOTE COUNTS

In a well-functioning democracy, every vote counts. That is, every vote is counted and counted exactly once. That is not to say individual votes are important. They are not. Individual votes are of little instrumental value in influencing electoral outcomes or the quality of government. In the next chapter, we look more closely at attempts to show otherwise. These attempts fail. Collectively, votes matter. Individually, they do not.

I am not going to argue that because your vote is insignificant, you should not vote. There are reasons to vote—and not to vote—even if individual votes do not matter much. Some economists (such as Mancur Olson) say it is irrational to vote. That is not my position.[23]

Instead, I introduce this issue here for the purpose of explaining how it affects my argument. From my perspective, the insignificance of individual votes is neutral in how easy it makes it for me to argue in support of this book's conclusions. Because I want to argue citizens have no duty to vote, the insignificance of individual votes is, at first glance, helpful. Arguing that someone lacks a duty to perform an action is easier when the individual action does no significant good. On the other hand, because I argue that people sometimes have a duty to abstain, the insignificance of individual votes is a problem for me. Arguing that people should not vote badly is much harder when individual bad votes do no significant harm. If, contrary to fact, individual votes did make a big difference, it would become easier for me to argue that bad voters should abstain but harder to argue that knowledgeable citizens lack a duty to vote well.

Justice and the Common Good

I argue that voters should vote for what they justifiedly believe to be in the common good. In a later chapter, I explain why voters should vote in a public-spirited way rather than for narrow self-interest. I also argue against skeptics who hold that we can make any sense of the notion of the common good.

That said, I am not planning to argue for a particular conception of the common good. The theory of voting ethics I give here is meant to be compatible with a wide variety of background theories of justice and of the common good. You can think of the term "the common good" as being a variable to be filled in by the correct political philosophy, whatever that is. Voters should justifiedly believe that they are voting for things that serve the common good, whatever that is. Their beliefs about what constitutes the common good must be justified as well.

Even if I do not take a stand on the common good, that does not make this book devoid of content. After all, I am going to argue for a number of controversial points, including:

1. Citizens have no civic or moral obligation to vote.
2. Citizens can pay their debts to society and exercise civic virtue without being involved in politics.

3. People who lack certain credentials (such as knowledge, rationality, and intellectual virtue) should abstain from voting.
4. Voters should not vote for narrow self-interest.
5. It can be permissible to buy and sell votes. It is not inherently wrong to do so.

Because this book is meant to present a theory of voting behavior that is neutral among different theories of the ends of government, for the most part I remain relatively neutral about what the common good is. I sometimes use examples of bad voting that rely on particular conceptions of the common good, but these are meant to be illustrations and should not be taken to be a definitive part of the theory presented here. For example, in the opening paragraphs I complained that bad voting could lead to homophobic laws. I happen to believe that homophobic laws, such as bans on same-sex marriage, are morally perverted and unjustifiable. I think defending this belief would be easy, though I do not defend it here. Still, it is not officially part of my theory of voting ethics. When I claim that voters should not vote for homophobic laws, this conclusion results from combining (A) my theory of voting ethics with (B) a theory of the common good and (C) a theory of moral epistemology (i.e., a theory of which moral attitudes can be justified). In this book, I am arguing for A, but not for B or C.

WHAT'S TO COME

In chapter 1, I examine whether we have a duty to vote. I show that most arguments for a duty to vote fail. However, I outline three arguments that seem more promising than the others. I take these to be the best arguments in favor of a duty to vote.

Still, in chapter 2, I explain why even these arguments fail. I do so by articulating a new theory of civic virtue and of paying debts to society. I show that citizens can exercise civic virtue and pay debts to society not only without voting but often without engaging in politics at all. So, by the end of chapter 2, I take it that I have established there is no duty to vote.

Chapters 3 through 5 concern how citizens ought to vote when they do vote. In chapter 3, I argue that citizens have to meet certain epistemic standards when they vote, or otherwise they ought to abstain. They must be epistemically justified in believing that the candidate or policy they support is likely to promote the common good, or otherwise they ought not vote at all. I chapter 4, I consider and rebut a variety of objections to this argument that hold that abstention involves a loss of autonomy for the individual. I examine and respond to other worries about abstention. In chapter 5, I argue that citizens should vote in ways that promote the common good rather than in ways that promote their self-interest at the expense of the common good.

Chapter 6 investigates whether vote buying and selling are morally wrong. I argue that vote buying and selling are morally permissible provided that selling votes does not lead to violations of the duties I described in chapters 3 through 5. Vote buying and selling are not inherently wrong.

Finally, chapter 7 concludes by reviewing some relevant social-scientific literature that suggests that voters and citizens are often ignorant, irrational, and systematically in error in their political beliefs. If these findings are correct, this means that many voters violate the standards of rightful voting explained in chapters 3 through 5.

CHAPTER ONE

Arguments for a Duty to Vote

WE BUILD SOME THINGS just so we can destroy them. When my son was
twelve months old, he liked to knock down block towers—the taller, the
better. Because he was better at smashing than building, I built the towers
for him. Sometimes, as I built, I realized I was making a defective structure, so I let him knock it over early. Ultimately, I tried to build the tallest
towers I could, even though they all were going to be knocked down.

What I do in this chapter is similar. This chapter has a constructive
purpose—to find arguments in favor of a duty to vote. At the end of
the chapter, the goal is to be left with a few good arguments in favor of
voting. Along the way, there are some false starts. Because some arguments lack promise, I knock them over early. Yet, by the end of this
chapter, a few remaining arguments in favor of voting stand tall. Still, I
erect these edifices only to destroy them in chapter 2, where I ultimately
conclude that citizens in contemporary democratic nation-states have
no duty to vote.

This chapter is the most technical of the book. To assess some of the
important arguments in favor of voting, it is necessary to make some calculations and discuss certain equations. However, I have tried to write in
such a way that readers who lack a technical background can understand
the material.

WHEN THERE WOULD BE A DUTY TO VOTE

Imagine that all citizens are about to vote. We can choose between candidates P and Q. The following conditions all hold:

A. There is a group of people to whom we each owe a strong duty of
   beneficence.
B. We each also happen to owe these same people a debt for all of the
   resources and effort they have invested in us.
C. For each of us, voting for candidate P or Q will pay our debt and is
   the *only* way we can do so.
D. Voting for P or Q is also the *only* way we can discharge our duty of
   beneficence toward these people.

E. If we each vote for P or Q, this will immensely benefit everyone to whom we owe duties of beneficence and reciprocity. However, it is also the case that voting for P is more beneficial than voting for Q.

F. Each individual voter knows that other voters will vote exactly as she does, and so her vote will not be defeated or overridden.

G. If anyone fails to vote, it will ruin everyone's lives. Justice and freedom will be lost forever.

H. As it turns out, that we should vote for P rather than Q is clear and obvious to everyone. It takes no effort or skill whatsoever to determine that P rather than Q is the best, and there is no chance any of us will make a mistake. Also, everyone knows, without any effort, that failing to vote leads to disaster.

I. Voting has no opportunity cost. It does not keep anyone from doing anything else of significant value for herself or for others.

If these conditions actually held in real life, we would each have compelling, overwhelming reasons to vote.

Imagine that some philosopher asserted that these conditions hold. That is, imagine some philosopher made what I call the Straw Man Argument:

Straw Man Argument:

1. Conditions A–I obtain.
2. Therefore, each citizen should vote.

This argument is a straw man because no one actually claims that all of these conditions hold. However, conditions A–I are exaggerations of the considerations people do offer in favor of a duty to vote. The fact that A–I are exaggerations of actual conditions is worrisome for anyone arguing for the existence of a duty to vote. After all, the less conditions A–I hold, the harder it is to show there is a duty to vote. When conditions A–I do not hold, competing considerations that might count against any argument in favor of a duty to vote are easier to find.

Problems with the Straw Man Argument include the following:

1. Individual votes do not have as much instrumental value as the argument presupposes.
2. Because there is some opportunity cost in voting, people could always do something else of value for themselves or for others. Sometimes voters should do these other things instead.
3. Rarely are voters presented with candidates of such high quality as, and as clearly differentiated as, P and Q. The stakes in get-

ting the right choice among the available choices are not nearly so high.

4. Abstention by one voter does not lead to catastrophic moral horror. In fact, even abstention by most citizens does not seem to have bad effects.

5. Acquiring the knowledge needed to evaluate candidates and policies is not easy and cost free. It takes time and effort. This time and effort could be spent on other worthwhile activities, including other activities that might benefit the common good.

6. The underlying duties that might ground a duty to vote—such as duties of beneficence or reciprocity—can be discharged in other ways besides voting. Showing that voting can be one way among others of discharging these duties is easy, but showing that voting is a necessary way or even an especially good way is difficult.

We examine each of these points over the next two chapters. The purpose of looking at the Straw Man Argument is this: it turns out the arguments people make on behalf of a duty to vote fail for one or more of the reasons the Straw Man Argument fails.

Arguments from the Instrumental Value of Individual Votes

In this section, I examine arguments that claim we should vote because each individual vote has significant value in terms of its expected impact on the quality of governance. These arguments fail because individual votes in fact have vanishingly small instrumental value in terms of their impact on the quality of governance.

Even if—contrary to fact—individual votes had significant instrumental value, this would not settle the issue. Proponents of a duty to vote would still need to prove that voting is mandatory, rather than optional or supererogatory. (An action is supererogatory if it is morally praiseworthy, but not morally obligatory.) Proving that each vote does significant good still leaves open the question whether doing such good is mandatory. Voting might just be one way among others of discharging a duty to act beneficently. Or voting might go above and beyond the call of duty. If voting turned out to be supererogatory, voters would be praiseworthy, but nonvoters would not be blameworthy. My argument in the next chapter shows that voting would not be mandatory, even if it turned out that individual votes had significant instrumental value.

Individual Votes and Electoral Outcomes

Here is one common argument in favor of voting:

The Prudence Argument:

1. All things being equal, you ought to promote your own interests.
2. Your individual vote, when cast correctly, significantly promotes your own interests.
3. Therefore, you ought to vote (correctly).

Defenders of a duty to vote usually argue from considerations of civic virtue and public-spiritedness rather than from self-interest. Still, it is a commonplace to say that unless you make your voice heard, the government will not look after your interests. So, on the folk theory of voting ethics, one reason you should vote is that voting helps produce favorable electoral outcomes for you.

A different version of this argument holds that individual votes can have significant utility for everyone:

The Beneficence Argument:

1. All things being equal, if you can perform an action that has a large expected benefit to the public good, you should do so.[1]
2. Voting the right way has a large expected benefit to the public good.
3. Therefore, you should vote the right way.

Notice that neither argument implies that citizens should vote however they wish rather than abstain. Rather, the arguments at best show citizens should vote a particular way as opposed to abstain. They leave open whether voting badly is worse than abstention.

Regardless, the arguments suffer from a more fundamental flaw. The second premises of both arguments are false, because they overstate the instrumental value of individual votes in terms of their effect on electoral outcomes.

Generally, individual votes have instrumental value in terms of their effect on the outcome of an election only if they change the outcome.[2] That is, individual votes have an effect only when they are decisive. After the election is over, determining whether single votes were decisive is easy. And, of course, individual votes are decisive only when the election is decided by one vote. In large-scale elections, this almost never happens.[3]

However, we have yet to show these arguments fail. Before the election occurs, an individual vote has some probability of changing the outcome of the election. By multiplying this probability by the expected value of the outcome for which the vote was cast, we generate the expected utility of individual votes in terms of their effect on the outcome.[4] If you vote the right way, the expected utility of your vote increases as the probability that you will be decisive increases. The expected utility of your vote also increases as the net value of the outcome you vote for increases.

On this point, Brian Barry once conjectured that even if one's vote has a low probability of being decisive, it must have high expected utility when the stakes are high. Was he right? He asks us to imagine a scenario in which we know that if our favored candidate wins, this will result in ¼ percent more GNP growth over the next five years.[5] To go further than that, imagine instead that if the right person were elected, this would lead to ¼ percent more GDP growth in just one year. The GDP of the United States in 2006, when corrected for purchasing power parity, was approximately $13.13 trillion. Its real growth rate was 3.2 percent. A 3.2 percent growth rate with a $13.13 trillion GDP is approximately $420 billion of growth. A 3.45 percent growth rate (¼ percent higher) is approximately $453 billion, for a difference of $33 billion. Suppose I plan to vote for the candidate who will produce the higher growth rate. What is the expected value of my vote?

In elections between two candidates, the answer to this question depends on two variables: the number of voters and their division between the candidates.[6] The more voters there are, the less likely my vote will be decisive. And if these other voters are not evenly divided in how they favor the candidates, if one candidate has an edge over the other, then the degree to which one candidate has an edge—the degree to which people tend to favor that candidate over the other—is the degree to which the leading candidate has an *anticipated proportional majority*. Once you do the mathematics, it turns out that the probability that an individual vote will be decisive decreases slowly as the number of voters increases, but it decreases dramatically when there is even a slight anticipated proportional majority.

To return to Barry's conjecture about individual votes, suppose my favored candidate (who is worth $33 billion more to the common good) enjoys a slight lead in the polls. She has a very small anticipated proportional majority. The probability that any random voter will vote for her is 50.5 percent. This is an election we would describe as "too close to call." Suppose also that the number of voters will be the same as in the 2004 U.S. presidential election: 122,293,332. I vote for my favored candidate.

In this case, the expected value (for the common good) of my vote for the better candidate is 4.77×10^{-2650}, that is, approximately zero. Even if the candidate were worth $33 billion to me personally, the expected value for me of my vote would be, again, a mere 4.77×10^{-2650}. That is 2,648 orders of magnitude less than a penny. In comparison, the nucleus of an atom, in meters, is about 15 orders of magnitude shorter than I am. In meters, I am about 26 orders of magnitude shorter than the diameter of the visible universe. In pounds, I am about 28 orders of magnitude less heavy than the sun. Even if the value of my favored candidate to me were dramatically higher, say ten thousand million trillion dollars, the expected value of my vote in our example—for a close election—remains thousands of orders of magnitude below a penny.[7] For an election in which the candidate has a sizable lead, the expected utility of an individual vote for a good candidate drops to almost zero.[8]

The Beneficence Argument appeals to the public utility of individual acts of voting. However, suppose all you care about is maximizing your contribution to the common good. If so, voting would not merely fail to be worthwhile—it would be counterproductive. It turns out that the expected disutility of driving to the polling station (in terms of the harm a driver might cause to others) is higher than the expected utility of a good vote. This is not hyperbole.

Aaron Edlin and Pinar Karaca-Mandic have estimated the expected accident externalities per driver per year in the United States—that is, the amount of damage the average driver imposes on others from accidents and reckless driving.[9] The expected accident externalities range from as little as $10 in low-traffic-density North Dakota to more than $1,725 in high-traffic-density California. Suppose a North Dakotan takes five minutes to drive to the polling station. The average expected accident externality of a five-minute drive in North Dakota is 9.5×10^{-5}, much larger than the expected benefit of a good vote in the previous example. So the voter imposes greater expected harm on her way to the polls than she could compensate for by a good vote.

The point is that in any large-scale election, an individual vote does little expected good or bad in terms of its propensity to affect electoral outcomes. Even when the right outcome is worth a huge amount, individual votes for that outcome are worth close to nothing. Votes have significant value collectively but not individually. In terms of impact on the result of an election, how *we* vote matters, but how any one of us votes does not.[10]

Note that there is some controversy over the best way of calculating the expected utility of individual votes. The preceding calculations use the formulae made popular by Geoffrey Brennan and Loren Lomasky in *Democracy and Decision*. Yet, even if there is dispute over just how small the expected utility of individual votes is, there is not much dispute over the claim that the expected utility is very small. Individual votes do not count for much, and so the Beneficence and Prudence Arguments fail.

Preventing Democratic Collapse

Anthony Downs suggested a different reason why individual votes might have significant instrumental value. Note that Downs never intended to prove that there is a moral duty to vote. He just wanted to explore whether voting might be prudent. Still, his argument, if correct, could easily and charitably be modified in an attempt to show there is a duty to vote. And, in fact, many people do use his kind of argument to defend a duty to vote.

I will call Downs's argument the Saving Democracy Argument. One advantage of this argument, compared to those we already examined, is that it gets us to the right target. That is, if successful, it shows it is right to vote rather than abstain, without imposing much of a restriction on how one votes. So this argument, if successful, would get us closer to the folk theory of voting ethics.

The Saving Democracy Argument:

1. A stable democratic government greatly promotes both the common good and the individual good of each citizen.
2. Voting, regardless of how one votes, tends to preserve stable democracy, but failing to vote threatens to undermine and destabilize democracy.
3. All things equal, one should perform activities that greatly benefit the common good and one's own interests.
4. Therefore, one should vote.[11]

Premise 2 is too strong, of course. In a 1932 election, a majority of Germans voted for either the National Socialist German Worker's Party (the Nazis) or the German National People's Party (the Nationalists). This allowed the two parties to form a ruling coalition. These voters did more to undermine democracy than any abstainers ever have. Thus, we should modify premise 2 so that it specifies that votes cannot be for antidemocratic parties.

There are two interpretations of premise 2. On one interpretation, the point of voting is to keep the number of votes sufficiently high so that democracy does not collapse. On a second interpretation, which I consider in the next subsection, the point of voting is that each individual vote marginally improves the democratic nature of society.

On the first interpretation of premise 2, the idea is that if no one or too few people voted, democratic government would collapse and be replaced with some far inferior form of government. There is some (perhaps unknown) determinate threshold of votes needed under which democracy falls apart. The point of voting is to help ensure this threshold is reached.

Downs wants us to conceive of casting a vote as a kind of insurance against this collapse:

> One thing that all citizens . . have in common is the desire to see democracy work. Yet if voting costs exist, pursuit of short-run rationality [i.e., abstaining from voting] can conceivably cause democracy to break down. However improbable this outcome may seem, it is so disastrous that every citizen is willing to bear at least some cost in order to insure himself against it. The more probable it appears, the most cost he is willing to bear.[12]

Downs might be exaggerating how bad it is to lose democracy. There is a continuum in the quality of governance between stable, well-functioning democracies and murderous totalitarian regimes or kleptocratic dictatorships. Living in a stable, decent, nondemocratic society is often less desirable than living in a stable democracy, but it need not be a disaster. (Is Qatar a disaster?)

For the sake of argument, however, assume that all nondemocracies are disasters. If we grant that, does that mean that my individual vote has enough expected utility to give me either self-interested or public-interest reasons to vote? Is it meaningful to say my vote "tends to preserve democracy"? No. The Saving Democracy Argument exaggerates the importance of individual votes.[13]

There are three possibilities of what my vote will do. First, it might be that enough other citizens vote such that democracy will be preserved regardless of whether I vote. In this case, my vote is superfluous. Second, it might be that so few other citizens vote that democracy will collapse regardless of whether I vote. In this case, my vote is futile. Third, it might be that my vote decisively saves democracy—with one less vote, democracy collapses.

Now, realistically, the first possibility is nearly always the case. The third possibility has never occurred in any large-scale election and probably never will. The third possibility seems dubious anyway. It would be strange if the survival of a democracy could depend on exactly one vote.[14] That there is some number of voters needed to preserve democracy is implausible. It is more plausible that if lower voter turnout tends to make democracies less democratic (in some morally important sense), it does so gradually. (This is why I consider the second interpretation of the Saving Democracy Argument in the next subsection.) However, for the sake of argument, let us assume there is such a determinate threshold, though we might not know what it is.[15]

Downs recognized that the probability that an individual vote will save democracy is low. He suggested that individual votes are a good deal because he thinks losing democracy is a disaster. The basic idea: low probability of saving democracy times very high value of preserving democracy equals significant expected utility of vote. Is this right?

To put this in an actual calculation, suppose there are N potential voters, other than I. Each can either vote or abstain. Suppose each potential voter has some probability p of voting. Suppose that exactly T voters are needed to save democracy. (T is the threshold at which democracy is saved.) If so, then the probability that my vote will decisively save democracy is the probability that one vote less than T will be cast. Define M = T − 1, that is, M is exactly one vote below the threshold needed to save democracy. If exactly M votes are cast, besides mine, then my vote will save democracy. If M − 1 or M + 1 (i.e., if T − 2 or T) votes are cast, then my vote will be futile or superfluous. So my vote saves democracy if and only if exactly M votes, besides mine, are cast. M is the magic number of votes that need to be cast such that my vote will decisively save democracy.

The probability that exactly M votes are cast is given by formula 1 (a binomial probability distribution):

$$(1)\ P(M\ voters\ vote) = \frac{N!}{M!\ (N-M)!}\ (p^M)(1-p)^{N-M}$$

where

> N = the number of other potential voters
>
> M = one vote less than needed to save democracy
>
> p = the probability that a potential voter will vote

Generously assume that American democracy will collapse when 30 percent or less of eligible voters vote. (In my view, this number is much too high.) Assume that the number of eligible voters is the same as in the 2008 presidential election: 231,299,589 voters. If so, American democracy will collapse if 69,389,877 or fewer votes are cast. My vote will thus save democracy if and only if exactly 69,389,876 votes are cast, other than mine. Also assume that each eligible voter has a 56.8 percent chance of voting. (This was the turnout in the 2008 presidential election, so I use it as an approximation of the probability that a potential voter will vote. It is a good approximation, because our sample set is in the hundreds of millions.)

On these generous assumptions, the probability that my vote will decisively save democracy is approximately $3.3 \times 10^{-14,704,390}$. So, even if we assume that saving American democracy is worth, say, 99 sextillion dollars, then the expected utility of my vote in terms of saving democracy is vanishingly small, millions of orders of magnitude less than a penny.[16] Thus, casting a vote as a form of insurance to prevent democratic collapse is a waste of time.[17]

Of course, normal, prudent people buy insurance. I pay about $1,000 per year for car insurance, but this exceeds my expected benefits. Does this make buying car insurance irrational? Presumably not. Most car insurance companies profit by charging more in premiums than they expect to pay in claims,[18] and any given individual should expect to pay more in premiums than she will receive in claims over her lifetime. However, I do not expect to save money by buying car insurance. Rather, I hope to prevent a catastrophic loss from occurring—to make sure I can keep my home if I accidently kill someone. This point might seem sympathetic to Downs's argument, because Downs suggested we vote in order to prevent the possible catastrophe of democratic collapse. Yet suppose car insurance cost a mere $1, but there were only a $3.3 \times 10^{-14,704,390}$ probability that the insurance would prevent a catastrophic loss. If so, I would be crazy to buy the insurance. Every time I changed my infant son's diaper, there was about a $3.3 \times 10^{-14,704,390}$ chance that he would quantum tunnel through his changing pad and crash to the floor, but I did not nothing to protect against that catastrophe. We simply ignore catastrophes that remote.

One might try to argue instead that losing democracy is infinitely costly. If losing democracy is infinitely costly and my vote has any chance, no matter how small, of saving democracy, I should vote. Suppose I had only a $1 \times 10^{-250,000,000}$ chance of saving democracy with my vote, but saving democracy is infinitely valuable. If so, this would give my vote infinite expected utility.

Yet, this argument proves too much. Not only would it show I should always vote, but it also implies that I should always perform any other activity that has any chance, no matter how small, of preserving democracy. For instance, it implies I should greet every stranger on the street with, "Hey, preserve democracy! It's important!" Doing this has a tiny chance of saving democracy, but if democracy is infinitely valuable, this makes the expected utility of each greeting infinitely high. In fact, if democracy is infinitely valuable, or losing democracy is infinitely costly, this means that I should always be working to preserve democracy, unless there is some other infinitely important activity competing for consideration. (Feeding my son would be permissible only insofar as it helps preserve democracy.)

Each Vote Improves Democracy

Now that the argument using the first interpretation of the Saving Democracy Argument has failed, we turn to the second interpretation of premise 2. The previous interpretation argued that the point of voting was to ensure that a sufficient number of votes was cast to preserve democracy. On that interpretation, each vote over the threshold was superfluous and each vote under it was futile. On the second interpretation, the argument instead is that each successive vote makes democracy more democratic, and this is a reason to vote. This version of the argument is more plausible than the last.

Obviously, the more people vote, the more democratic society is. So what? We could make society more democratic by holding elections daily.[19] This would not do us any good.

For the sake of argument, suppose that the quality of governance, in terms of the government's tendency to promote each citizen's interests, is a direct function of the number of voters. (We have little or no empirical evidence that this is the case.) That is, let us grant that each additional vote improves social well-being by some margin or improves the quality of governance by some margin. Would that imply that individual citizens should vote?

To answer this question, we should first ask what kind of function the quality of governance is in terms of the number of voters. One possibility is that government quality is a linear function of the number of voters, as shown in figure 1. Here, axis Q represents the quality of government; axis N represents the number of voters. Q is a linear function of N, here shown simply as $Q = mN$. (The constant m is the slope of the line. Fig. 1 shows $m = 1$ for simplicity's sake.)

If the quality of governance were a linear function of the number of voters, then at least every successive vote would do as much good as any other. No matter how many people have voted, my vote always would do as much good as the one before it.

We would still need to know how much good votes do. Suppose Q were a slowly increasing linear function of N; that is, suppose that m were very small. In this case, while each vote would do as much good as any other, they still would do very little good. Any given public-spirited potential voter might still have better ways to serve the common good than by voting. If an individual vote were worth $1 to the common good, it would be hard to explain why voting would be morally mandatory. On the other hand, if it could be shown that each vote were worth $1 million or $1 billion to the common good, there would a better case for morally mandatory voting.

However, even if we generously grant that the quality of governance directly increases with each vote, there is no reason to think that it does

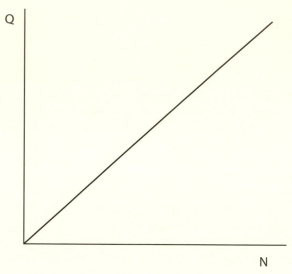

Figure 1

so in a linear fashion, as in figure 1.[20] Anyone familiar with economics knows that nearly all inputs (and goods) have diminishing marginal
returns. For example, in standard production functions, the quantity of
a firm's output is represented as a function of the various factors of production, and it nearly always has diminishing marginal returns. The first
laborer at McDonald's is worth more than the second or third is. In fact,
at some point, adding an additional unit of a factor of production often
yields negative returns—for example, at some point adding an additional
worker at McDonald's costs more than the worker is worth. (At some
point, additional workers just make the restaurant too crowded to serve
customers.)

In this version of the Saving Democracy Argument, the quality of governance is, in effect, a production function with one factor of production:
the number of votes. Nearly every good and every factor of production
has diminishing marginal returns. It would be surprising if voting were
an exception to this rule.[21] In the absence of any empirical evidence that
it is an exception, we should assume it is not. Defenders of this version
of the Saving Democracy rarely try to overcome the worry that votes
might have rapidly decreasing diminishing marginal returns. In part, this
is because the argument is almost never formulated in anything like a
rigorous way.

So, if the quality of governance were a function of the number of voters, figure 2 would be a more plausible representation of that function

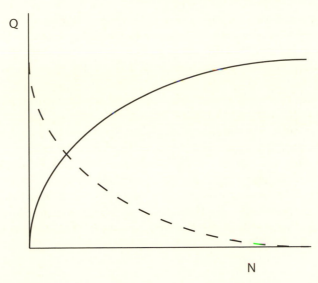

Figure 2

than figure 1. In figure 2, the solid curve represents the quality of governance as a function of the number of voters. The dotted curve represents the marginal value of each additional voter.[22]

If figure 2 rather than figure 1 more closely represents the successive value of each individual vote, this leads to some intuitive results. If very few people are voting, this gives individuals more reason to vote, because their votes are more important. If nearly everyone is voting, this gives individuals less reason to vote. Eventually, though each additional vote continues to add to the quality of government, the addition becomes vanishingly small, and so individuals can always serve the common good better through some means other than voting.[23]

For this version of the Saving Democracy Argument to succeed, its defenders need to provide empirical evidence that every vote does significant good. They need to show that the value of votes does not diminish so rapidly such that it makes sense for some but not all eligible voters to vote. They have not done that. Also, for them to substantiate the empirical assumptions of their argument, it will not be enough to show that high-quality governance *correlates* with high voter turnout. They need to show that high turnout *causes* good government. (I have not been able to find an empirical study showing that high voter turnout causes higher-quality governance,[24] but there are studies suggesting that good-quality governance causes high turnout.)[25] Finally, those who make this version of the Saving Democracy Argument oblige themselves to refute people such as Bryan Caplan, who have provided empirical evidence that increasing the number of voters can sometimes be harmful. We should not assume on behalf of the Saving Democracy Argument that adding additional votes always increases the quality of governance rather than lowers it.

I have not proved here that this version of the Saving Democracy Argument cannot succeed. Rather, I have shown that we lack any reason to accept it, as it rests on unsubstantiated, implausible empirical claims. People making this argument owe us empirical evidence that its central premise—each vote improves the quality of governance—is true. They owe us evidence that each vote has significant value. They owe us evidence that it makes sense to have everyone vote rather than just a significant portion of voters vote. They have not provided such evidence. That any such evidence will be forthcoming is unlikely, because the empirical claims are implausible.

Summary

Individual votes have low expected utility in terms of their effect on the outcome of the election and their ability to prevent democratic collapse. After a certain point, they most likely have low expected utility in terms of their impact on the quality of government. If there is a duty to vote, it cannot be because individual votes have significant instrumental value in terms of their impact on government.[26]

Causal Responsibility

In the recent book *Free Riding,* Richard Tuck wants to show that it is rational to vote.[27] I argue here that Tuck fails. Tuck does not try to prove there is a duty to vote. However, because his book has been receiving significant praise, it would not be surprising if in the coming years someone attempts to use his arguments to show there is a duty to vote. I want to preempt this attempt. Thus, it is worth looking at his argument that voting is rational to see if it could be modified to show there is a duty to vote.

Mancur Olson argued that voting is irrational because individual votes have little or no causal power over electoral outcomes.[28] Tuck wants to prove that Olsen is mistaken, because some votes are causally efficacious. However, even if Tuck succeeds in showing that some votes are causally efficacious toward the outcome of an election, all this does is undermine part of Olson's worry about whether voting is instrumentally rational.

Showing that votes are causally efficacious is not sufficient to show that voting is rational.

The Causal Efficacy of Individual Votes

Tuck argues that individual voters can cause an electoral outcome, even when their votes were not necessary to cause the outcome, because their votes have a chance to belong to the "causally efficacious set of votes." The causally efficacious set of votes is the subset of votes needed to win the election. Suppose that 10,000 people vote for A and 3,999 people vote for B. If so, 4,000 votes for A were necessary for A's victory; the other 6,000 votes were superfluous. The causally efficacious set of votes totals 4,000—these are the votes that won the election. The probability that a random voters' vote formed part of the causally efficacious set is 40 percent.

Tuck relies on two controversial claims about causation. For the sake of argument, I assume the claims are true. Tuck's first claim is that everyone who forms part of the causally efficacious set has some sort of causal responsibility for the outcome.[29] His second, more controversial claim is that C is the cause of E provided C is minimally sufficient for E, even if C is not necessary for E (i.e., even if E would have happened without C). A set of factors C is *minimally sufficient* for E provided (1) C is sufficient for E, and (2) there is no proper subset of C sufficient for E. More formally, C is *minimally sufficient* for E iff $[(C \rightarrow E) \cdot \sim \exists D((D \subset C) \cdot (D \rightarrow E))]$. Note that for any given E, there may be many distinct sets of factors $(C_1, C_2, C_3, \ldots)$ minimally sufficient for E.

Tuck argues that when elections are close, the probability is high that one's vote is in the causally efficacious set. The idea of the causally efficacious set is meant to diffuse the common worry that a voter wastes his time casting a vote with no causal affect on the outcome of the election. On Tuck's view, the voter can tell himself, "There is a high probability that my vote, when combined with the others, helped produce the desirable outcome. It was important that we reach 4,000 votes, and given that I knew others would be voting for A as well, this gave me a good instrumental reason for voting for A, even if my vote wasn't necessary." Voting is an effective way of producing an outcome the voter desires.

To see if Tuck's argument works (in showing that it is rational to vote), we need to consider two kinds of potential voters. A *Type-1 Potential Voter* desires not merely that a good electoral outcome occurs but also desires that she be causally responsible for the outcome of the election. A *Type-2 Potential Voter* cares only that the good electoral outcome occurs. He attaches no special value to being the agent of causation. I argue that Tuck can sometimes show that it is rational for Type-1 Potential Voters to vote, but he cannot show that it is rational for Type-2 Potential Voters to vote.

The Desire to Be Efficacious

Let's say I am a Type-1 Potential Voter. I desire not only to see a good electoral outcome occur but also to help bring about the outcome. Tuck argues that it can be rational for me to vote provided I have high enough probability of being in the causally efficacious set.

Tuck claims that voting is necessary to satisfy the desire to be casually efficacious over electoral outcomes. (Even this is not obviously true, because one way I can cause electoral outcomes is to influence others to vote.) If we grant his account of causation, he is right that voting provides a chance of being efficacious. However, this does not yet show that it is rational to vote. Many people who desire to be efficacious might still rationally choose not to vote, because the value of being efficacious discounted by the probability of being efficacious might be low compared to other available actions.

Tuck cannot use the probability of being efficacious alone to determine whether voting is rational. If performing some action Φ has a high probability of achieving my goal G, that does not automatically imply it is rational for me to Φ. Instead, we would need to know how important or valuable G is. It might be rational to forgo G, even if one has a 100 percent chance of achieving G through Φ, if G is not very valuable, and if there are more valuable goals that could be achieved instead.

Thus, to determine whether it is rational for people who care about being causally efficacious to vote, we need to multiply (A) the probability that one's vote will be in the causally efficacious by (B) the value of being in the efficacious set. That is, we use a formula such as 1:

$$(1) \ U_i \ = \ p(i \in K) \times V_i(i \in K)$$

where

$$U_i \quad = \text{ the expected utility of voting}$$

$$p(i \in K) = \text{the probability that my individual vote is a} \\ \text{member of the causally efficacious set}$$

$$V_i(i \in K) = \text{the utility of my individual vote being a} \\ \text{member of the causally efficacious set}$$

One problem with this formula is that there is no obvious way to determine what $V_i(i \in K)$ is or should be.[30] How much value is there in my vote being in the causally efficacious set? This will vary from person to person, depending on how much they happen to care about being efficacious. At best, Tuck's argument so far shows only that it is rational for some people to vote sometimes, if they happen to care enough about being causally efficacious.

However, this depends on opportunity cost (something Tuck does not consider). It is rational for any given person to vote only if her U_i in formula 1 is higher than the expected utility of other available actions. Suppose that I value being causally efficacious at $50, I value watching the three *Godfather* movies on election day at $41, and the probability my vote will be in the causally efficacious set is less than 80 percent. If so, then the expected utility of voting is less than the expected utility of watching the movies. If so, then it is not rational to vote, even though I care about being in the causally efficacious set. So Tuck can show that it is rational to vote provided (1) one desires to be efficacious, but only if (2) one has nothing better to do with one's time when one votes.[31]

Tuck Has the Wrong Theory of Rational Choice

Type-2 Potential Voters have no desire to be causally efficacious, but they have preferences over which electoral outcome obtains. Tuck cannot show that it is rational for Type-2 Potential Voters to vote, except in unusual circumstances.

If people have no desire to be casually efficacious, then formula 1 cannot explain why they should vote. Still, Tuck wants to prove that it is rational to vote, in many cases, even when people have no desire to be causally efficacious. That is, he wants to show it can be rational for me to vote even if for me $V_i(i \in K) = 0$, that is, even if I am a Type-2 Potential Voter. Suppose I desire that candidate A is elected but attach no value to my helping to cause A's election. Tuck wants to argue that it is rational for me to vote simply because I have a good chance of producing the outcome by voting. Tuck says that by voting I (sometimes) have a high enough probability of doing something sufficient to produce the outcome I desire.

Tuck wants to show that voting is rational without jettisoning or modifying common theories of rational choice. Tuck wants to prove Olson is wrong about the rationality of voting not because Olson has the wrong theory of rational choice but because Olson is wrong about the causal efficacy of votes.[32] Tuck says that Olson has incorrectly assumed that the causes of events must be necessary for those events. In contrast, Tuck wants to show that causes must only be minimally sufficient. Yet, even if individual votes do have the causal efficacy Tuck claims they have, this does not prove that voting is rational. In fact, Tuck accepts the wrong theory of rational choice.

Tuck says to the second kind of potential voter (the one who wants an outcome to occur but attaches no value to producing it) that he should vote because voting will achieve his goal. Tuck thinks that if Φ-ing is sufficient to produce a desired outcome, then it is rational to Φ. Tuck claims that it is rational to vote, even if you do not care about being casually efficacious, because by voting (if enough others also vote) you can do something sufficient to produce the outcome you desire. Tuck says that the "essence of instrumental action is . . that we do what is a *means* to an *end*, that is, *causes* it."[33]

This is an incorrect account of rational choice. Rational agents are not defined simply as creatures who do what is sufficient to produce their ends. Tuck appears to subscribe to a problematic view of rational choice, which Gerald Gaus calls "Rationality as Effectiveness":

> Alf's action [Φ]is instrumentally rational if and only if Φ-ing is an effective way for Alf to achieve his desire, goal, end, or taste, G.[34]

The problem with Rationality as Effectiveness is that the mere fact that Φ suffices to produce a desired outcome does not make it rational to Φ or irrational not to Φ. Rationality as Effectiveness is both too restrictive and too permissive an account of rationality.

It is too restrictive because it implies that even if you have overwhelming evidence that Φ-ing will lead to G, if you Φ and Φ-ing happens to fail, then you were irrational to Φ. For example, suppose you have cancer, but you take SuperCure MiracleDrug, which costs $1 and is 99.9999 percent effective at curing cancer. You take the drug, knowing that there is only a 1-in-1,000,000 chance it will not work. After taking it, alas, you are not cured—you are the unlucky one out of a million who is not helped. According to Rationality as Effectiveness, this means it was irrational for you to take SuperCure. But that is absurd. Rather, taking SuperCure was the rational choice, but not all rational choices pay off.

Rationality as Effectiveness is also too permissive a theory of rational choice. Suppose you want to be richer. You spend all of your money, $100,000, on a bet that has a 1-in-1,000,000 chance of earning you an additional $1. Fortuitously, you win, and so now have $100,001 instead of $100,000. Rationality as Effectiveness implies that it was rational for you to make this bet, but clearly it was not. It was a dumb bet, but dumb bets sometimes pay off.

So one problem with Tuck's argument that it is rational for Type-2 Potential Voters to vote is that, contrary to Tuck's intentions,[35] he appears to be working with a different theory of rationality from Olson's. Tuck sees himself as criticizing Olson's theory of causation but as working with Olson's theory of rational choice. However, in fact, Tuck appears to accept Rationality as Effectiveness, but this is an unpopular theory of rational choice, which Olsen likely rejects. After all, Olson complains not only that voting is causally inefficacious but also that the expected costs of voting are less than the expected benefits. Olson most likely subscribes to a theory of rational choice closer to what Gaus calls "Instrumental Rationality":

> Alf's action Φ is instrumentally rational only if Alf chooses Φ because he soundly believes it is the best prospect for achieving his goals, values, ends, etc.[36]

Instrumental Rationality is a more plausible theory of rational choice because it takes into account opportunity costs in decision making. Rational agents do not merely desire to be effective in securing their ends; rather, they wish to economize among their goals.

Tuck's Theory Implies Abstention Is as Good or Better Than Voting

Nevertheless, this is not the main problem with Tuck's argument. Recall that the Type-2 Potential Voter prefers that A be elected instead of B, but he attaches no special value to his helping to cause A to be elected. Suppose we grant Tuck that voting is rational because it is sufficient, given how other voters vote, to produce a desired outcome. Tuck has not thereby shown that it is irrational for this second kind of voter to abstain. For this second kind of voter, given how other voters are voting, abstention is also sufficient to achieve his goal. Given what other voters are doing, voting for A and abstaining from voting for A are both sufficient for A to be elected. (Recall that Tuck is not trying to argue that one should vote because there is some small chance one's vote will be decisive.) So Tuck's argument seems to imply that Type-2 Potential Voters have reason to vote but equally good reason not to do so.

Actually, this is too charitable to Tuck. Suppose Alf has exactly one goal—to see A elected. Tuck may have shown that it is rational for Alf to vote, though it is not irrational for him to abstain. However, suppose Bob has two goals—to see A elected and to watch television. It is thus *irrational* for Bob to vote. Voting and abstaining are both sufficient to produce his first goal, but voting takes time away from achieving the second goal. Bob best satisfies his two goals by watching television and abstaining from voting. Voting for A and abstention are not equally rational for Bob. Voting has an opportunity cost, but watching television has no opportunity cost. So, if Bob follows Tuck's theory of rational choice and does whatever is sufficient to produce his goals, he will abstain. Abstention is sufficient to realize his two goals, but voting is not.

Thus, Tuck's argument implies that it is rational for Type-2 Potential Voters to vote only if they have no opportunity cost whatsoever in voting, and even then, it implies that voting for one's preferred outcome and abstention are equally rational strategies for achieving one's preferred outcome.[37]

Summary

If we grant Tuck his theory of causation, he has at best shown that voting can be rational under these limited conditions: (1) The agent desires that an electoral outcome occur; (2) by voting, there is a high probability that the agent's vote will be causally efficacious; (3) the agent attaches significant value to being causally efficacious, such that (4) the value of being efficacious discounted by the probability of being efficacious results in voting having an expected utility equal to or higher than the expected utility of any other available action. He has also shown that it can be rational to vote even (5) if one attaches no value to being efficacious, but only on the condition (6) that voting has no opportunity cost at all. Even then, he cannot show that it is irrational not to vote—abstention is as good as voting. Of course, voting always has *some* opportunity cost, and so Tuck has not shown that it is rational for people who do not care about being efficacious to vote.

A DUTY TO VOTE?

If someone were to attempt to use Tuck's argument to prove there is a duty to vote, the most obvious way to do this would be to argue that it is morally important to be causally efficacious in producing some outcomes. Sometimes the point of acting is not merely to ensure that some desired result occurs but also to ensure that the actor causes that result.

Robert Goodin says that to care about someone typically means not just that you desire that her life go well but that you also want to help cause her life to go well. There is something strange about the idea of being concerned with someone else's welfare but being indifferent to whether one's own actions make any difference to her welfare.[38]

Can this point be extended to voting? Suppose voting for A will greatly benefit the citizens at large. Suppose I know also that A is likely to win—most people recognize that A is a better candidate than B. If I evaluate my action solely on its expected utility (in generating electoral outcomes), I have no good grounds for voting. However, we might argue that citizens should be public-spirited. They should not merely desire that good electoral outcomes occur; rather, they should try to make them occur.

So consider the Agency Argument:

Agency Argument:

1. (Given that you are a citizen,) you should be a good citizen.
2. In order for you to be a good citizen, it is not enough that good electoral outcomes occur. Rather, in addition, you should help cause those outcomes.
3. Therefore, you should vote.

I will assume premise 1 is true for the sake of argument. Premise 2 is problematic. Why should we believe that citizens should each help cause electoral outcomes?

Consider a clear case where it is important not merely that a good thing happens but that I cause it to happen. Consider a version of the Agency Argument, applied to the case of parenting:

1. (Given that I am a parent,) I should be a good parent.
2. In order to be a good parent, it is not enough that one's child be well cared for. Instead, one needs to cause or be among the causes of the child's being well cared for.
3. Therefore, I should care for my child or otherwise provide for his care.

That I should *cause* my son to be well cared for is clear. The reason, from a moral standpoint, is that *I owe him a duty of care.* I have a preexisting obligation to make sure that he is well cared for. Arguably, this duty is not discharged unless I am sufficiently causally responsible for his welfare. For example, if I were to abandon him, but his mother provided excellent care in my absence, I would fail to discharge my duties as a father.

In the case of parenting, the Agency Argument does not *prove* that I have a duty to care for my son. Rather, it *presupposes* this duty. Premise 2 is true only because the conclusion (3) is true. If someone were to offer the Agency Argument as proof that parents should care for their children, she would beg the question.[39]

So there is a worry that the Agency Argument begs the question when applied to voting. Consider premise 2 of the Agency Argument again:

2. In order for you to be a good citizen, it is not enough that good electoral outcomes occur. Rather, in addition, you should help cause those outcomes.

The best explanation for why I would have a duty to be causally responsible for electoral outcomes is that I have a duty to vote. So it looks like this argument begs the question.

To avoid begging the question, an alternative formulation of the Agency Argument might make premise 2 broader:

1. You should be a good citizen.
2. In order for you to be a good citizen, it is not enough that other citizens obtain adequate levels of welfare and live under a reasonably just social order. Rather, in addition, you need to be an agent who helps to cause other citizens to have these adequate levels of welfare, etc.
3. In order to do this, you must vote.
4. Therefore, you must vote.

In this version, the Agency Argument does not beg the question. However, now premise 3 looks questionable. Even if we grant premise 2—that as a citizen you owe it to other citizens to cause them to have adequate levels of welfare, etc., it is not obvious why you must vote in order to do this. Prima facie, voting appears unnecessary to discharge the duty described in premise 2. You could discharge the duty described in premise 2 in any number of ways besides voting. So, at best, this argument is incomplete—we need a subargument for premise 3. At this point, if someone offered the alternative formulation of the Agency Argument, we would not have reason to accept the conclusion until she offered some defense of premise 3. However, in the next chapter, I show that no such defense can be provided. Premise 3 is false. So for now we can regard the Agency Argument as at best potentially showing there is a duty to vote, but in the next chapter, I show it does not succeed.

THE PUBLIC GOODS ARGUMENT

Lomasky and Brennan say the most common justification for a duty to vote is the Generalization Argument (an argument they reject):

> What if everyone were to stay home and not vote? The results would be disastrous! Therefore, I (you/she) should vote.[40]

This commonsense argument gropes toward a kind of Kantian reasoning. Kant's moral theory claims that we should act only on those plans of action which we could consistently will that everyone act on (in relevantly similar contexts). If we assume for the sake of argument that universal abstention would be disastrous, then we cannot rationally will that everyone act on maxims such as "I won't vote" or "I won't vote unless doing so generates significant expected utility." Does that mean I should vote? Of course, using Kant's first formulation of the categorical imperative the right way is tricky. So finding the proper way to turn this commonsense argument into a good one will be hard, if possible at all.

It would be bad if no one voted, but that does not imply that everyone should vote. Lomasky and Brennan draw a parallel example: it would be bad if no one farmed, but that does not imply that everyone should farm.[41]

Many activities are strategic from a moral point of view. Sometimes, what I ought to do depends on what others do. For instance, I have a moral duty to provide food for my son. Right now I discharge that duty by buying food from supermarkets. I can discharge my duty this way only because I can count on others to grow food and offer it for sale. If no one else farmed, it would become morally imperative that I find other ways of obtaining food. I would owe it to my son to give up my job as a college professor and instead learn to hunt, scavenge, and garden. However, because I can reliably count on others to farm, I have no obligation to produce food on my own. (Note that I am not free-riding on the provision of food. I do not steal it. Rather, I offer services in exchange for cash and cash in exchange for food.)

On the other hand, suppose we live in a just political regime. The regime provides public goods, such as roads. The rest of you pay your taxes. I might think, "My taxes won't be missed. The roads will still be provided. My contribution is negligible. So I won't pay." If I do not pay, I free-ride on the provision of public goods. For me to enjoy the roads without paying my fair share is unfair. Similarly (to use another example of Lomasky and Brennan's), if everyone else observes a norm of not walking over a newly seeded lawn, I might be able to walk over it as I please without causing any noticeable damage. By doing that, however, I free-ride on others' restraint. We all get to enjoy the new lawn, but it is unfair for me not to bear part of the cost of the lawn (by having to walk around it) that the rest of you bear.

Lomasky and Brennan respond to the question, "But what if nobody did it?" by pointing out that there are two kinds of activities. For some activities—such as being a farmer—it is morally important that *enough* people do them, not that everyone does them. (In fact, it would be bad if everyone farmed, because that would take time away from other valuable pursuits and lower the standard of living.) For other activities, such as paying taxes for public goods, avoiding littering, or keeping off the lawn, it is morally important that everyone do them, not just that a certain number of people do them. With this distinction in hand, Lomasky and Brennan then ask the defender of the duty to vote to show them that voting is the second kind of activity, not the first.

How could someone show that voting is the second kind of activity? Suppose we could show voting is morally equivalent to paying taxes for public goods. A well-functioning democracy is a public good.[42] As with other public goods, at least under normal circumstances,[43] it is immoral to free-ride on their provision. This insight leads to the Public Goods Argument for voting.[44]

The Public Goods Argument:

1. Good governance is a public good.
2. No one should free-ride on the provision of such goods. Those who benefit from such goods should reciprocate.
3. Citizens who abstain from voting free-ride on the provision of good governance.
4. Therefore, each citizen should vote.

Lomasky and Brennan claim that the Public Goods Argument misunderstands voting. They claim that abstaining from voting is not like failing to pay taxes but more like choosing to be a dentist rather than a farmer.[45] They claim that voting is the kind of activity where it is morally important that enough people do it but not that everyone does it. So they dispute premise 3 of the Public Goods Argument. They claim that nonvoters do not free-ride on the provision of good governance any more than I (working as a philosopher) free-ride on the provision of food (by farmers). While I agree with Lomasky and Brennan that the Public Goods Argument fails *for this very reason*, I think their response to it is inadequate. So, for the rest of this section, I explain their objections and then respond on the Public Goods Argument's behalf. In the next chapter, I provide a better explanation of why premise 3 is false.

If you benefit from an activity others perform, but do not perform that activity yourself, how do you know whether you are free-riding on that activity? Lomasky and Brennan suggest that someone free-rides on others' activity when she benefits from that activity, abstains from doing the activity herself, and her abstention imposes a differential burden on those who continue with the activity.[46] For example, if you pay taxes for national defense and I do not, then while we both enjoy national defense, you are rendered worse off by having to pay for defense, while I am not. And, as more and more people stop paying taxes, the burden on those who continue to pay increases. In contrast, when Farmer John stops farming, this does not typically impose a greater farming burden on the remaining farmers. On the contrary, it *benefits* the remaining farmers, because it reduces the competition they face and thus raises their profits.

Lomasky and Brennan argue that failing to vote is more like retiring from farming than like failing to pay taxes. If one voter abstains, this lowers the size of the electorate. Lomasky and Brennan conclude that abstention benefits rather than hurts other citizens, because it decreases the competition they face. If I do not vote, your vote counts more. My abstention increases the probability that your vote will be decisive and you will get your way.

It is not clear that this is an adequate response to the Public Goods Argument. If I abstain, I do not necessarily compensate the remaining voters by increasing their electoral effectiveness. If I tend to vote for the Prosperity Party, then, by abstaining, I make it (very) slightly more likely that the Tradition Party will win. Prosperity Party voters now have more power as individuals, but, at the same time, the chances that they will get their way have diminished rather than increased. Though as individuals they now have more power, as a group they have less, and their success depended on their power as a group.

If the point of voting should be to provide good governance (in a later chapter, I argue this is so), then whether my choice to abstain compensates fellow citizens depends on the quality of the remaining voters relative to me. Suppose Charles is active-minded, self-critical, highly educated in philosophy and the social sciences, well informed about current events, and votes for the public interest rather than narrow self-interest. If he decides not to vote, this makes it more likely that relatively ignorant, misinformed, immoral, or irrational people will decide the electoral outcome.[47] On the other hand, if David Duke abstains, we can be glad he thus increases the electoral effectiveness of other voters. To summarize: the choice to abstain compensates others (by increasing their probability of being decisive) only if increasing their probability of being decisive benefits them.

There is another reason to worry about Lomasky and Brennan's claim that abstaining automatically compensates other voters. Many people (e.g., deliberative democrats) who think there is a duty to vote hold that everyone ought to be adequately conscientious, rational, and well informed in how they vote. Suppose that the majority of voters in the last election were adequately conscientious, rational, and well informed. Lomasky and Brennan agree that being conscientious, rational, and well informed about politics takes significant investments of time and effort. If I abstain, I increase the probability that these other good voters will be decisive. However, they had to undertake some significant costs in becoming good voters. Many philosophers think it is plausible that by abstaining I free-ride on the good governance these other voters provide. While my abstention makes it easier for voters to provide good governance (because it removes the threat that I will vote badly), they might complain that it is unfair that I did not do my part in providing good governance. It is not clear that I have compensated them for their investments of effort and time simply by increasing the expected utility of their individual votes. Of course, this argument works only to the extent that real voters are conscientious, well informed, and rational. So Lomasky and Brennan might be able to claim that if others are voting badly, then the Public Goods Argument cannot show that you have a duty to vote. However, if others are voting well, then Lomasky and Brennan have not shown us that we do not similarly have a duty to vote well. We all benefit from good governance, but the good voters had to suffer costs in providing it, while (it appears) I get it for free.

Lomasky and Brennan have not yet refuted the Public Goods Argument. In the next chapter, I refute the Public Goods Argument by showing that citizens can avoid free-riding on the provision of good governance without themselves directly providing for good governance.

ARGUMENTS FROM VIRTUE

Previous sections involved arguments about what we owed each other and ourselves. In this section, we consider arguments relying on what it takes to be virtuous or to lead a worthwhile life.

One way to argue for a duty to vote, or least to argue that failing to vote shows a deficiency of character, comes from virtue ethics. Consider the simple Civic Virtue Argument:

The Civic Virtue Argument:

1. Civic virtue is a moral virtue.
2. Civic virtue requires voting.
3. Therefore, citizens who do not vote thereby exhibit a lack of civic virtue and are to that extent morally vicious.

Premises 1 and 2 are widely shared. They seem commonsensical. And so, it seems as if we have a quick and easy argument to show that abstention is morally subpar.

Notice that this argument, as presented, does not conclude that there is a duty to vote. We could easily modify it to generate that conclusion, but virtue theorists often worry that other moral theorists place too much weight on duty. Perhaps we do not really need to show that there is a duty to vote. Rather, maybe all we need to show is that there is something subpar about the character of the nonvoter.

In parallel, in the field of environmental ethics, there are a variety of attempts to respond to Richard Sylvan's Last Man thought experiment.[48] Sylvan asks you to imagine that you are the last person alive. Somehow, you know that no other sentient beings (including animals) will inhabit Earth ever again. Next to you is the last remaining redwood tree.

A thought occurs to you—you could destroy it, just for fun, or for no reason at all.

Sylvan then asks us to consider if it there is something wrong with destroying the tree. Many people have a gut reaction that there is. Still, they are at a loss to explain why, because most people tend to think that we can owe obligations only to other humans or to sentient animals. By hypothesis, destroying the tree will not cause any suffering or pain. So, what is wrong with destroying it, if anything? This question has led many environmental ethicists to explore the idea that we can owe duties to nonsentient beings.

Another alternative, though, is not to argue that it is wrong to destroy the redwood but simply to argue that anyone who would be willing to do so lacks good character. Perhaps we have no duty to preserve the tree—it is not, strictly speaking, wrong to destroy it—but a person who would destroy a majestic redwood for sheer enjoyment or for no reason at all must be to some extent morally vicious. Thomas Hill Jr. has a paper arguing that *the kind of person who would do such a thing would almost always be someone of bad character, even though the action is not wrong*.[49]

Similarly, we could just argue that civic virtue is a significant moral virtue (which most people will grant) and then argue that failing to vote shows a lack of civic virtue (which most people will also grant). It follows that failing to vote shows some deficiency of moral character, even if, strictly speaking, abstaining is not wrong. One can show a deficiency of character even when one does not violate any duties. For example, suppose a colleague's child dies. I go through the normal motions of consoling him. I buy flowers. I tell him, sincerely, that I will provide any help he requests. Still, I do not feel any actual sympathy for him. Here, my failure to sympathize implies I have some moral deficiency, even though I have discharged all my duties toward him.

However, because this chapter is about searching for arguments in favor of a duty to vote, here is a second version of the Civic Virtue Argument.

The Modified Civic Virtue Argument:

1. You ought to have moral virtue and perform those activities necessary for virtue.
2. Civic virtue is a moral virtue.
3. Therefore, you ought to perform those activities necessary for civic virtue.
4. Civic virtue requires voting.
5. Therefore, you ought to vote.

In both the modified and the original version of the Civic Virtue Argument, the key premise is this: "Civic virtue requires voting." In the next chapter, I refute both versions of the Civic Virtue Argument by showing that this premise is incorrect. It relies on a widely held but nonetheless mistaken conception of civic virtue.

Note that it might in fact be the case that all or most actual nonvoters choose not to vote as a result of a character deficiency. Even if so, this would not necessarily vindicate the Civic Virtue Argument. Suppose it turned out that all nonvoters are cowards and are indifferent to the welfare of others, and this causes them to refrain from voting. In that case, they would indeed lack good character. However, this allows that one could still have good character and not vote. To succeed, the Civic Virtue Argument requires that civic virtue is intimately connected to voting, much as integrity is intimately connected to standing up for one's principles. That is where the argument is mistaken. In the next chapter, I argue that there is no such intimate connection between civic virtue and voting.

CHAPTER TWO

Civic Virtue without Politics

> The duties of citizenship will not necessarily drag us out
> of private life into politics, administration, or philan-
> thropy, though it may well be that everyone ought at
> least to be prepared to participate in such functions if
> the occasion should arise.
> —Bernard Bosanquet, *Aspects of the Social Problem*
> (1895)

THREE ARGUMENTS FOR VOTING

THE PRECEDING CHAPTER left us with three arguments on behalf of a duty
to vote: the Agency Argument, the Public Goods Argument, and the Civic
Virtue Argument.

The Agency Argument held that citizens should bear some causal responsibility in helping to produce and maintain a just social order with
adequate levels of welfare. The Agency Argument asserts that voting is
necessary to do this.

The Public Goods Argument holds that nonvoters unfairly free-ride
on the provision of good governance. Failing to vote is like failing to pay
taxes—it places a differential burden on others who do the hard work of
providing good government.

The Civic Virtue Argument holds that voting is an essential way to
exercise civic virtue, and civic virtue is an important moral virtue.

In this chapter, I outline a theory of civic virtue and of paying debts to
society. (It is only an outline, not everything there is to say about civic
virtue but enough to make my argument.) On my view, commonsense
and popular philosophical theories of civic virtue are overly political.
They fail to recognize that there is a division of labor in how civic virtue
is and should be exercised in liberal democratic societies. Because much
of this chapter is about explaining my theory of civic virtue, I postpone
discussing the issue of voting; however, at the end of the chapter, I return
to the three arguments and show why they fail.

The most popular views of civic virtue hold that active political participation and community-based volunteering are essential to civic virtue. In

this chapter, I argue instead that a person of exceptional civic virtue can exercise civic virtue through stereotypically private activities and need not participate in politics at all.

Toward a Liberal Theory of Civic Virtue

I defend the *extrapolitical conception* of civic virtue. According to the extrapolitical conception, political participation is not necessary for the exercise of civic virtue. Citizens can have exceptional civic virtue despite disengagement with politics. Most ways to exercise civic virtue in contemporary liberal democracies do not involve politics, or even activities on the periphery of politics, such as community-based volunteering or military service.[1]

In contrast, the most popular conception of civic virtue holds that active political participation is essential to civic virtue. This conception is rooted in civic humanism and civic republicanism.[2] Though most people are not republicans, the commonsense conception of civic virtue more or less is the republican conception. Republicans claim civic virtue requires heavy, active political participation, including but not limited to voting.[3] For instance, Adrian Oldfield says that citizenship on the republican model is "a practice or activity . . . underpinned by an attitude of mind" and demonstrated by "public service of fairly specific kinds," including military service, political deliberation and participation, and raising children to participate in politics.[4]

The republican conception of civic virtue is so dominant that the extrapolitical theory of civic virtue might seem paradoxical. Claiming that civic virtue need not involve politics might appear to be a contradiction in terms. It is not a contradiction, though. We should distinguish between the political virtues and the civic virtues more generally.[5] The degree to which civic virtue requires political engagement should be something we investigate, not something we stipulate.

In liberal societies, there are many ways to be a good citizen. Some of these ways are the stereotypical republican ones: voting well, campaigning, pushing for institutional improvements, or engaging in national, military, or political service. But many activities stereotypically considered private, such as being a conscientious employee, making art, running a for-profit business, or pursuing scientific discoveries, can also be exercises of civic virtue. For many people, in fact, these are better ways to exercise civic virtue.

The impact of this theory of civic virtue is threefold. It shows that there may be more civic virtue among citizens than theorists have realized; that, insofar as we think of citizens as having debts to pay to society, there are many ways to pay these debts; and that common arguments for political participation are misguided.

WHAT "CIVIC VIRTUE" LEAVES OPEN

In this section, I argue that political participation is not built into the concept of civic virtue. Whether political participation is necessary for the exercise of civic virtue is an open question and one not settled by the concept of civic virtue. I illustrate this point by examining a number of definitions of "civic virtue" offered by philosophers and political theorists.

Concept versus Conception

The distinction between the *concept* of something and various *conceptions* of it is now familiar. For example, Rawls says that assigning rights and duties and determining the proper distributions of benefits and burdens are built into the concept of justice.[6] Different conceptions (theories) of justice—utilitarian, liberal, communitarian, etc.—disagree about what the various duties, rights, and distributions are, but they are each conceptions of justice because they each concern Rawls's two points.

Similarly, David Schmidtz says that giving people their due is built into the concept of justice.[7] If you are not talking about giving people their due, you aren't talking about justice. Again, different theorists hold different conceptions of justice. They disagree about what people are due, though they recognize that justice is about what people are due. You cannot resolve their disagreements simply by appealing to the concept of justice—the concept of justice leaves open which conception of justice is best.

Take the distinction between concept and conception over to the realm of civic virtue. What is built into the concept of civic virtue? On what issues may different conceptions disagree while still being conceptions of civic virtue?

Defining "Civic Virtue"

Most central to the concept of civic virtue is this: civic virtue makes one a good member of a community. The concept of civic virtue settles that much.[8] Different conceptions of civic virtue offer different accounts of what it takes to be a good member of a community.

Here are some definitions of civic virtue that other theorists have offered, as they attempt to articulate more fully what's built into the concept of civic virtue. Shelley Burtt defines "civic virtue" as the "disposition to further public over private good in action and deliberation."[9] Richard Dagger uses this same definition in his defense of republican liberalism.[10] William Galston defines a civic virtue as "a trait that disposes its possessors to contribute to the well-being of the community and enhances their ability to do so."[11] Jack Crittenden says that to be "civic-minded" is to "care about the welfare of the community (the commonweal or *civitas*) and not simply about [one's] own individual well-being."[12] Geoffrey Brennan and Alan Hamlin analyze civic virtue as being able to determine the common good and having the motivation to act appropriately toward it.[13] There seems to be consensus that civic virtue is best understood as being something like the disposition and ability to promote the common good (of the relevant community) over purely private ends.[14]

We could of course press certain objections against these definitions or ask difficult questions about them.[15] For instance, we could ask whether virtues are best understood as dispositions. We can ask whether the person of civic virtue is concerned to promote the common good of the local community, the nation-state, or the entire world. We can ask exactly how much public-spiritedness is sufficient for civic virtue. These are worthy topics, but I do not explore them at length here. Answering these questions will not help us decide between the extrapolitical and the republican conceptions of civic virtue. So we can take the answers to these questions as neutral to the dispute at hand.

None of these definitions imply, simply as a matter of logic, that civic virtue requires political participation. If civic virtue requires political participation, this is an interesting, substantive philosophical claim rather than a tautology. To say that justice requires that we give people their due is a tautology, but to say that justice does or does not require free speech is an interesting, substantive philosophical claim. Likewise, to say that civic virtue makes you a good member of a community is a tautology, but to say that civic virtue does or does not require political participation is an interesting, substantive claim.

Still, many seem just to assume that civic virtue requires political participation. For instance, almost immediately after Dagger says that civic virtue is the disposition to further public over private good, he concludes that a person of civic virtue will want to participate in government in order to help maintain the liberties needed for a good society.[16] Later, after emphasizing again that civic virtue concerns promoting the common good, Dagger concludes that a *real* citizen will thus take an active part in public life.[17] Dagger seems to claim repeatedly that if civic virtue is about promoting the common good, this rather straightforwardly means that civic virtue requires significant political engagement.[18]

Similarly, Crittenden says, "Civic education, whenever and however undertaken, prepares people of a country, especially the young, to carry out their roles as citizens. Civic education is, *therefore*, political education or, as Amy Gutmann describes it, 'the cultivation of the virtues, knowledge, and skills necessary for political participation."[19] Notice the "therefore" in Crittenden's quotation. Crittenden thinks that carrying out one's role as a citizen more or less *just is* participating in politics. This point seems uncontroversial to him and probably to most people.

Dagger, Crittenden, and others make such inferences too quickly. Their definitions of civic virtue leave open what exactly the civic virtues are. These definitions leave open whether civic virtue requires (significant or any) political participation or the skills necessary for political participation. They also leave open whether everyone ought to exercise civic virtue in the same way, or whether some people should have one subsidiary set of civic virtues while others should have a different set.

Many agree that to exercise civic virtue requires that one engage in activities that contribute to the common good of the community. This prompts a question: what activities contribute to the common good? Even after one settles on some normative account of the common good, it requires further investigation to determine which traits best contribute to the common good, whether it is best if everyone contributed to the common good through politics, and whether everyone ought to contribute to the common good in similar ways. Determining the answers to such questions cannot be done by definition or stipulation. One should not simply assume that the only or best way for each citizen (or most citizens) to contribute is through political involvement, or even through other stereotypically "civically minded" activities, such as volunteering or military service.

There is a gap between the uncontroversial conceptual claim that civic virtue involves the disposition to promote the common good and the substantive claim that civic virtue requires citizens to promote the common good through political participation. If one wants to defend the view that civic virtue is tightly linked to political participation, more work must be done.[20] In the next section, I argue instead that the common good is often best promoted through extrapolitical means, through activities that do not fit the stereotype of civic virtue. Exercising civic virtue need not involve politics. Being an exceptional citizen need not involve *any* political participation.

The Common Good

If the republican and I dispute what it takes to promote the common good, this might be due to differences in our conceptions of the common good. Here, I provide a brief account of what I take the common good to be. I say more in chapter 5, including whether my theory of voting ethics depends on my conception of the common good.

In my view, something is presumed to be in the common good if it promotes the interests of most people either without harming others' interests or, if it does harm them, without exploiting them.[21] I do not assume there is some common good over and apart from the interests of individuals in society. I certainly do not assume that political participation is good for its own sake or is constitutive of a flourishing life, but then, neither do most republicans. On my view, promoting the common good will tend to mean advancing the interests of community members by helping to provide and maintain the background institutions, social practices and norms, economic and social conditions, and public goods (such as police protection and roads) under which people are likely to have good lives.

This rough characterization of the common good is going to seem controversial to some, in particular to some (but not most) of the republicans whose model of civic virtue I am arguing against.[22] Some republicans' arguments for political participation rely on more controversial notions of the common good that liberals and even other republicans would be inclined to reject.[23]

One might worry that the only reason I can argue for a nonpolitical conception of civic virtue is that I rely on an individualistic conception of the common good. One might think that if the common good stands over and apart from individual interests, or is not reducible to the aggregate of such interests, then this would vindicate the republican concept of civic virtue over mine. In the next section, I argue this is not so. The extrapolitical conception of civic virtue does not depend on any particular conception of the common good.

"Schlivic" Virtue versus Civic Virtue

Suppose someone rejects these definitions of civic virtue and rejects the conception I offer below. Suppose one pounds that table and insists that to exercise civic virtue, by definition, requires significant political engagement.

I take it that civic virtues make one a good community member. If one insists that civic virtue requires political engagement simply as a matter of logic, my response is that that one can be a good community member by engaging in public-spirited nonpolitical activity. A public-spirited person who promotes the common good through nonpolitical means might lack civic virtue but instead have "schlivic" virtue. Schlivic virtue is the disposition and ability to promote the common good by nonpolitical activity.

So, not much is gained by insisting that civic virtue requires political engagement as a matter of logic. If one insists that it is not an open question whether civic virtue involves political engagement, this just implies that it is an open question whether good citizens should have civic virtue, schlivic virtue, or some combination of the two.

The Extrapolitical Conception of Civic Virtue

In this section, I outline the extrapolitical theory of civic virtue and argue that it is superior to the republican view. I also articulate part of an account of how citizens can pay their debts to society, so as to avoid free-riding on the good governance provided by other citizens.

Note that my purpose is simply to explain how we should best understand civic virtue. I do not attempt to argue here that civic virtue is particularly important or valuable, or that everyone should have civic virtue as I describe it. (The question of what civic virtue *is* is more fundamental than the question of how important it is.) I do not argue that pursuing the common good is more important than, say, pursuing justice (insofar as these pursuits come apart) or pursuing private ends for private reasons. Once we are clear on what civic virtue is, we can ask how important it is, but that is a separate, secondary task.[24] I see us as not yet able to undertake this secondary task because we have been working with an incorrect conception of civic virtue.

The Public Goods Argument relies on something like the notion of a debt to society. The idea is that citizens receive a particular good—good government—from society, and they have an obligation to pay for that good. In contrast, the Civic Virtue Argument does not rely on the idea of debts to society but merely on what it takes to possess and exercise civic virtue.

At times I discuss what it takes to possess civic virtue. At other times, I discuss what it takes to pay one's debts to society. These are not the same thing. A person can have excellent civic virtue but, through bad luck or misfortunate, fail to pay her debts to society. For instance, imagine that a recent college graduate sets out to promote the common good but is killed in a car accident before she does any good. In this case, she had civic virtue but perhaps failed to pay her debts. Alternatively, a person might pay her debts, but lack civic virtue. For instance, imagine a politician has done much to promote the common good but did so out of a lust for power rather than out of concern for his fellow citizens. In this case, she may have paid her debts to society but lacked civic virtue.

I am unsure whether citizens really do have debts to society, as opposed to particular people. Though if I am unsure whether citizens have debts to society, I do have a theory of what it takes to pay these debts. If that seems weird, consider: I am also unsure whether intelligent extraterrestrial life exists, but I am sure that nuclear weapons can kill it, if it does exist.

An Expansive Conception

The extrapolitical conception of civic virtue is an expansive conception of civic virtue. An expansive conception of civic virtue allows that stereotypically private arenas can be arenas to exercise civic virtue. A good example of this comes from the USSR. Gary Becker describes the expansive list of constitutional duties held by (i.e., imposed upon) Soviet citizens. Beyond the obvious political obligations (e.g., obeying the law, respecting others' rights), citizens were expected, in their capacities as citizens, to raise their children well, to "protect nature and safeguard its riches," to promote friendship with foreigners, and to do productive work that adds to the social surplus.[25] The USSR had an *expansive* conception of civic duty. That is, many personal activities liberals regard as beyond the purview of the state were regarded by the Soviets as obligations held in virtue of being a citizen. Activities that liberals would generally consider private were considered by the Soviets as arenas to exercise civic virtue.

Surprisingly, liberals have good reason to adopt certain aspects of the Soviet view. Of course, liberals should not adopt the entire Soviet view of civic duty—for example, that citizens hold an extensive list of obligations and that most of these obligations are to be enforced by state sanction. The USSR rejected the distinction between private and public arenas—it thought all aspects of life are political—but liberals will want to preserve some such distinction. Yet, the liberal should agree that the USSR's constitution was correct to recognize that there are many ways for citizens to contribute to the common good. Some of these ways are (what the liberal would call) political, but not all are. Some of the ways are through what the liberal considers private activities.

John Rawls says, "Society is a cooperative venture for mutual advantage."[26] Liberals view society as a positive-sum game, a web of interaction in which each participant is made better off as a result of participating. Liberal society is a partnership of private individuals pursuing largely private visions of the good. However, liberals recognize that many of these private pursuits also contribute to the common good. Individual citizens benefit from liberal society not merely because they are free to pursue their activities in peace. Rather, they benefit (sometimes directly, sometimes indirectly) from the activities of others.

The systematic effect of private citizens' pursuit of private ends is to create background conditions of wealth, opportunity, and cultural progress. Each of us does as well as we do because of the positive externalities created by an extended system of social cooperation. This extended system of cooperation explains why each of us in contemporary liberal societies has a high standard of living and easy access to culture, education, and social opportunities. We are engaged in networks of mutual benefit, and we also benefit from other people being engaged in these networks.

On a related point, Schmidtz says that "any decent car mechanic does more for society by fixing cars than by paying taxes."[27] By extension, we can add that a decent mechanic typically does more for society by fixing cars than by voting or writing senators. By fixing cars, she is helping to create and sustain the cooperative networks that promote the common good.

My point is not to deny that governments help promote and sustain the common good or to assert that extended cooperative networks do not need governmental support. Rather, just as it would be mistake to discount the role of politics in promoting the common good, it would be a mistake to discount the role of nonpolitical activities in promoting the common good.

One might say that private actions cannot benefit the common good without governmental support and regulation. Perhaps, but the converse is also true. Philosophers often use state-of-nature thought experiments to help illustrate how politics contributes to the common good. They ask us to imagine how life would go in the absence of government and conclude that life would be solitary, nasty, poor, brutish, and short. If so, then government contributes to the common good. However, we can also imagine an "inverse state of nature"—a political society that lacks private, nonpolitical activity. In the inverse state of nature, people try to gather together for public deliberation, voting, and law creation, but no one engages in private actions. In the inverse state of nature, life would also be nasty, poor, brutish, and short, because there would be no food, music, science, shelter, or art. Political activity alone does not create the common good any more than private, nonpolitical activity alone creates the common good.

How Liberal Citizens Do Their Part

Freedom of thought, freedom of association, freedom of occupation, the division of labor within firms, and the specialization of roles that evolves between firms result in society becoming an unimaginably complex web of cooperation. In a liberal society, nearly all citizens participate in the process of social construction, of creating and maintaining a society together, but not all do it directly through politics.

Consider the famous essay "I, Pencil," by Leonard Read.[28] "I, Pencil" is written as if it were the autobiography of a pencil. It describes at length

56426

all of the knowledge, skill, and labor used to produce a single pencil. Each component has to be mined, manufactured, and shipped to the factory. Countless machines and tools are used both in the final production of the pencil and in the production of its components. Read concludes, quite literally, that pencil production is so complicated that no single person on earth knows or could know how to make a pencil from scratch; and that millions of people participate in producing a single pencil, though only few of them know they are doing so. Read's second conclusion is germane to our discussion here. When you write with a pencil, you benefit from the input of millions of people around the world. Most of them have no idea that they have helped produced a pencil and that, in virtue of doing so, they are helping you write or draw. Yet the benefits of their labor and knowledge are far-reaching. This holds for most of us. We each do a small part, but our actions benefit millions. We do not simply benefit our customers or employers.

A citizen of a liberal society receives a bundle of goods: economic, cultural, social, political, and the like. Most liberal citizens contribute to the bundle others receive, but they do it in different ways. Liberalism encourages a division of labor in how citizens contribute to creating this bundle.

Some citizens provide political goods by voting, rallying, supporting causes, fighting in just wars, writing to senators, writing letters to editors, running for office, and so on. Others attempt to provide for the public welfare by volunteering or community organizing. These sorts of activities more or less exhaust the republican conception of civic virtue.

However, one can also contribute to the social surplus by working at a productive job that provides goods and services others want. One makes society more interesting, more worthwhile, by creating culture or counterculture. One promotes the common good by raising one's children well (and not just by instilling in them the democratic or political virtues). And so on.

Consider artists, entrepreneurs, small-business owners, venture capitalists, teachers, physicians, intellectuals, stock traders, stay-at-home parents, working parents, chefs, janitors, grocery clerks, and others. Each of these kinds of people in one way or another contributes to fostering a worthwhile society. They each help create the bundle of goods others in their society receive. Through their different kinds of work, they engage in the process of social construction. They help create the common good of a well-functioning liberal society, of the background conditions of opportunity and wealth that make it so that other citizens' lives go so well. Many firefighters, police, volunteers, civil servants, military members, activists, voters, and the like promote the common good, but they are not the only ones to do so.

Though good governance is a public good (i.e., a non-rivalrous, non-excludable good), it does not follow that every member of society benefiting from that good must contribute directly to it. Each citizen receives a bundle of goods from society, but this does not imply each citizen should pay for each of those goods in kind. Suppose for the sake of argument that citizens have debts to pay to society for the goods they receive. Even if so, there are many ways of paying those debts. Some citizens pay by providing good governance, others by providing good culture, and others by providing economic opportunity. Citizens who provide these other kinds of goods are not free-riding on the provision of good governance. Rather, they pay for that good with a different kind of good.

Suppose Michelangelo, Louis Pasteur, or Thomas Edison never voted, never participated in politics, never volunteered, and, by clerical error, never paid any taxes. This alone would not imply he failed to contribute to the common good. On the contrary, each contributed far more to the common good than the average political officeholder or active, participatory democrat. If Michelangelo, Pasteur, or Edison did not vote or participate in politics, this might mean that he had less than perfect civic virtue, but he might still have had extraordinary civic virtue. (This would depend in part on his motivations.) Each has done far more for the common good in virtue of focusing on his particular excellences than he would have through politics.

In his famous funeral oration, Pericles says that private actions can be harmful to the polity, but one can compensate by performing useful public service. If so, there seems to be little reason not to accept something like the inverse. Private actions can be good for the polity, and one can compensate for a lack of direct public service through socially beneficial private activity. We should not think that only people such as Pericles advance the common good. Lives other than "lives of service" serve others.

Citizens' investing time and effort into political activities can potentially come at the expense of the common good.[29] Consider, as a hypothetical case, Phyllis the Physician. Phyllis is a genius. She produces new medical breakthroughs hourly. Society may want Phyllis to contribute to the common good but not by taking time away from medicine—not even by volunteering at the local free clinic. And if Phyllis is public-spirited, she probably will not waste her time with politics. She would do more good by spending that time on medicine instead.

Phyllis's case is an extreme one, but elements of it can be generalized. Engaging in politics always has some opportunity cost, and sometimes this opportunity cost will mean that engagement produces a net loss for the common good. Getting citizens more involved in politics (or other stereotypically "civic" activities) often means getting them less involved in other activities where they would do more good. For any given citizen, when judged against what other citizens are doing and are good at doing, there will be an optimal mix of political and nonpolitical ways for her to contribute to the common good. For some citizens, this will mean heavy political engagement at the expense of other pursuits. For other citizens, it will mean complete political disengagement so as to free the citizen to pursue nonpolitical activities. For most citizens, the optimal mix will be some combination of political and nonpolitical engagement. Though each citizen might contribute in different ways, they can all exhibit the same overall degree of civic virtue.

The example of Phyllis is not intended to suggest that public-spirited citizens will engage only in those activities where their engagement has positive expected marginal utility. On the contrary, it is important that some number of citizens vote well. However, if individual citizens decided whether to vote based solely on their expected utility to the common good of their individual votes, no one would vote. There are some activities—including voting well—that are collectively beneficial to the common good even though individual inputs are not significantly beneficial. Presumably any good theory of civic virtue will need to explain when a public-spirited citizen should choose to engage in these collectively beneficial activities as opposed to individually beneficial activities. A full theory of civic virtue would solve this problem. I do not attempt to solve it here.[30] Rather, my point is to show that there are opportunity costs to the common good from having everyone participate in politics, and so we will want to balance out different ways of contributing to the common good. How best to achieve that balance is an interesting question, but if we are asking that question, we have already moved away from the republican theory of civic virtue toward the extrapolitical theory.

Indirect Contributions to Good Governance

Someone stubbornly clinging to the republican conception of civic virtue could, perhaps, insist that civic virtue is about promoting not merely the common good but the *political* part of the common good. Suppose we grant this claim. It still would not follow that citizens should promote the political part of the common good directly through political means. Even if one narrowly defined "civic virtue" as the disposition to promote political goods, this would not imply that citizens possessing civic virtue must, as a matter of logic, engage with politics. Instead, it would remain an open question whether the best way for citizens to promote the political good is to do so though political participation.

One point of the division of labor is to free people to do what they are good at or, at least, to allow them to become good at doing something useful. Suppose people need both fish and apples to live well. If Peter specializes in growing apples while Quentin specializes in catching fish, and they agree to trade, this typically allows them both to enjoy more apples and fish than they would were they working independently. Peter's specializing in apple growing *enables* Quentin to specialize in fish catching, and vice versa. Peter produces apples directly, but he indirectly contributes to the production of fish. Quentin produces fish directly, but he indirectly contributes to the production of apples.

The reason citizens can excel at their separate tasks is that the others enable them to specialize. This mutual enabling extends to politics. Those who focus on directly producing good governance receive assistance from those who provide the goods that make this focus possible (and vice versa).

Martin Luther King Jr. had exceptional civic virtue. But he could not have rallied for political reform if others had not provided food, clothing, shelter, transportation, and even much of the basic philosophy underlying his movement. Liberal society creates a system of mutually beneficial trades. One result of this network of mutual enablement is that when a citizen contributes directly to producing one kind of good, she thereby contributes indirectly to producing the others. The businessperson who directly contributes to economic opportunity can at the same time, in virtue of this contribution, indirectly contribute to good governance. The college professor who directly contributes to discovering knowledge can at the same time, in virtue of this contribution, indirectly contribute to good governance. And so on.

Thus, even if we insisted civic virtue is about promoting political goods, it would remain an open question whether citizens should promote these goods directly or indirectly. Political goods might be like most other goods (such as food, art, and technology), where it is not valuable to have every individual provide for each of them directly. For any given citizen, there will be the optimal degrees to which she should provide directly and indirectly for political goods. For some citizens, this will mean focusing on direct contributions; for others, it will mean ignoring direct contributions entirely and focusing on indirect contributions. For the vast majority, it might mean occasionally contributing directly to political goods—perhaps by voting well every few years—but most of the time leading the kind of lives we see average citizens lead.

We can grant, also, that those citizens who are not directly involved in politics might have reason to become more involved if conditions change. It does not make sense to have everyone in the military, but under the threat of invasion from a powerful foreign power, it makes sense for citizens to move from private activities to military service. Similarly, it might be that day-to-day politics requires little political activity from citizens, but unusual crises might call for more involvement.

I have argued that citizens can repay their debts to society by providing any number of goods and services in return. A citizen does not have to repay cultural goods with cultural goods or political goods with political goods; she can exchange political goods for cultural goods or economic goods for political goods. That said, I am not arguing that you can make up for murder by raising the GDP, or compensate for theft by producing nice art. When I talk about paying debts to society in this chapter, I am discussing what it takes, in general, to avoid free-riding on the bundle goods and services one receives over one's lifetime as a citizen. This is not a theory about rectificatory justice, about compensating others for the harm one has done to them or atoning for past mistakes.

Nonindividualistic Conceptions of the Common Good

I accept an individualist conception of the common good. For instance, I regard peace as being the common good because it benefits almost everyone, not because it benefits society apart from the individuals that constitute society. As I mentioned in the previous section, this is one area of dispute between some (but not all) republicans and me. At first glance, one might think that if some more strongly collectivist notion of the common good were correct, this would vindicate the republican conception of civic virtue over the extrapolitical conception. Not so.

In a recent article, Brennan and Lomasky survey a number of conceptions of the common good and of things that might be said to be in the common good. They note that there is significant agreement between liberals and republicans. For instance, both liberals and republicans can accept that certain public goods—that is, non-rivalrous, non-excludable goods like military defense—can promote the common good. They can both agree that one can promote the common good by increasing opportunities to enjoy "inherently social goods," that is, goods that can be enjoyed only with others, such as the experience of watching a Metallica concert together. They can both agree that social capital is important.

What most liberals do not accept, but some republicans do, are what Brennan and Lomasky call "strongly irreducible social goods."[31] X is said to be a strongly irreducible common good for some society S just in case X is good for S, and X's being good for S is not conditional upon S's being good for any member of S. For instance, perhaps ancient Sparta's exceptional military prowess was a strongly irreducible common good. Maintaining its military prowess impoverished the city and stunted the moral development of its citizens, but perhaps it was good for Sparta, if not for any of the Spartans. Liberals tend to think that no such strongly irreducible common goods exist. (Liberals tend to think societies are not the kinds of things that can have goods of their own.) However, even those few liberals who accept that strongly irreducible common goods exist tend to deny that such goods should form a basis of social policy, unless these goods also happen to be good for individuals. Liberals, more or less by definition, think that political policies have to be justified in terms of individual interests, not societal interests that stand apart from individual interests.

However, suppose one believes (I think mistakenly) that there are strongly irreducible common goods, that these goods ought to be pursued, and that these goods can be achieved only through politics. Even this would not imply that an extrapolitical conception of civic virtue is incorrect or that the republican conception is correct. As I have already argued, citizens who engage in nonpolitical activities can thereby indirectly promote political goods. This holds even if the common good is understood to include strongly irreducible common goods. Classical Sparta provides an obvious example of this. The Spartan citizens were able to maintain Sparta's military might only because they relied upon the helots to provide food and shelter. Even if one held that ancient Sparta's common good was its military might, it is still the case that the helots indirectly provided that might. If Sparta's soldiers had had to farm, they would not have been so mighty.

This point will probably extend to other strongly irreducible social goods. Even if those goods are produced though political action, the people who produce those goods can do so only because they are aided and enabled by those who produce other goods. Thus, it appears that my argument for the extrapolitical conception of the civic virtue does not rest upon my individualistic, aggregative conception of the common good.

Personal Costs versus Public Benefits

One reason it is easy to overlook private contributions to the common good is that such contributions are often very obviously profitable, or at least of low cost, to the contributors. Yet, there is a difference between the benefit conferred by an activity and the cost the agent bears for that activity. One cannot measure the value of a contribution by the cost of making it. Jane might spend $100 to buy a gift for Kelly that Kelly values at only $40. Or Jane might spend $10 for a gift that Kelly values at $40. Jane might spend $10 making a gift that Kelly values at $40, but Jane might have so enjoyed making the gift that she would gladly have paid $80 for the experience of making it. In each case, the value of the gift to the receiver is $40, though the cost to the giver varies.

If Luke decides to contribute to society by becoming a policeman rather than an investment banker, he will probably bear higher personal costs, given the differences in pay and risk. However, it does not follow that society gains more from Luke's choosing to become a policeman, or even that the average policeman does more good for society than the average investment banker. If Luke wants to contribute as much as possible to society, he will not search for the role that costs him the most. He will search for the role in which he will do the most good.

At the extreme, consider the soldier who "dies in vain." This soldier has sacrificed everything for his country, but that does not mean his country benefited from the sacrifice. Perhaps the average soldier has more civic virtue than the average private citizen, as shown by the soldier's willingness to accept danger for the sake of the common good. But, still, it does not follow that the average soldier does more good than the average civilian. Or, even if the average soldier does do more good, it does not follow that for any individual citizen, she will do more good as a soldier than as a civilian. The personal cost of an activity does not reliably track the public benefit it confers.

To have civic virtue requires that one be disposed to bear certain costs in order to promote the common good. That does not mean that one must actually bear these costs. Instead, one just needs to be disposed to bear them. The amount one suffers is not a reliable measure of how much civic virtue one has. One can have high degrees of civic virtue without ever having to sacrifice one's own interests on behalf of the common good. In parallel, to have parental virtue requires that one be disposed to bear certain costs in order to promote the interests of one's children. However, a dad who is properly disposed to sacrifice his interest to his children's might never have to make any such sacrifices, because they are well behaved, he enjoys parenting, and he has fortuitous financial and social circumstances. So, if we see that some citizens never bear any significant personal costs when they promote the common good, we cannot immediately infer they lack civic virtue. It might be that they are properly disposed to promote the common good, even at their personal expense, but circumstances have not required this of them.

Also, to pay your debts to society does not always require that you sacrifice your self-interest. It just requires that you provide sufficiently valuable goods and services to society in return. If you happen to enjoy providing those goods and services, then you might be able to repay your debts without ever sacrificing your self-interest. That does not change your level of debt or whether you have paid your debts. (Consider in parallel: If I owe you dinner, I repay you by taking you to dinner. If I happen to enjoy your company enough that I feel I have profited by taking you, I still repay my debt.)

There is a possible view that holds that whether citizens have paid their debts is determined not by the value of their contributions but by the costs they incur in making contributions. This view leads to some perverse results. It implies that an altruistic, ambitious, motivated person who *enjoys* politics, volunteering, working a productive job, and being a good neighbor would have to do a lot to repay her debts. Or perhaps she would have to find some publicly beneficial activity that she hates doing and do that instead, even if that activity is not as publicly beneficial as the activities she enjoys. Alternatively, consider my wife's friend Katrin. (Katrin is a pseudonym.) Katrin has had many resources invested in her, has attended excellent schools, and consumed many expensive goods over her lifetime. However, she has worked only a total of six months, part-time, in her lifetime. (She has not done much else to benefit society either.) Katrin is lazy and unmotivated. She dislikes being productive. Though she has hardly done anything, what little work and volunteering she has done, she has hated. If you thought that the way to pay your debts to society is to suffer a certain amount, then you might conclude that Katrin has paid her debts, because she has suffered enough. This seems implausible. It is more plausible to think that the way to repay your debts is not to suffer for society but to make society better off by your presence.

The Motivational Component of Civic Virtue

Civic virtue has a motivational component. One can greatly contribute to the common good but still lack civic virtue. The virtuous agent must have the right motivations about what she is doing. For instance, a person who helps others merely out a desire for personal profit is not benevolent. For a citizen to exercise civic virtue through private activities, it is not enough that she contributes to the common good. Contributing to the common good must be one of her principal goals, if not her only goal. To have civic virtue, a citizen must be disposed to promote the common good even at the expense of her self-interest. (Just how strong this disposition must be is up for debate and need not be settled here.) A person indifferent or antagonistic to the common good cannot have civic virtue, even if she in fact greatly advances the common good.[32]

So, if Michelangelo turns out to have been indifferent to making the world better for others and cared about art only for art's sake or only about getting paid, then his artistic endeavors, however valuable, would not be exercises of civic virtue. However, if in addition to his other concerns (money, fame, aesthetics, pleasure), he was significantly motivated to promote the common good of the polity, then he was acting out of civic virtue. To the extent that one's goal is to make a difference or to improve society, then one is starting to exercise civic virtue.[33] Thus, the extrapolitical conception of civic virtue implies that a wide array of publicly beneficial private activities *could* be exercises of civic virtue provided that people have the right motivations. The extrapolitical conception does not have the silly implication that anyone who promotes the common good has civic virtue.

How Demanding Is the Extrapolitical Conception of Civic Virtue?

To possess civic virtue, one needs to have a sufficiently strong motivation to promote the common good. This leaves open two kinds of questions. First, just how important is civic virtue? Should everyone have civic virtue, and just how much civic virtue should everyone have? Second, for a person to possess civic virtue, just how strong must her motivation to promote the common good be? That is, just how much of her self-interest must a person be willing to sacrifice in order to qualify as possessing civic virtue? These are important questions, and a full theory of civic virtue would answer them. Because the answers are not needed for my purposes in this chapter, though, I do not answer them here.

Readers might be tempted to conclude that the extrapolitical conception of civic virtue is not sufficiently *demanding*. A virtue or norm is demanding to the degree that it constrains and limits the options available to an agent, or to the degree that it is costly to the agent to possess the virtue or abide by the norm. For instance, hedonistic act utilitarianism is often accused of being demanding. Hedonistic act utilitarianism holds that an agent should perform the action that generates the most net pleasure for all sentient beings. This view tends to be constraining because it greatly limits the actions available to the moral agent, and it tends to be costly because it often requires agents to undertake serious sacrifices on behalf of others.

Whether the extrapolitical conception of civic virtue is demanding depends on the answers to the questions I raised earlier. On its face, the extrapolitical conception of civic virtue seems less demanding than the republican conception. After all, the extrapolitical conception opens up more ways of exercising civic virtue, and thus allows those citizens who do not enjoy politics to choose other, more enjoyable activities that contribute to the common good. So, on its face, it is a less constrained view of civic virtue. In light of giving citizens more options in how to exercise civic virtue, it also gives them the option of choosing less costly ways of exercising civic virtue.

However, suppose we do a little more moral philosophy and try to answer the questions I raised. When we answer them, we discover that citizens ought to have maximal civic virtue and that they should be prepared to undertake great sacrifices for the common good. If so, then the extrapolitical conception of civic virtue, when *combined* with these *other* claims about civic virtue, might imply that a particular citizen must be a surgeon rather than a poet, must choose to work in a poor area rather than a wealthy area, and so on. In principle, the extrapolitical conception of civic virtue could be highly demanding, even more demanding than the republican conception of civic virtue. Whether the extrapolitical conception is demanding depends on how much civic virtue is necessary to be a good person, and how much of a sacrifice one must be willing to undertake to have civic virtue. Rather than try to answer these other questions about civic virtue here, which are not necessary for the argument I want to make, I just want to show that political activity is not essential for civic virtue and that one can avoid free-riding on political goods without directly providing political goods back in turn.

That said, suppose instead we discover that civic virtue does not require a citizen continually to subvert her interests for society. (I think this conclusion is correct, though I have not argued for it here.) If so, the extrapolitical conception of civic virtue would have some attractive features, which I now discuss.

Liberal societies have the goal of helping people live together in peace and prosperity while they pursue their differing visions of the good. Liberals want to minimize the obstacles they impose on reasonable citizens in achieving their conceptions of the good and try to improve the opportunities for citizens to succeed in their pursuits.

Political participation speaks to many people—they find themselves at home there. Yet, for many, it is an alien place. They want to make a difference, but not there, and not that way. For many, politics is stressful, aversive, or simply boring. A liberal would want to avoid, as much as she can, creating institutions that require significant political engagement from all. Liberalism allows citizens the freedom to discover their own ways of making a contribution. The liberal project is, among other things, about constructing institutional frameworks under which the best way to promote one's own interest is to figure out ever better ways of increasing one's value to one's fellow citizens. But it is also about leaving people free to choose their own path.

Political philosophers, political scientists, and many other social scientists often advocate greater participation.[34] They often envision a good society as one where every citizen spends significant time deliberating about and engaging with politics. They might be right. Still, they should be suspicious, and self-critical, when they make such claims. For these so-cial theorists, politics, in one way or another, is where they feel at home. Accordingly, they should be wary of recommending everyone act in simi-lar ways, for it is easy for them to overlook how aversive politics can be to others. (If personal trainers wrote political philosophy, I suspect they would deemphasize political deliberation and instead stress the value of exercise.)[35]

My conception of civic virtue is more egalitarian than most. On my view, civic virtue is not the kind of thing exemplified by lawyers and poli-ticians. Instead, anyone can have civic virtue, even if he lacks the ability to do politics.

As Lomasky and Brennan say, "Statesmanship is no trivial calling, ei-ther with regard to the magnitude of its effect on others or the depths of expertise required for success."[36] Political participation—especially par-ticipation that helps rather than harms the common good—takes time and effort. Consider activism: to be a good activist, supporting a cause is not enough; one must support the right cause. This requires having some sig-nificant knowledge of social-scientific and philosophical matters in order to assess the cause one supports. While political science, economics, and philosophy are all worthwhile endeavors, studying them to develop even a basic level of comprehension requires serious investment.

This investment has major opportunity costs for the individual.[37] Time is scarce. Time spent developing the political virtues often is not spent on private pursuits, such as playing with one's children, working toward a college degree, learning guitar, gardening, developing artistic talent, and the like. Some citizens will of course enjoy studying and engaging in politics (in particular, the kinds of citizens who end up writing political theories arguing that everyone should study politics). For many, however, politics is loathsome, just as working as an auto mechanic or a mathema-tician is loathsome to many.

This might seem like an unfair complaint about political engagement. Yet we find republicans making even stronger claims. Oldfield says that "the practice of citizenship . . . *is* an unnatural practice for human be-ings" and agrees with Rousseau that people's "'natural' character has to be 'mutilated' before they will engage in it."[38] Oldfield approves of this mutilation but recognizes that liberals will find it repugnant. However, the liberal can respond that Rousseau's ideal of citizenship requires such mutilation only because the ideal is too narrow. A broader, more expan-sive conception like the extrapolitical theory finds room for more people without having to chop off as much of their natural selves.[39]

To live in a well-functioning liberal democracy is a great gift and some-thing citizens should be thankful for. Yet, for many citizens, what makes liberal democracies so valuable is, in part, that they do not demand everyone spend significant time participating in politics. They even permit people to opt out of politics altogether. Democratic politics is not the point of democratic politics. Ideally, a liberal democracy makes people safe enough in their status as free and equal citizens that many could freely choose to avoid politics. Liberalism embodies the hope that an average person could be unconcerned with politics—perhaps not the hope that all *will* be unconcerned, but that an average person *could* be unconcerned with little threat to her status as a free and equal citizen. Actual liberal societies fall short of their ideals, but at the same time, they do remarkably well at protecting citizens' statuses as free and equal.

The extrapolitical view of civic virtue allows liberals to respond to a criticism by J.G.A. Pocock and other communitarians. Pocock, favorably citing Polybius, says that modern liberal societies tend to undermine civic virtue by pulling people toward private ends.[40] Citizens fly homeward rather than to the assembly. In contrast, the extrapolitical theory of civic virtue shows how citizens' pursuit of private ends can also be a way to exercise civic virtue.

Modern liberalism's success is that it finds many ways of reconciling the private and common good (at least, more so than competing regimes) and so lowers the personal cost of benevolence. Liberal society is an institutional framework in which individuals can generally best serve their vision of the good by also serving others' different visions.[41] Liberal institutions try to economize on moral motivation, for example, by working with rather than against self-interest. The extrapolitical theory of civic virtue allows that citizens can choose to promote the public good in the manner they find most congenial, provided that promoting the public good is itself a strong motivation in making that choice.

Suppose we did some surveys of citizens of liberal societies and discovered that many citizens seem unconcerned about the public good. We might then reasonably wonder how much of this results from citizens' mistaken acceptance of the republican model of civic virtue. We can imagine a citizen saying, "Well, if the only way I can be a good citizen is by participating in politics, I guess I do not want to be a good citizen." That citizen might mistakenly regard herself as not caring about the common good because she has internalized the view that caring requires political engagement. Instead, she might very well care about the common good but just not want to contribute to it that particular way.

Michael Walzer asks, "What *was* citizenship?"[42] He says citizenship was possible only in classical republican societies. He contends that contemporary hand-wringing over citizenship comes from the feeling that something has been lost, because citizens seem to care so little about politics. He says this feeling of loss inspires many to try to resurrect the republican conception.[43] However, he adds that citizenship so described was not really lost, because it never really could find a home in liberal societies. Perhaps so, but this need not be because liberalism fails to encourage concern for the public good. Rather, it may be that liberalism encourages a different, more diverse, and better kind of citizenship than republican societies ever could.

Why There's No Duty to Vote

I have outlined my view of civic virtue and of how citizens do their part in liberal societies. In light of this theory, I now return to the three surviving arguments for voting and explain why they fail.

Recall the Agency Argument:

1. You should be a good citizen.
2. In order for you to be a good citizen, it is not enough that other citizens obtain adequate levels of welfare and live under a reasonably just social order. Rather, in addition, you need to be an agent who helps to cause other citizens to have these adequate levels of welfare, etc.
3. In order to do this, you must vote.
4. Therefore, you must vote.

In light of the argument made in this chapter, we can conclude that premise 3 is false. Voting is just one way among many that I, as a citizen, can be causally responsible for producing a just social order and for helping to cause other citizens to have adequate levels of welfare. So premise 3 is false because it is overly strong. Voting is not necessary to discharge the obligation described in premise 2.

Recall the Public Goods Argument:

1. Good governance is a public good.
2. No one should free-ride on the provision of such goods. Those who benefit from such goods should reciprocate.
3. Citizens who abstain from voting free-ride on the provision of good governance.
4. Therefore, each citizen should vote.

In light of the preceding discussion, it should be clear how the extrapolitical theory of civic virtue challenges this argument. Premise 3 is false. Citizens can contribute in other ways and thus not be guilty of free-riding. They can pay for the political goods they receive by providing nonpolitical goods. Moreover, providing nonpolitical goods is an indirect way of providing political goods.[44]

Suppose you are not fully on board with my account of civic virtue and of how citizens do their part. However, even if you just find it a plausible alternative, this poses a problem for the Public Goods Argument. Someone making the Public Goods Argument has the burden of proof, because she is asserting the positive claim that there is a duty to vote. So, to succeed, the defender of the Public Goods Argument needs to prove that a view like mine is wrong. She would need to show that citizens cannot pay for good governance by supplying nonpolitical goods. She needs to show that providing nonpolitical goods is not an indirect way of providing political goods. Until she shows this, she has not discharged her burden of proof.

Suppose you reject my conclusion that one can have civic virtue and pay any debts to society without participating in politics. Suppose you insist that in order to avoid free-riding on good governance, one must *directly* provide for good governance. Even then, my argument is a challenge for defenders of the duty to vote. Just as there are many ways of contributing to society without participating in politics, there are many ways of promoting good governance without voting. At best, it seems that the Public Goods Argument could derive a duty to promote good governance directly, but voting is not necessary to discharge this duty. One could run for office, make campaign contributions, or volunteer at city hall instead.

Consider again the Civic Virtue Argument:

1. Civic virtue is a moral virtue.
2. Civic virtue requires voting.
3. Therefore, citizens who do not vote thereby exhibit a lack of civic virtue and are, to that extent, morally vicious.

This argument relies upon something like the republican conception of civic virtue. But in light of the preceding discussion, it should be clear how the extrapolitical theory of civic virtue challenges this argument. Premise 2 is incorrect. Citizens can exercise civic virtue in any number of ways besides voting.

The defender of the Civic Virtue Argument needs to show not merely that voting can be an exercise of civic virtue, but that failing to vote is, in almost all cases, a failure of civic virtue. She has not shown this. And, as with the Public Goods Argument, she bears the burden of proof.

Note that even if I were incorrect in claiming that one can exercise civic virtue through nonpolitical means, much of this chapter would still pose a problem for the Civic Virtue Argument. I have been emphasizing the importance of the division of labor in how citizens promote the common good. So suppose you insist that civic virtue requires political engagement.

(You reject my claims that public-spirited citizens need not provide political goods and that they can provide them indirectly.) Even so, it is one thing to show citizens ought to engage in politics or that doing so is necessary for civic virtue but another to show that they have to do it in any particular way. Perhaps there is a division of labor in how citizens should best directly provide political goods. Some citizens can exercise civic virtue through writing letters to editors, others through activism, others through political philosophizing, and others through voting.

Revisiting the Straw Man Argument

We have examined a variety of arguments in favor of there being a general duty to vote. The most plausible arguments relied upon ideas of doing one's part and civic virtue. Yet, in this chapter, I have shown that they relied on mistaken ideas of civic virtue.

I attacked three arguments for voting in this chapter. They suffered from many of the failings of the Straw Man Argument. The arguments ignored that there is some opportunity cost in voting, especially in voting well. Public-spirited citizens who want to do the most good sometimes can do more good by disengaging with politics and pursuing some other activity. Also, the underlying duties that might ground a duty to vote—such as duties of beneficence or reciprocity—could plausibly be discharged in ways other than by voting. It is easy to show that voting can be a public-spirited act. But it is hard to show that voting is morally mandatory or necessary for civic virtue.

I cannot advance a general nonexistence proof of a duty to vote. However, the argument in this chapter has the potential to undermine a wide range of arguments for a duty to vote besides those I examined here. Many arguments for voting rely upon the idea of "doing one's part," but they fail to recognize just how many different ways there are to do one's part. In general, arguments for a duty to vote are based on underlying duties of beneficence, fairness, or reciprocity, but these underlying duties can be discharged in ways other than voting.

It is consistent with my view to hold that, under special circumstances, a duty to vote might arise. I have not argued that there can never be a duty to vote. Instead, I have argued that a citizen in a modern democratic polity generally has no civic duty to vote, or even to participate in politics.

A final word on nonvoters: as a matter of fact, most people believe that there is a duty to vote. Consequently, when you discover that a person abstains from voting, this information gives you some defeasible reasons to suspect that she lacks certain admirable character traits. Most people subscribe to the folk theory of voting ethics. So, when you learn that a person chooses not to vote, you have some reason to presume that she believes she has a duty to vote but has chosen not to abide by that duty. Even if a person in fact lacks a duty to X, if she believes she has a duty to do X but does not do it, this can be evidence of bad character. Even though I think there is no duty to vote, I suspect that most people who abstain do so either because it is too costly for them, given their circumstances, or because they have somewhat deficient character.

It is also consistent with my view to hold that for some citizens, voting, even if it is not obligatory, is at least a good idea, morally speaking. Suppose it would be easy for you to vote well (as described in the next few chapters). You are already well informed and rational and have a justified belief about what it takes to promote the common good. It would be of no great cost to you to vote; you do not have some pressing prior obligation or activity. If so, voting seems like a good idea (if you will vote well), even if strictly speaking it is not required.

The folk theory of voting ethics holds that in general, citizens should vote rather than abstain. This claim has not withstood scrutiny. In the next few chapters, I attack a different part of the folk theory. I argue that, while citizens have no duty to vote, if they do vote, they must vote well. In fact, they have a duty to abstain rather than vote badly.

CHAPTER THREE

Wrongful Voting

IN THIS CHAPTER, I argue that citizens have an obligation not to vote badly. They should abstain rather than pollute democracy with bad votes.

I use "bad voting" as a term of art. By "bad voting," I do not mean "the kind of voting that by definition one ought not to do." So, when I say people ought not vote badly, I say something interesting and substantive, rather than something trivial and tautological. I am concerned with two kinds of bad voting, which I label "unexcused harmful voting" and "fortuitous voting."

Unexcused harmful voting occurs when a person votes, without epistemic justification, for harmful polices or for candidates likely to enact harmful policies. (I discuss what it means for policies to be harmful more in depth in chapter 5.) For example, a person who votes to ban gay marriage because she finds it disgusting would, except in extraordinary circumstances, be guilty of harmful voting. This kind of voting is collectively, not individually, harmful, because individual votes have insignificant expected utility or disutility. *Fortuitous voting* occurs when citizens vote for what are in fact beneficial policies or candidates likely to enact beneficial policies, but they lack sufficient justification to believe that these policies or candidates are good. In other words, fortuitous voting occurs when a person makes the right choice for the wrong reasons or for no reason at all. For example, suppose David Duke mistakenly believes that (someone who is in fact a good) candidate will impose racist policies, and so Duke votes for that candidate. In this case, Duke voted for the right person, but for the wrong reasons. I argue Duke should abstain instead.

The arguments for why harmful voting and fortuitous voting are wrong are slightly different. I first explain why there is a moral duty not to engage in harmful voting and then explain why there is a moral duty not to engage in fortuitous voting. If I am wrong about one, I might still be right about the other. The upshot is that people have to be justified in believing that the candidates or policies they vote for will promote the common good.

Irresponsible individual voters ought to abstain rather than vote badly. This thesis may seem antidemocratic. Yet it is really a claim about voter responsibility and how voters can fail to meet this responsibility. On my view, voters are not obligated to vote, but if they do vote, they owe it to others and themselves to be adequately rational, unbiased, just, and informed about their political beliefs. Similarly, most of us think we are not obligated to become parents, but if we are to be parents, we ought to be responsible, good parents. We are not obligated to become surgeons, but if we do become surgeons, we ought to be responsible, good surgeons. We are not obligated to drive, but if we do drive, we ought to be responsible drivers. The same goes for voting. Political virtue is hard.

My view contrasts with those who think we have no obligations regarding voting; we are obligated to vote, but any or nearly any vote is acceptable; we must vote well; and (the comparatively rare view that) we ought not vote at all.

Unexcused Harmful Voting

Harmful voting occurs when people vote for harmful or unjust policies or for candidates likely to enact harmful or unjust policies.[1] However, I am not going to argue that all such instances of harmful voting are morally wrong.

One might vote for what is in fact a harmful policy but be justified in doing so. For instance, imagine that the past two hundred years of work by thousands of epistemically virtuous, independent political scientists points toward a particular policy being good. The policy might still end up being harmful, though everyone was justified in thinking it would not be.

So, let us say that unexcused harmful voting occurs when people vote, without sufficient reason, for harmful policies or candidates likely to produce harmful policies. The label "unexcused harmful voting" sounds moralized. However, unexcused harmful voting is not by definition morally wrong. In the next section, I make a substantive argument that shows that such voting is wrong. So, when I say that voters ought not to cast unexcused harmful votes, this is a substantive claim, rather than a tautology.

One might vote for a harmful policy but not be negligent in doing so. I have compared voters to surgeons: not everyone has to be a surgeon or a voter, but if a person is a surgeon or a voter, she should be a good one. Surgeons make mistakes. Some mistakes are excusable. We do not typically blame them when they misdiagnose an unknown, extremely rare disease that has all the symptoms of a common disease. We do not hold it against a surgeon today that she is not using better techniques that will not be invented until the next century. Because she has performed properly by a reasonable standard of care appropriate to the current level of knowledge, she is not culpable. On the other hand, some mistakes result from negligence, from falling below a reasonable standard of care.

In medicine and other professions, standards of care are usually defined as what a normal, prudent practitioner would do in similar circumstances. However, note that typical quality of care from a surgeon 1,000 years ago was so low that one might reasonably claim that all surgeons at that time were culpable for doing surgery. Accordingly, this definition of a standard of care in medicine presupposes that average levels of competence are generally high. Thus, we should not use this definition of standard of care for voting—it might be that normal, prudent voters are incompetent.

Instead, voters can be said to have voted well, despite having voted for what turned out to be harmful policies, only if they have a sufficient epistemic justification for their votes. They vote well when they vote for policies or candidates who they are justified in believing will promote the common good. (In chapter 5, I explain why the common good, rather than self-interest, should be the proper target of votes. In this chapter, I take it for granted.) Otherwise, they make unexcused harmful votes when they vote without sufficient reason for harmful policies or candidates who are likely to enact harmful policies.

Rather trying to settle the exact standards for justified belief here, I leave that to be determined by the best epistemological theories. My argument then rests upon there being such a thing as unjustified political beliefs, but it need not be committed to any particular epistemology. On any reasonable epistemological view, there will be such a thing as unjustified beliefs about political matters.[2] On any reasonable epistemological view, the kinds of beliefs I use as examples of unjustified beliefs are counted as unjustified beliefs. For example, no plausible epistemological theory holds that beliefs are justified when such beliefs are based on wishful thinking, motivated reasoning, or despite overwhelming countervailing evidence.

The most common forms of unexcused harmful voting are voting from immoral beliefs, from ignorance, or from epistemic irrationality and bias. I do not mean to give a new formula for bad voting. Sometimes, as per the characterization of bad voting given here, voting on the basis of these three forms does not count as bad voting.

For an instance of voting from immoral beliefs, suppose Alex believes that blacks are inferior and should be treated as second-class citizens. This is an unjustified, immoral belief. If Alex votes for policies because he wishes to see blacks treated as inferiors, he votes badly.

As an instance of voting from ignorance, suppose Bob is *completely* ignorant about a series of propositions on a ballot. While he desires to promote the common good, he has no idea which policy would in fact promote the common good. In this case, if he votes, he votes badly.[3]

As an instance of voting from epistemic irrationality and bias, Candice votes with the goal of increasing the nation's material prosperity. However, she formed her beliefs about what stimulates economic growth via an unreliable, biased process. She finds a candidate espousing a regressive neomercantilist (i.e., imperialist, protectionist) platform emotionally appealing and votes for that candidate despite the evidence showing that the candidate's platform is inimical to the goal of creating prosperity. In this case, Candice has false means-ends beliefs on the basis of irrational belief formation processes. When she votes on these beliefs, she makes an unexcused harmful vote.

THE DUTY TO REFRAIN FROM COLLECTIVE HARMS

I argue that one has the duty not to vote on unexcused harmful beliefs because this violates a more general duty not to engage in collectively harmful activities. A collectively harmful activity is a harmful activity caused by a group or collective, where individual inputs into the harmful action are negligible. (Note: I do not define a "collectively harmful activity" as an activity that *would be* harmful *were* many people to do it.)[4] For instance, producing air pollution is a collectively harmful activity. As a group we do a lot of damage, but as individual polluters we do negligible harm.

Note that my argument relies on the empirical premise that politicians generally attempt to give people what they ask for.[5] I do not defend this premise here (though I offer citations for it in the notes).

An outline of my argument is:

1. One has an obligation not to engage in collectively harmful activities when refraining from such activities does not impose significant personal costs.
2. To cast an unexcused harmful vote is to engage in a collectively harmful activity, while abstaining imposes low personal costs.
3. Therefore, one should not cast an unexcused harmful vote.

Later in this chapter I make the argument in a more complete manner and consider various objections. I consider additional objections in the next chapter.

The duty to refrain from harmful voting is not generally grounded in the harmfulness of individual votes. As we saw in chapter 1, individual votes have vanishingly small expected utility. This means that a bad vote has vanishingly small *dis*utility.

Harmful voting is collectively, not individually, harmful. The harm is not caused by individual voters but by voters together. (In this respect, voting is unlike surgery or driving.) When I refrain from harmful voting, this does not fix the problem. Still, it is plausible that I am obligated to refrain from collectively harmful activities, even when my contribution has negligible expected cost, provided I do not incur significant personal costs from my restraint. I argue that this is the reason I ought not vote for harmful policies and candidates.

Consider, as an analogy, a thought experiment called Firing Squad:[6]

> A ten-member firing squad is about to execute an innocent child. All shots from the squad will hit the child at the same time. Each shot, by itself, would be sufficient to kill him. You have the option of joining the squad and shooting the child with the others. No one is forcing you to join the squad—you are free to walk away.

Most people have the intuition that joining the squad and participating in killing the child is wrong, even though he will die regardless of whether you shoot. Why would they think this? It is not clear that by shooting him you cause him to die. After all, he would die anyway. Still, most people have a strong intuition that it is wrong to join the squad and shoot the child. Here is one plausible explanation of why joining the squad is wrong: there is general moral prohibition against participating in these kinds of activities, even if one's individual inputs do not make a decisive difference. I wish to explore this idea in my argument against bad voting.

What does morality require of us in a collective action problem, especially in cases where we are acting in collectively harmful ways? Suppose the problem can be solved only if everyone or the vast majority of people acts differently. Morality does not require me, as an individual, to solve the problem. One reason is that I am unable to solve it. If, for example, I am in a prisoner's dilemma or a tragic commons (see appendices I and II at the end of this chapter), restraining myself from contributing to the problem fails to solve the problem. Rather, my restraint exposes me to exploitation as a sucker and can exacerbate the problem.

In some cases, I might be able to solve the problem through extraordinary personal effort. Suppose I live in a small village where everyone except me litters. If I spend ninety hours a week picking up litter, the town will be clean. Here I can solve the problem as an individual, but it is implausible to think morality requires me to do so. That I have to clean up after everyone else is too much of a burden and is unfair.

It is more plausible that morality requires something weaker. When there is a collective action problem, I do not have to solve the problem, but I should not be part of the problem, provided I can avoid being part of the problem at a low personal cost. When people are engaged in a collectively harmful activity, I should not participate in the activity, provided I can avoid participating at a low cost to myself. Morality requires me to have clean hands when the cost of having clean hands is low. We can dub premise 1 (from the preceding outlined argument) the *Clean Hands Principle*:

> One has an obligation not to engage in collectively harmful activities when refraining from such activities imposes no significant personal costs.

Recall that a collectively harmful activity is harmful activity caused by a group or collective, where individual inputs into the harmful action are negligible.

In classic prisoner's dilemmas, I cannot avoid being part of the problem. (See appendix I.) My attempt to avoid causing the problem opens me up to exploitation. Also, in cases of tragic commons, I often cannot avoid being part of the problem without incurring a high personal cost. (See appendix II.) If the only way I can feed my children is to join in exploiting a common resource others are already turning to dust, arguably I am permitted to do so. However, in the preceding firing squad example, no one is forcing me to shoot the little boy. I can walk away. I should not join in.

Unexcused harmful voting, at least when there is a lot of it, is a collectively harmful activity. (I discuss voting for fringe candidates later.) But unexcused harmful voting is not generally like a prisoner's dilemma or a tragic commons. In the prisoner's dilemma or tragic commons, for me to engage in collectively harmful behavior is individually rational. A fortiori, for me to engage in the behavior is often downright necessary. If I do not contribute to the problem, I suffer a personal disaster. But harmful voting is not like that. Refraining from harmful voting has little personal cost.

Why does morality require me not to be part of the problem, at least in cases where there is little personal cost in not being part of the problem? The principle that one should not engage in collectively harmful activities (when the cost of restraint is low) need not be grounded in any particular moral theory. It is a freestanding idea that is implied by a variety of plausible background moral theories.

For example, here is what a rule consequentialist might say about the Clean Hands Principle. Brad Hooker's sophisticated rule consequentialism holds that an action is wrong if it violates the code of norms whose internalization by the overwhelming majority of people would lead to the best consequences.[7] A pro tanto norm against engaging in collectively harmful activity when the cost of restraint is low would almost certainly form part of this code.[8] For any two codes that are otherwise identical, if one code has a requirement against engaging in collectively harmful activity when the cost of restraint is low but the other code lacks such a requirement, the first code can be expected to generate better consequences than the second. (After all, people abiding by the first code will do less frivolous pollution, will not participate in firing squads, etc.) So a norm against engaging in collectively harmful activity when the cost of restraint is low would be in the code selected by Hooker's rule consequentialism.

Kant's moral theory holds that an act is wrong if and only if it is based on a plan of action that a rational agent cannot will to be universal law. A Kantian might argue that engaging in collectively harmful behavior is not universalizeable. Imagine a maxim of the form, "I shall feel free to engage in collectively harmful behavior when there is little personal benefit to doing so." If everyone followed this maxim, it would be harmful to almost everyone. The maxim would thus fail the "contradiction in the will" test, because no rational agent would will that everyone behave according to that maxim.[9]

Eudaimonistic virtue theory holds that an action is wrong if it is not the kind of action that a virtuous agent, acting in character, would perform in that context.[10] A virtuous agent would not be willing to engage in collectively harmful activities without good reasons. Instead, only a person of defective character would participate in collectively harmful activities when the cost of restraint is low.

For illustrative purposes, I discuss at greater length how a duty to avoid engaging in collective harms could be grounded in plausible views about fairness. Consider that the problem of harmful voting is analogous in many respects to the problem of air pollution. Rita Manning asks: "Why then does it sound odd to suggest that each driver is morally obligated to control air pollution? Presumably because air pollution is not caused by any one driver and cannot be ended by the single actions of any one driver. If I were the owner of the only car in America, I could drive to my heart's content and not cause any [significant] air pollution."[11]

Of course, polluting and bad voting are not completely analogous. (The surgery and driving analogies are not perfect either.) If I am the only small-scale polluter, my pollution makes no significant difference. However, if I am the only voter, my vote makes all the difference. Still, when I am one of many bad voters or many polluters, my individual contribution is negligible, but I am nonetheless part of the problem. Yet, if I stop voting badly or polluting, the problem does not go away.

Individual drivers are part of the group causing the problem. Individual obligations derive from finding fair ways to solve the problem. Suppose pollution would be at acceptable levels if cut in half. One way to achieve this could be to require half the population not to drive, while the other half may continue to drive at its current levels with its current highly polluting cars. One could be assigned driver or nondriver status by lottery. This solution is unfair because it burdens some but not all who cause the problem. The default moral position is that everyone causing the problem should bear at least some of the burden of correcting it. More controversially, one might claim that people should bear this burden either equally or in proportion to how much they contribute to the problem, at least in the absence of countervailing conditions.

Fairness is one way to bridge the gap between collectively harmful behavior and individual action. *We* should pollute less because pollution harms us all, but *I* should pollute less because, all things being equal, it is unfair for me to benefit from polluting as I please while others suffer the burden of polluting less. Ceteris paribus, we should share the burdens of not polluting. The duty not to vote badly could follow this pattern. *We* bad voters should not vote because it is harmful to everyone, but *I*, the individual bad voter, should not vote because it is unfair that I benefit from polluting democracy as I please while others suffer the burden of polluting democracy less. Ceteris paribus, we should share the burdens of not polluting the polls.

If restraining oneself from voting caused significant personal harm, then individuals might be permitted to vote in harmful ways. In fact, such restraint does have costs. Individual voters receive various psychological payoffs from voting—it makes them feel good about themselves for a short time. If they were prohibited (by morality) from voting, they lose this payoff. However, elections decided by harmful voters mean that people have to live with racist and sexist laws, unnecessary wars, lower economic opportunities, and lower levels of welfare. The type of harm or loss of pleasure suffered by the voter from abstention seems relatively trivial compared to the type of harm suffered by the person who bears the burden of bad policy. The voter's pleasure in voting is not sufficient to counterbalance a potential duty to refrain from polluting the polls. By voting, bad voters consume psychological goods at our collective expense.

In parallel, an individual might drive a gas-guzzling Hummer to promote his self-image and get real pleasure from this activity. I do not take his pleasure to be sufficient to counterbalance the harms imposed on all by smog and global warming. This is not to say that one must never drive, or even that one may not pollute in the pursuit of pleasure. We all have reason to favor principles that allow us to lead happy lives. Rather, it is to say that at some point, the pursuit of individual pleasure is outweighed by the need to preserve the healthy environment that makes pleasurable lives possible.

There are also possible collective costs from bad voters staying home. Perhaps widespread voting produces greater social cohesion. Perhaps when bad voters vote, this tends to make them care about voting more, and this may inspire them to become better voters. I think these opportunity costs are likely to be outweighed by the benefits of reducing bad voting, but it is hard to say without something like an empirical study of the indirect positive effects of bad voting.

Another complaint is that taking democracy seriously is hard when most voters abstain from voting. Perhaps so, but it is even harder when most voters vote badly. Regardless, democracy performs better, even with low voter participation, than its competitors (oligarchy, etc.) do. So, at worst, low voter participation means we are not able to take democracy as seriously as some people would like to, but this does not mean we must replace democracy with something else.

Note that this argument allows that one might sometimes be justified in voting for the lesser of two (or more) evils. Putting Mussolini in power is harmful, but not as harmful as putting Hitler in power. We can imagine scenarios under which voting for the equivalent of Mussolini is the best alternative as compared to abstaining from voting or voting for the equivalent of Hitler. If the individual voter has sufficient justification in believing that this is so, then she may vote for Mussolini.

This argument also allows that one might be justified in voting for a policy or candidate whose probable degree of harmfulness is unknown, provided this helps prevent a known-to-be dangerous policy or candidate from winning. So, if I had to choose between Stalin and a random unknown person, I could be justified in voting for the unknown person as opposed to abstaining or voting for Stalin. This characterization might also allow that a good voter can sometimes vote for otherwise unknown candidates on the basis of party affiliation, if the voter has sufficient reason to believe that most members of that party would promote the common good if elected.

This argument also allows that one might be justified in electing someone, even if one does not know which policies are good. Suppose I know that Aubrey is omniscient, omnibenevolent, and good at getting things done. I thus know that she will make a good leader, without knowing what she will do as a leader. So I am justified in thinking that she will promote the common good, without knowing how she will do it.

Note also that there is a difference between casting a blank ballot and voting per se.[12] These two actions are different and should be evaluated separately. Suppose my theory implies that you should abstain rather than vote, because you are too irrational or ignorant to choose a candidate. If so, it might still be permissible for you to cast a blank ballot. (It might also be impermissible to cast a blank ballot, if doing so violates the Clean Hands Principle).

THE FRINGE VOTER AND THE INDIVIDUAL LITTERER

Some people vote for fringe candidates who have no significant chance of winning. John Taylor Bowles was the National Socialist Movement's candidate in the 2008 U.S. presidential election. Had Bowles been elected, this would have been a disaster, though probably not as much of a disaster as when Hitler came to power. Would it be wrong to vote for Bowles, given that he had so little chance of winning? (I am not sure how many write-in votes Bowles received, but I am sure it was fewer than 10,000.)

Someone might claim that votes for Bowles do not count as real votes, any more than the sixty-two votes for Santa Claus count as real votes. However, Bowles's supporters presumably wanted him to be president. When they voted, they were sincere. Perhaps the sixty-two Santa Claus voters were also sincere (or deluded), though it's more likely that they intentionally spoiled their ballots. For the sake of argument, I count all sincere votes for real, living people as genuine votes. Otherwise, we are faced with the problem that any vote for a minority candidate with a significant disadvantage could be counted as "not a real vote." Green Party candidate Ralph Nader did not have a real chance in 2008, and in some sense, the Republican Barry Goldwater did not have much of a chance in 1964, but I want to count their supporters as making genuine votes.

So, what should we say about voters for fringe parties? Votes for bad candidates with a real chance of winning have insignificant expected disutility, so clearly votes for terrible fringe candidates have no significant expected disutility either. But the argument I have been making does not rely on the disutility of individual votes.

The Public Goods Argument held that everyone has a duty to vote because good government is a public good (i.e., a non-rivalrous, non-excludable good), and not voting free-rides on the provision of this good. In the preceding chapter, I showed that abstention did not necessarily count as free-riding, and so even if members of the community have a duty to do their part, this does not necessarily show that it is their part to vote.

However, the Public Goods Argument's first premise is correct. Good government is a public good. Some obligations arise from the fact that the good government is a public good. Consider that parks are a public good. This does not imply that everyone who benefits from the good must actively maintain it by mowing the lawn, cleaning up litter, spreading fertilizer, and the like. However, everyone (including even those who do not benefit from the good) has an obligation not to despoil the park. Littering in the park is wrong. For you to litter in the park is wrong, even if you are the only litterer, and even if you litter in an obscure spot where it is unlikely someone will see the litter. Littering is not horribly wrong, as committing rape or murder is, but it is wrong.

If we want the park to remain clean, we do not want people to take it upon themselves to judge whether their litter will not be discovered. A rule of the form "feel free to litter provided that you believe others won't see the litter or be bothered by it" invites people to litter too much. The way we get clean parks is by having a more categorical prohibition against littering.

If you litter in an otherwise clean park, you take advantage of others' good behavior. For others to bear the cost of putting trash in its proper place when you do not is unfair. People who litter take advantage of the rest of us who do not. We bear the costs of keeping the park clean. They enjoy the benefits but do not bear the costs.

Sincere voters for bad fringe candidates are litterers. Good government is a public good. Even though they do not have a duty to provide good government, they should not pollute the system. When they vote for harmful candidates, this imposes a differential burden on other voters (to use Lomasky and Brennan's term). Every time someone votes for John Taylor Bowles, it becomes imperative that at least two other people vote for some better candidate. People who vote for Bowles take advantage of the rest of us who vote for worthy candidates.[13] The Bowles voters enjoy the benefits of living under a system of decent governance, rather than having to suffer under the social system they think they prefer. While most of the rest of us bear the cost of being sufficiently rational to provide decent governance, they do not bear this cost. We do not want people to feel free to vote for harmful candidates, just because they think it will not lead to bad consequences. The fact that people feel free to do so is itself likely to lead to bad consequences, just as it will lead to bad consequence if people feel free to litter when they believe it will not have bad consequences.

Voters for bad fringe candidates also sometimes can be seen as *expressing* morally bad attitudes through the act of voting. As Brennan and Lomasky say, to "cast a Klan ballot is to *identify oneself* in a morally significant way with the racist policies that the organization espouses."[14] They compare this to when the audience in the Roman coliseum cheers as lions devour Christians. Cheering does not harm the Christians any further, but cheering is still wrong. It is wrong to express approval of wrongful actions. If I sincerely say, "I think the KKK should run the country," I express racist attitudes and thereby do something wrong. A single vote for a KKK party candidate is inconsequential, but it is morally repulsive of me to *endorse* that candidate's values through my vote. (Note: Freedom of speech is not an issue here. We are not discussing whether one *has the right* to express contemptible attitudes, but instead whether expressing contemptible attitudes is right.)

FORTUITOUS VOTING

Sometimes voters vote the right way for the wrong reasons. This is not unusual. People believe the right things or do the right things for the wrong reasons all the time. Unreliable methods of reasoning need not always arrive at the wrong answer. Mathematics teachers have students show their work because students often accidently arrive at the right answer through a series of fortunate mistakes. A person who treated *Mein Kampf* as a sacred, indubitable text would come to have some correct beliefs about politics, because Hitler sometimes says true things.

For the sake of argument, assume Obama was the better of the two major U.S. presidential candidates in 2008. Still, many of his supporters were not in a position to judge his or McCain's policy proposals or character. They voted for him because of his rhetoric, because of his emotional appeal, for self-image, or because they were pressured to do so by their peers. Or, to take a hypothetical case, suppose a deluded person votes for Obama because he is convinced Obama will destroy the United States, and this deluded person wants to see the United States destroyed.

In this case, people vote the right way for the wrong reasons. I refer to this as fortuitous voting. Fortuitous voting occurs when citizens vote for what are in fact beneficial policies or candidates likely to enact beneficial policies, but they do not have sufficient justification to believe that these policies or candidates are good.

Fortuitous voters do not know they are voting fortuitously. To know they are voting fortuitously, they would have to know that they are not justified in believing that their vote will serve the common good, but also to know—and therefore to be justified in believing—that it will serve the common good.

THE DUTY NOT TO IMPOSE UNACCEPTABLE RISK

People have an obligation not to vote fortuitously, even though, by hypothesis, if most people do vote that way, good things will happen. Fortuitous voters by definition pick a good choice. Still, they have an obligation to abstain from voting rather than to vote fortuitously.

Fortuitous voting is wrong because it imposes unacceptable risk. Sometimes people should refrain from certain activities—even when those activities lead to good consequences—because engaging in those activities usually leads to bad consequences. When good things happen, it is by accident.

Suppose I have severe bronchitis. My physician consults a witch doctor for treatment advice. The witch doctor burns some animal fat, then tosses in some alphabet soup, and reads the patterns of letters. Miraculously, the letters spell "prednisone." My physician writes me a prescription for prednisone, which just happens to be the right medicine. Here, the physician's prescription is fortuitous. Following her treatment will lead to good consequences. However, she has done something wrong. She used a highly unreliable decision method to arrive at her prescription. Her use of this method puts me at serious risk. In this case, I was just lucky.

Or suppose I decide to build a nuclear reactor in my basement, despite having little training in nuclear engineering or physics.[15] This reactor has a 90 percent chance of exploding and killing my neighbors, but, fortunately, it does not do so. Here I have done something wrong—exposing my neighbors to too much risk of harm—even though I did not in fact harm them.

Now, suppose government leaders used similarly unreliable and risky methods to make political decisions. If so, they act negligently toward citizens, much as my physician was negligent toward me in the previous example. Even if they accidently pick a good policy, they still have done something wrong. By using unreliable decision-making procedures, they exposed citizens to undue risk of harm.

When voters vote for good things for bad reasons, they are behaving wrongly in much the same way as the people in the foregoing examples. They impose undue risk on their fellow citizens, but luckily no one is harmed.

The electorate has a collective obligation to the governed not to expose them to undue risk in the selection of policy. The governed have a right not to be exposed to undue risk. When elections are decided on the basis of unreliable epistemic procedures or on the basis of unjustified moral attitudes, this exposes the governed to undue risk. Therefore, the electorate (as a collective body) ought not to decide elections that way.

The argument for why individual voters should not vote for bad reasons works much the same as the argument for why individual voters should not vote harmfully. The ethics of participation in collective activities applies here. Individuals should not participate in collective activities that impose undue risk provided that refraining from such behavior imposes little personal cost. Refraining from voting fortuitously imposes small personal costs. Therefore, individuals should not vote fortuitously.

While the majority of the electorate owes it to the governed not to impose unnecessary risk upon them, we individual voters owe it to each other to avoid participating in collectives that impose undue risk.

These arguments rely on the notion of undue risk, but what counts as undue risk? Robert Nozick asks, "Imposing how slight a probability of a harm that violates someone's rights also violates his rights?"[16] More broadly, we can ask how significant a probability of harm we are allowed to impose on others before the imposition counts as wrong.

We need to allow some risk imposition if we are going to live and flourish together. Every time I drive I impose some risk on innocent bystanders and other drivers, but that does not normally count as wrong. However, drinking and driving is wrong.

I am not going to give a full theory of acceptable risk here. The argument against fortuitous voting relies upon the notion of unnecessary, unacceptable risk, but I cannot give necessary and sufficient conditions for something to count as unacceptable risk. (That said, we are sometimes adept at distinguishing things even though we cannot give necessary and sufficient conditions for them. I can distinguish dogs from cats with near perfect accuracy despite not being able to articulate necessary and sufficient conditions for doghood and cathood.)

Still, other philosophers have made some advances on producing a theory of unacceptable risk. Sven Ove Hansson, a leading theorist on risk, argues for a principle like this:

> Exposure of a person to a risk is acceptable if and only if this exposure is part of an equitable social system of risk-taking that works to her advantage.[17]

I'm not sure if Hansson's view is right. However, if need be, I will just piggyback on his work here.

We need to allow risk taking. Risky behaviors are morally assessed as a kind rather than as individual acts. We ask, "Does a norm of allowing that kind of behavior tend to hurt people or help them? Of those it harms, does it harm them as a means to benefiting others, or is the harm accidental? How bad are the harms and how good are the benefits? Is allowing this kind of risk a form of exploitation?"[18] A given kind of behavior that imposes risks on others is justified to the extent that it is beneficial to all (especially to those upon whom the risk is imposed) and nonexploitative.

When people with political power make decisions using unreliable belief-forming procedures (such as wishful thinking or forming beliefs on the basis of peer pressure), this imposes a high level of risk on the governed. It tends to harm the governed, though it sometimes works to their benefit.

REDUNDANCY

The explanation of why fortuitous voting is wrong also implies that unexcused harmful voting is wrong. Unexcused harmful voting also involves imposing undue risk. Harmful voting occurs when people vote using unduly risky decision-making methods, and the methods lead to bad results. Fortuitous voting occurs when people vote using unduly risky decision-making methods, and the methods lead to good results.

However, this redundancy should be excused. One reason for redundancy is that the argument against fortuitous voting relies upon complicated, controversial issues of undue risk. So, if that argument fails to show that fortuitous voting is wrong, the previous argument might still succeed in showing that unexcused harmful voting is wrong.

Unexcused harmful voting arguably has an additional count against it. Taken collectively, fortuitous voting and unexcused harmful voting both impose undue risk, but unexcused harmful voting also imposes harm.

The difference between harmful voting and fortuitous voting is much like the difference in tort law between mere negligence and liability. One is negligent when one violates a duty of care toward a person. But one is liable when one is negligent *and* this negligence results in damages toward a person. Fortuitous voting is negligence that does not result in damages, but unexcused harmful voting is negligence that does result in damages. In tort cases, in general, one owes compensation for the latter but not the former. For example, suppose we are in a car accident, and I am at fault. If the collision does not hurt you or your property, then you cannot collect against me. If, somehow, the collision not only did not damage you but made you better off, you could not collect against me. But if it damages you or your property, then you can collect against me.

RELIGIOUS VOTING

There is considerable debate right now about whether citizens may use religious convictions in political deliberation and decision.[19] Religious voting is nothing special. The same norms that govern nonreligious voting govern religious voting. If a voter votes for X but is not justified in believing that X will promote the common good, then she does something wrong, regardless of what role religion played in her vote. If she is justified in believing that X will promote the common good, she acts rightly, regardless of what role religion played in her vote.

For the purposes of this argument, I consider a religious voter to be someone who votes on the basis of beliefs in any kind of supernatural or magical entity or property. This broad definition can include, among others, Abrahamic monotheists, Hindus, most Buddhists, New Age spiritualists, and believers in qi or Chakras. (Note that a person who has religious beliefs, but whose beliefs do not influence her vote, does not count as a religious voter on this definition.)

Consider four different religious voters:

1. Betty believes in supernatural stuff on the basis of faith, that is, without evidence or despite overwhelming contrary evidence. Betty is thus unjustified in her beliefs about the supernatural.

2. Chris rejects faith as a means to belief. He believes in supernatural stuff on the basis of evidence, using reliable methods of reasoning. His belief in the supernatural is no different from a physicist's belief in quarks. According to normal epistemic standards, Chris is justified in his beliefs about the supernatural.

3. David tries to be like Chris but fails. He rejects faith as a means to belief. Instead, David believes that the evidence points strongly to supernaturalism. However, David has misinterpreted the evidence such that he is not justified in his beliefs. While David has made a mistake, it is an honest one. He has had a slip of irrationality, but he has a genuine commitment to rationality and overall is of high epistemic virtue.

4. Edward sees himself as being like Chris, but is not. Edward is deluded about his own rationality. Edward regards himself as believing on reason but in fact believes on faith. Edward spends much of his time rationalizing his supernatural beliefs, but his arguments are unsound and his evidence is poor. While David makes an honest though culpable mistake in his reasoning, Edward is intellectually dishonest and corrupt.

We might characterize these four voters as follows: Betty is a faith-based theist, Chris is a successful rational theist, David is an unsuccessful rational theist, and Edward is a pseudorational theist. Note that when I say David is unsuccessful, I do not mean that his beliefs are false. Rather, I mean that given his evidence, he should not believe in supernatural entities. My concern here is not with the truth of their beliefs but their level of justification for those beliefs, regardless of whether the beliefs are true.

According to my theory of voting ethics, Betty, David, and Edward vote wrongly when they vote on the basis of their religious beliefs. Betty, David, and Edward are all unjustified in their religious beliefs. When they vote, they are either unexcused harmful voters or fortuitous voters. In contrast, according to my theory of voting ethics, Chris does nothing wrong in voting from his religious beliefs.[20]

In the abstract, religious voting is not particularly interesting. The test of whether one may vote from religious convictions is no different from the test of whether one may vote from social-scientific beliefs. The more interesting question is what real religious voters are like. What proportions of them are like Betty, Chris, David, or Edward? My theory just says that Chris is a good voter and the others are not. Officially, this book takes no stand on what actual religious voters are like. To take that stand, I would need to take the correct epistemological theory and use it to evaluate real voters using good social-scientific surveys and interviews.[21]

Objection: People Vote for Character, Not Policies

One objection to my position is that voters tend to vote for character, not for policies. They might be quite good at judging the character of candidates, even if they are bad at judging the efficacy of different proposed policies for achieving different ends. If so, the objection goes, then most voters do not act wrongly when they vote.

To a significant degree, voting for character is voting for the wrong reasons.[22] When we elect someone, we give him power. That power can be used for good or bad. The office of the presidency is not an honorific meant to show we respect that person's character. Giving someone the presidency is not bestowing a medal or a certificate of commendation but giving him (some) control of the state, an institution that makes rules, and forces innocent people to comply with these rules using violence and threats of violence. We need to be sure he will do a good job controlling it.

So character-based voting is acceptable only insofar as it is a proxy to the quality of the governance a candidate is likely to produce. To what degree good character and good policies are correlated is largely an empirical question. If someone is morally corrupt, there is a pretty good chance he will use the power of the state for personal benefit rather than to promote the common good. Yet, a virtuous politician with a powerful sense of justice might still be deeply misguided and committed to all sorts of counterproductive, harmful policies. Having the right values is not sufficient for making good policy, because it requires social-scientific knowledge to know whether any given set of policies is likely to achieve those values. Just as an incompetent surgeon can be still be a virtuous person, so an incompetent politician can be a virtuous person. If there is good evidence that a politician is likely to enact harmful policies, one should not vote for her (without sufficient reason) even if she is a good person. Voting on the moral virtue of a candidate counts as good voting only to the extent that the candidate's moral virtue is evidence that she will enact good policies.

The objection might be recast in terms of political skill rather than moral virtue. Politicians extol their years of experience and ability to work across party lines in generating outcomes. Still, even if voters are good judges of such political skills and vote accordingly, such skill could mean bad policies will be enacted. A senator might excel at getting bills passed, but perhaps all of the bills have been harmful. Just as voting on moral character is not obviously a reliable way of generating good policy outcomes, neither is voting on this kind of political skill.

OBJECTION: EXPRESSIVE VOTING

Jerry Gaus argues that voters do not have a duty to vote for good political outcomes. He says that this takes too narrow a view of the purposes of voting. Sometimes voting is not about producing good outcomes but about expressing attitudes.

Gaus is a justificatory liberal, that is, he thinks laws must be justified to the reasonable people subject to those laws. Given this, one might expect him to hold that citizens should not vote for laws that cannot be publicly justified. Surprisingly, he argues *against* what he calls a "minimal duty of civility":

> *The Minimal Duty of Civility*: If Alf thinks that *L* is not publicly justified, Alf violates the duty of civility if he publicly advocates *L* (in a political forum), votes for *L*, etc., unless Alf [justifiedly] thinks that advocating *L* (voting for it, etc.) would help bring about a publicly justified outcome.[23]

(Note that the purpose of the "unless" clause in this definition is meant to allow for strategic voting.)

Gaus complains that not all voting is instrumental. People do not always vote in order to produce good policy outcomes. Sometimes they vote for expressive and symbolic reasons. Sometimes they vote to express dissatisfaction with the current state of affairs or to express concern for the poor. Sometimes the point of voting is simply to communicate one's interests.

I agree with Gaus that, as a matter of fact, voters often vote for expressive and symbolic reasons. However, even if true, that does not imply it is acceptable for them to do so. On my view, they should vote instrumentally or not vote at all. Or, more precisely, they may have whatever motive they please when they vote, but they are required to vote in ways that they justifiedly believe will promote the common good.

Gaus says, "Voters have expressive political concerns, and precluding them from politics needs strong justification: given the indirect links between voting and legislative outcomes, it is not obvious that such a justification is forthcoming."[24] Gaus adds, "Voters employ their political liberties to convey their concerns and aspirations. In this sense, [the political arena] is an information-collecting system as well as a decision-making system."[25]

So Gaus's argument seems to rest on two claims. First, because voting does not lead directly to legislative outcomes, why voters would have a duty of civility is unclear. Legislators, not voters, pass the laws. (Of course, sometimes voters do directly decide laws, as in California's 2008 Proposition 8.) Legislators, not voters, bear the ultimate responsibility for the laws. Second, voting provides information for political leaders. Leaders can use this information to determine what to do.

Even when voters choose among candidates rather than among potential laws, they choose who governs. My argument in this book relies on the empirical premise that candidates generally try to give voters what they want. Empirical work shows that this to be so.[26] Candidates of course routinely break promises and misrepresent themselves. Yet, in general, electing candidates of certain ideological bents tends to produce outcomes conforming to those bents.

The voters who put the National Socialists in power in Germany in 1932 cannot be held responsible for everything the new government did, of course. But much of what the government did was foreseeable by any reasonably well-informed person, and so their supporters were blameworthy.

Gaus's second claim is that voting is an information-gathering system. Unfortunately, what Gaus means by this is unclear. An example of something he might mean is this: if there is higher-than-average participation during the election, elected officials should see this as showing discontent and should make some changes to alleviate this discontent. The changes they should make might not be the ones that the voters ask for—after all, Gaus is arguing that voting should not always be regarded instrumentally. However, Gaus's second claim is as problematic as the first. When voters vote to convey their concerns and aspirations, but do not vote well, this tends to harm the common good.

Because voting "determines outcomes as serious as war and peace, liberty and oppression, poverty and equality," we should not "regard individual votes as a form of flamboyant self-expression."[27] Citizens should vote for instrumental reasons, rather than expressive ones, because voting decides who leads. Voters have other, better opportunities to express themselves. They can write letters to newspaper editors, protest, attend rallies, send money to causes, write books and articles, blog, make movies, paint, talk to one another. They have many outlets for self-expression that do not lead as directly to political outcomes as voting does.

Suppose the majority of you vote for an obviously bad presidential candidate for expressive reasons. Perhaps you were rightly dissatisfied with the status quo. Still, you did not bother to research the candidate, his preferred policies, and the likely outcomes of those preferred policies. As a result of your vote, the candidate now has significant power. He implements a number of harmful policies, some of which harm me. I have a moral complaint against you: how dare you impose bad governance on me as a means to expressing yourself! If you're upset, write a poem![28]

Or consider another case.[29] Suppose Sanda is a Burmese immigrant to the United States who has recently become a U.S. citizen. The next election will be her first chance ever to vote. Sanda wants to vote but does not know enough to qualify as a good voter. (Though she recently passed the U.S. citizenship exam, most of the questions on the civics portion of the exam consisted of trivia and fun facts, which are irrelevant to assessing potential policies.) She is excited about living in a democracy, because she sees democracies as a good means for promoting the common good and securing social justice. She wants to express a commitment to the democratic system of government. Voting will enable her to feel a sense of solidarity with her fellow Americans. Though she will vote badly, the probability that this will harm anyone is vanishingly small. Is it permissible for Sanda to vote?

The subject matter of morality is not just the rightness and wrongness of actions but also the goodness and badness of different motives. You can do the right thing for the wrong reasons, and even sometimes do the wrong thing for the right reasons. According to the theory I have presented here, if Sanda votes, she acts wrongly. Even if so, this does not imply that she has badly defective moral character. She might be doing the wrong thing for the right reasons. Her action is strictly speaking wrong, but her motives are not contemptible.

Sanda votes in part as a means to express *good* attitudes—a commitment to democracy as a means to producing social justice. Despite that, her behavior is also somewhat bizarre. She wants to express a commitment to democracy, but for whatever reason, in her very first chance *ever* to vote, she failed to place herself in a position to vote well. This is somewhat perverse. If someone wanted to express a commitment to democracy through voting, we might expect her to invest the time to vote well. Imagine I told you, "I want to express a commitment to democracy. In order to express my commitment, I'm going to vote tomorrow for a bunch of candidates I know little about who take various stances on issues I do not understand. For all I know, it would be disastrous for the country if I got my way. Good thing I'm not the only voter!" If I said that, you would find my behavior repellant or at least odd. Sanda would not describe herself this way, but nevertheless, this is what she is doing.

By voting badly, Sanda participates in a collectively harmful activity. In general, taking pleasure in voting or having the desire to express one-self does not excuse bad voting. Taking pleasure or having the desire to express oneself does not excuse littering in public parks or participating in the Firing Squad either. It may seem that voting badly is not so bad as littering in public parks or participating in the Firing Squad. However, we need to remember that democracies make life and death decisions and impose rules upon innocent people through violence and the threat of vio-lence. Sometimes voting for the wrong candidate is very much like being an extra shooter in the Firing Squad thought experiment. For example, if you elect a candidate who intends to criminalize an activity that the state should not criminalize, then however noble your intentions and expres-sive desires might be, you are helping to oppress innocent people.

That said, sometimes voting expressively is also a way of voting instru-mentally. Sometimes, a group of voters might justifiedly believe that vot-ing for a fringe party (even a bad one) or for certain candidates is a way of serving the common good, because voting this way can be expected to make mainstream parties behave better. Sometimes, voters justifiedly believe that expressing discontent through voting will promote the com-mon good. In these kinds of cases, voters are said to vote strategically. My theory of voting ethics allows for strategic voting. (See chapter 5 for further discussion of this issue.) The kind of expressive voting that Gaus defends and which I criticized here is different from this more sophisti-cated form of expressive voting. In this section, we have been discussing voters who vote to express themselves, but do not have any idea what effect their self-expression will have.

Objection: This Thesis Is Self-Effacing

I argue that people who would vote badly should not vote. However, the people I describe as bad voters are unlikely to recognize that they are among those obligated not to vote. To confirm this in at least one in-stance, as an unscientific experiment, I discussed my thesis with a person who I believe exemplifies bad voting. He agreed that *other* people should not vote. Even worse, if good voters were to hear that bad voters should not vote, they might stop voting out of fear of doing wrong.

Thus, my position in this chapter might be self-effacing. However, even if this were so, my thesis is simply that people should not vote badly. I do not claim that advertising this thesis to the general public would make the world better. Whether telling the truth about morality makes the world a better place depends on many contingencies. Sometimes people are corrupt enough that hearing the truth inspires bad behavior.

A self-effacing position need not be false. For instance, suppose certain critics of utilitarianism are correct when they claim that if people accepted utilitarianism, this would make the world worse by utilitarian standards, simply because most people are not good at employing such standards. If so, this does not show that utilitarian standards are false. Rather, it just shows that we should not advertise them. As David Brink notes, there is a difference between a *criterion of right* and a *method for making decisions*.[30] The former is about what makes actions right or wrong, but the latter is about figuring out how to do what is right or wrong. A good method for Alex might be different from what is good for Bob because they have different cognitive abilities. Alex is good at making calculations while Bob is not. But the standard of right action is the same for both. The point of the decision-making method is to help them get to the right action.[31] In this chapter, I articulate a criterion of right, not a method for making decisions.

Despite this, one might still argue that self-effacement harms my position because *ought* implies *can*: people ought to X only if they can X. People have a duty only if they can follow the duty. One might pose the following dilemma. Either people cannot recognize they are bad voters, in which case they cannot obey the principle and thus are not subject to it, or if they do recognize they are bad voters, they use this recognition to turn themselves into good voters, and thus are no longer subject to the duty.

This appears to be a false dilemma. In moments of clarity we sometimes recognize that we have bad character or tend to act badly in certain ways. But realizing our errors does not fix them—we easily slip back into old behaviors. For instance, one might notice that one has been repeatedly dating people with the same flaws, but this rarely fixes the problem.

Another worry is that my theory requires irrational voters to possess knowledge about themselves, which they might be unable to possess. If so, then my theory violates *ought* implies *can*—it asks people to do something they cannot do. Philosophers generally conclude that a person cannot have an obligation to do X if it is impossible for her to do X. So, if the theory presented here asks voters to do something they cannot do, then the theory is false. For instance, suppose Bonnie votes regularly but is so deeply irrational about politics that she could not stop being irrational even if she tried. She is so irrational that she is unable to know that she is irrational. She believes herself to be a good voter and is unable to think otherwise. One might worry that my theory requires her to know that she is irrational and thus know that she should not vote. Yet, by hypothesis, Bonnie cannot know this—it goes beyond her abilities. If so, then my theory appears to violate the principle that *ought* implies *can*.

This objection is mistaken. I have argued that irrational voters ought to abstain from voting. This does not imply, and I have not argued, that they have a duty to know that they are irrational, or to know that they should abstain from voting. Similarly, I have argued that voters should justifiedly believe they are voting for things that would promote the common good. This does not imply, and I have not argued, that they should know they are good voters. My theory says that citizens should vote well or abstain. It does not say that they should know that they are good or bad voters. Thus, this theory does not ask citizens to do anything that they cannot do. The theory says that Bonnie should not vote, which is easy to do. It does not say that she should *know* that she should not vote, which is hard to do.

Still, one might object that one cannot have a duty unless one knows that one has a duty. This does not seem right. Suppose I am a soldier and receive orders from my superior in an envelope. The orders require me to X. I never bother to open the envelope, and so never learn that I have a duty to X. Despite that, I still have a duty to X, even though I am unaware that I have a duty to X.

In another version of the objection, suppose one cannot have a duty to X unless one *can* know that one has a duty to X. (After all, the soldier in the preceding example could know what his duty is, but perhaps irrational voters cannot know they have a duty not to vote.) This version of the objection also seems wrong. Suppose I am driving drunk and a child is crossing at a crosswalk. Because I am so drunk, I am unable to see the child, and so I am unable to recognize that I have a duty to stop. Still, I have a duty to stop. Though I am unable to know I have a duty to stop, I am not relieved of the duty, because I had a responsibility not to make myself unable to recognize my moral duties. That I cannot know that I have a duty to stop is my fault, and thus I still have a duty to stop. Insofar as Bonnie is like the drunk driver, she is still blameworthy for voting.

A final variation on this objection holds that one cannot have a duty to X unless one can know, in principle, that one has a duty to X. (After all, the drunk driver could have known, in principle, that he had a duty to stop, if only he had not been drunk, and he could have chosen not to drink so much.) This seems more plausible than the other versions of the objection. If Bonnie cannot know, even in principle, that she has a duty not to vote, and if it is not her fault that she cannot know this (i.e., if it is not her fault she is irrational), then perhaps she might be excused from the duty not to vote badly. Still, very few bad voters will be like that. Most bad voters can know that they are bad voters, and even among those who cannot know they are bad voters, most of them are at fault for not being able to know this. Most people could be more rational if only they chose to put in the effort.

The view that bad voters should not vote does have a practical upshot. We sometimes can minimize the effects of some vices even when we cannot rid ourselves of them. For example, overeaters sometimes realize that in future moments of temptation, they will rationalize eating any junk food in easy reach. Thus, some overeaters do not keep junk food in their homes and take alternative routes to work to avoid passing fast-food restaurants. If a person could recognize that she tends to be a bad voter, she might take action to improve her voting behavior, or at least choose to abstain, just as I have in cases where I was not in a position to vote well.

Summary and Conclusion

Voters should justifiedly believe that the policies or candidates they support would promote the common good. Otherwise, they should abstain from voting.

This chapter presents a theory of when it is morally permissible for a person to vote. However, it is not a theory of whether it is permissible to induce others to vote, or whether one might have an obligation to try to stop them from doing so. So suppose Steve is an irrational but fortuitous voter. He happens to support the right candidate for the wrong reasons. My theory says Steve should not vote—it is wrong for him to do so, and he would be blameworthy for voting. Still, even if it is wrong for Steve to vote, it might be permissible for Terrence to encourage Steve to vote (because Terrence happens to know Steve will vote fortuitously). More broadly, it might be acceptable to be a community organizer who induces lots of irrational, ignorant voters to vote, provided one is sufficiently justified in believing they will vote fortuitously. My theory says that the fortuitous voters are blameworthy for voting, but it does not say that *you* are blameworthy for inducing them to do a blameworthy thing.[32]

I see myself as a defender of democracy. I wish to keep the voting process free of pollution, and what defender of democracy wishes to see her favored system polluted? Many democrats are concerned with both democratic procedures and democratic values.[33] Not just any outcome produced by democratic procedure is acceptable, nor is every outcome aligning with democratic values acceptable regardless of what procedure produced it. Universal voting by bad voters might make procedures more democratic than massive abstention by people who would vote badly. Yet this does not mean the outcome of this procedure will align better with democratic values, and thus does not mean that opposing universal voting is inherently undemocratic.

When people call for universal or extended participation, we have to ask what would be the point of the institution of universal participation. If we are passionate lovers of democracy, we might celebrate what universal participation would symbolize. Yet, in the real world, we have to ask how institutions would function. Institutions are not people. They are not ends in themselves. They are not paintings, either, to be judged by their beauty, by what they symbolize, or who made them. Institutions are more like hammers—they are judged by how well they work. Good institutions get us good results; bad institutions get us bad results.

APPENDIX I

The Prisoner's Dilemma

THE PRISONER'S dilemma game gets its name from a hypothetical story in which two suspects are given the opportunity to stay silent or rat on one another. In the abstract, the game works as follows. There are two players, each of whom has two moves, *cooperate* or *defect*. They move at the same time. The payoffs are depicted in figure 3.

In the prisoner's dilemma, cooperation is a win-win scenario. Both parties are made better off if they cooperate with each other and remain silent. Nevertheless, if both players try to maximally benefit their self-interest, the players do not cooperate. They both defect. Player 1 defects because no matter what player 2 does, player 1 is better off defecting. If player 2 cooperates, player 1 gets a huge gain by defecting. If player 2 defects, player 1 would suffer a huge loss if she cooperates, and so is better off taking the smaller loss from defecting. This holds for player 2 as well; she is also better off defecting no matter what. In the language of game theory, defection is the *dominant strategy*—the optimal move regardless of what the other player does. The prisoner's dilemma interests political philosophers because it shows something seemingly paradoxical: both players, in the attempt to arrive at an optimal result for themselves, arrive at a suboptimal result.

	Player 2 cooperates	Player 2 defects
Player 1 cooperates	*2 gets small gain* 1 gets small gain	*2 gets large gain* 1 suffers major loss
Player 1 defects	*2 suffers major loss* 1 gets large gain	*2 suffers small loss* 1 suffers small loss

Figure 3

APPENDIX II

The Tragedy of the Commons

ECOLOGISTS describe land as having a "carrying capacity," the maximum population that land can sustain indefinitely. Once the carrying capacity of land is exceeded, resources are depleted faster than they can be renewed, and the terrain starts to become wasteland.

The ecologist Garret Hardin found that when land is held in common by many different people, this could often lead to what he dubbed "the tragedy of the commons."[34] For example, suppose a pasture is held in common by a 10 different ranchers. Each owns 1 steer. The carrying capacity of the pasture is 10 head of steer—it can sustain 10 cattle indefinitely without degradation. With the pasture at or under carrying capacity, there is plentiful grass. The cattle are fully fed and can sell for $10 each on the market, for a total of $100 in output from the land. However, suppose one of the ranchers decides to add a second steer to the pasture, bringing the total cattle up to 11 and exceeding the land's carrying capacity. At this point, there is not quite enough food for the cattle, and the pasture starts to die. Because the cattle are not fed well enough, they now sell for only $8.00 each on the market. Yet, for the rancher that added the second steer, this is a good deal. He has increased his sales from $10 for one steer to $16 for two. However, everyone else has lost $2, and the total output of the land is now only $88.00 (down from $100). What do the other ranchers do? They will probably put additional cattle up themselves in the attempt to make up for the loss, but this eventually turns the ground to dust.

The problem is much like the prisoner's dilemma. Even if an individual rancher wanted to preserve the land, he could not, because he cannot control it. He cannot prevent other ranchers from abusing it. Accordingly, because he needs to feed his family, he might have to abuse the land himself, *preemptively*.

CHAPTER FOUR

Deference and Abstention

I HAVE ARGUED that citizens have duties to abstain rather than vote badly. This chapter considers a number of objections to the argument of the previous chapter. Each objection is related to issues of deference and abstention.

OBJECTION: DOES ABSTENTION IMPLY EPISTOCRACY?

My position is elitist. Some forms of elitism are bad. Some are not. Yet claiming that only competent people should undertake certain activities is not obviously a bad sort of elitism. While it is elitist to claim that a person with an unsteady grasp of comparative advantage should not vote on trade policy and immigration reform, it is also elitist to claim that a person with an unsteady hand should not perform surgery.

David Estlund defines "the epistocracy of the educated thesis" (a view he rejects) as the view that when "some are well educated and others are not, the polity would (other things equal) be better ruled by the giving the well educated more votes."[1] This seems to be a bad form of elitism. I am not here arguing on behalf of unequal voting rights. Instead, I am arguing that some citizens should not exercise their right to vote by voting. "I have the political right to X" does not imply "It is morally right for me to X." However, because I claim that some people should not vote, perhaps Estlund's arguments against epistocracy would count against my position.

Estlund says to the potential epistocrat, "You might be correct, but who made you boss?"[2] Good voters have no more right to rule than bad voters. Estlund argues that universal suffrage is a default because any other system invites "invidious comparisons." Making political wisdom a condition of the right to vote would not be generally acceptable to the people under the government's authority.[3] The theory I have presented here is compatible with Estlund's view. My position is not that the good voters should rule by right, or that the bad voters are by right forbidden from ruling. Rather, bad voters should exercise their equal right to rule in the way that is most advantageous to themselves and others: by abstaining from politics. I have argued that people should not vote badly, but I have not argued that someone should force them not to vote badly.

Some philosophers worry about people having unequal voting power. Yet one can hold that people should *have* equal voting power, but many people should not *exercise* the power they have. Still, someone might object that not exercising power is equivalent to not having power. Thomas Christiano worries that when citizens allow others to make decisions, this results in a society in which the few rule and the many obey.[4]

This need not be so. In committees, clubs, and at the polls, I have been asked to vote on issues I did not understand, have much knowledge about, or about which I was biased. My concern was to do the right thing and help make sure the best policy goes through. If I do not know what I am talking about, or if I know that I am prone to error and bad judgment about a given issue, one way of respecting my fellow citizens, committee members, and the like is to abstain. The times I have abstained were not losses of power. While I permitted other people to make the decisions, they did not rule me. After all, *I* permitted them to make the decision.

Abstention is not like relinquishing one's right to rule. On the contrary, abstention can be a way of voting indirectly. Suppose I am from out of town and visiting all of you. We are deciding on a restaurant. I prefer that we eat at the best place. However, I know little about the local restaurants, while you all are connoisseurs. Despite your greater knowledge, a concern for fair and respectful procedure entails that we should each get an equal say. You do not have the right to tell me where to eat. You know better, but no one made you boss. Though ignorant, I could vote directly for a specific restaurant. Yet, because I want to pick the best restaurant, I could also say, "I vote for the best restaurant, but I do not know which one that is. Because the rest of you know better, I vote that my vote reflects your collective wisdom." I then abstain but, in effect, vote indirectly.

Objection: Abstention Causes a Loss of Autonomy

Some might see abstention as a violation of autonomy, perhaps even slavelike. To abstain means to cede political judgment to others and to give up one's own independent judgment.

This seems mistaken. First, deferring to others does not always involve a troubling loss of autonomy. Second, the idea that voting gives the voter significant autonomy or control is implausible anyway.

The first problem with this objection is that deference is not necessarily a loss of autonomy. So long as I have an equal right to vote, choosing not to vote can be an autonomous act, a way of expressing my will that the best outcome be achieved. Because I retain a right to vote, I am an equal citizen and the democratic decision-making procedure remains generally acceptable.

Julia Driver considers a similar issue, asking whether deferring to moral experts shows a lack of autonomy:

> When an agent decides to accept the testimony [of the moral expert] the agent is acting autonomously. There is an autonomous decision not to make one's own decision. So, one does display independence of thought at this level. If the worry is that one is failing to make up one's own mind, then the worry involves a confusion over levels of decision-making. If I *decide* to trust the expert, I have made an autonomous decision. The trust is not like infant trust nor does it involve the blind deference of one who has been cowed.[5]

Driver acknowledges that some people are overly deferential or indiscriminately cave in to pressure or to putative authority. These people are not autonomous. However, that does not mean that all deference shows a lack of autonomy.

Deference can be autonomous when done the right way. When I was a graduate student, I received plenty of practical advice (about writing, presenting, networking, etc.) from my dissertation supervisor and other faculty. I was in a position to grasp the truth of some of this advice but not all of it. Some of the advice could be shown true only through experience. Still, when I accepted this latter kind of advice, I was not thereby acting non-autonomously. I did not just take their word for it. Rather, I accepted their advice because I came to an independent, autonomous judgment that they were trustworthy and reliable advisers. Even as I followed their advice, I remained prepared to stop following if I came upon strong enough evidence that they were wrong.

The second problem with this objection is that it appears to overstate the degree of autonomy that voting confers. I take it for granted that in some sense a person who lacks a right to vote is, all things being equal, less free than a person who has the right to vote. I am not sure if the kind of freedom in consideration here has much to do with autonomy. A person who lacks the right to vote might still be a self-controlled, self-legislating person, just as a person who has the right to vote might be slavish and blindly deferential.

However, the issue here is not whether having a right to vote makes one more autonomous, but whether the act of voting makes one more autonomous. A person who abstains might still be self-controlled, self-mastered, and self-legislating, just as a person who votes might be slavish and blindly deferential. Indeed, many of the people I have argued should not vote should not vote precisely because they are slavish and blindly deferential—they vote on the basis of peer pressure and emotional impulses rather than on good reasons. They unjustifiedly defer to others.

If there is a connection between voting and autonomy, it must be something like this: by voting, a person is in part the author of the laws. If she abstains, then she has no authorship over the laws, and thus the laws are in some way imposed upon her. I have already explained why the claim that "the laws are imposed upon her" seems false. But the claim that a voter is in part the author of the laws needs further examination. First of all, if abstainers cannot be considered authors of the law, then it seems that neither can voters for losing candidates and policies. So, at best, voting confers autonomy on you only if your side wins. However, even then, it does not confer any significant autonomy.

I have made many autonomous decisions in my life. I have made autonomous decisions over petty things: what to wear each day, what to eat, what color toothbrush to have, what to watch on television. I have made autonomous decisions over important things: what to write about for my dissertation, where to go to college and graduate school, which job offers I would accept. I have made autonomous decisions over momentous things: whom to marry, whether to have a child, what to choose for a career.

Suppose these choices had been subject to democratic decision making. We would regard that as taking the choice away from me and giving it to the democratic body. Even if I had an equal vote in this body, it would be a severe loss of autonomy. Even if the democratic body did not just vote, but actively deliberated over the best choices (and listened to me give my reasons), having it make the decisions would mean a severe loss of personal autonomy for me.

It is not just that I have more autonomy when I make decisions alone as opposed to when a democratic assembly (of which I am a member) makes the decisions. Rather, when a democratic assembly (of which I am a member) makes the decisions, I don't have much autonomy at all. Making decisions collectively requires me to submit to and appeal to the judgments of others rather than to my own judgment.[6] This is one of the main reasons why liberal societies recognize and protect an extensive set of private rights for each citizen. To protect citizens' autonomy, certain things—such as what to believe, where to work, what to worship—have to be taken off the political bargaining table.[7] When people come together as a deliberative democratic body to decide these things, this strips citizens of their autonomy.

Robert Nozick illustrates this point with a story called the "Tale of the Slave."[8] Nozick describes the changing conditions under which a slave lives and asks his readers to point out when the slave stops being a slave.

Say you are the slave. At first, you live under a cruel master, who beats you arbitrarily. Then the master posts a set of rules and punishes you only when you violate the rules. The master then starts allocating resources among all of his slaves on kindly grounds, considering their needs, merit, and other factors. The master then decides to allow the slaves to spend four days doing whatever they please and requires them to work only three days on his manor. The master then decides to allow the slaves to live in the city or wherever else they like, as long as they send the master three-sevenths of their income. The master also continues to regulate many of their activities and can call them back to the manor for defense. The master decides to allow his 10,000 slaves—other than you—to make decisions among themselves about how to regulate their behavior and how much of their income they must send the master. You are bound by their decision, but cannot vote or deliberate.

When the master dies, he leaves all of his slaves, including you, to each other as a collective body, except for you. That is, his 10,000 other slaves collectively own everyone, including you, but you own no one. The other 10,000 slaves decide to allow you to advise them about what rules they should pass. These rules govern both their behavior and yours. Eventually, as a reward for your service, they allow you to vote whenever they are evenly divided—5,000 to 5,000—over what to do. You cast a ballot in an envelope, which they agree to open whenever they are split. Finally, because they have never been evenly split, they just include your vote with theirs all the time.

At the end of the story, many readers think the slave never stopped being a slave. This is disturbing because by the end of the story, the situation very much resembles modern democracy. I don't invoke the story here to prove that we are all slaves in modern democratic societies. Even though I agree that modern democratic societies abuse their citizens in certain ways and do not afford them as much freedom as citizens by right should have, we are clearly more free than the slave at the beginning of the story. (Notice, for one, that Nozick's tale does not mention whether the 10,000 slaves recognize and protect rights.)

Instead, what I think we should learn from Nozick's story is that being a member of rule-making body, especially a large one, does not give one much control. Each slave in the tale of the slave can legitimately claim that *everyone else makes all the decisions* and that *the decisions the body makes would have occurred without her input*. Democratic politics can sap us of autonomy in part because democratic bodies often rally around charismatic leaders and split into warring tribes. But even when political power remains equal, and even when democratic outcomes result from the equal input of all, there can be feeling of an utter lack of power. Our voices and votes are lost.

In parallel: I went to Mardi Gras one year. At night, the streets were so congested that I could lift my feet and be carried along by the crowd. It took serious effort to move against the current. Everyone in the crowd had the same predicament. We were all equals. Our individual movements equally decided the collective movement of the crowd. Yet, we were each powerless.[9]

Benjamin Barber, a longtime proponent of what he calls strong democracy, does not seem to grasp this point. He says, "We want what we want privately, but we want even more to be able to choose the public agenda that determines what our private choices will be."[10] Barber provides no empirical evidence that this is so. (That is, he did not do or cite any surveys, etc., to establish that this is what people want. Instead, he simply assumed that most people want what he wants.) However, if we grant that having the power to choose the public agenda is important, it is still unclear how modern democracy provides me with any significant ability to choose the public agenda. As Michael Walzer says, "Isn't the vote itself a kind of power, distributed by the rule of simple equality? A kind of power, perhaps, but something well short of the capacity to determine destinations and risks. . . . A single vote . . . represents a 1/n share of sovereignty. . . . in a modern mass democracy, it is a very small share indeed."[11] When I make a choice about what to wear, I end up wearing what I choose. When I make a choice about the public agenda and express this choice through voting, it makes no significant difference. It never has and it never will.

One further point about deference and autonomy: we cannot control or have a say over everything that happens in our lives, so we have to choose where we make a stand, where we think it's important to be authentic. Politics is one place to make a stand, but it is not the only or obviously best place.

Consider an analogy. Chris was a punk rock kid who rode the bus with me in ninth grade. One day Chris complained about my manner of dress: "You wear the Gap just like everyone else. You don't try to be original or true to yourself." Chris, in contrast, had chosen to conform to the punk rock subculture. I responded with something like this, "I don't care that much about how I dress. So I go along with how others dress. It's not that important to me, and how they do it is good enough." (In contrast, it was very important to Chris to dress a certain way.) In this case, it is implausible to say that I was inauthentic or lacked self-control because I deferred to the crowd on how to dress. Sometimes this deference is a way of being authentic, or as authentic as it is reasonable to be, because deferring prevents one from wasting time on unimportant things.

There is no obvious reason why politics cannot be like that. A self-controlled, authentic, autonomous individual might defer to others on politics because she recognizes that others will produce good enough outcomes, and within that range of likely outcomes, the outcomes just are not that important to her. Or she might defer because she accepts not having control over everything and finds more important places to make her stand.

In summary, to make a conscious decision to abstain does not involve any serious loss of autonomy—in part because one can autonomously choose to defer to others' decisions and in part because the act of voting does not confer any significant degree of autonomy upon the voter, so abstention has little opportunity cost in terms of autonomy.

OBJECTION: SHOULD I ALWAYS DEFER TO SUPERIOR VOTERS?

Another objection to my argument is this: my theory implies that we should always defer to voters who are epistemically and morally superior. After all, if the bottom 1 percent of voters (in terms of their morality, rationality, and knowledge) should defer to those above them, should the next 1 percent also defer, once the bottom 1 percent drops out? If so, this cycle of abstention and deference would continue until only the very best voters remain.

This objection seems to be confused about what I have argued. I have not argued that the bottom 1 percent should defer to just anyone with better epistemic and moral credentials. My theory implies that if people in the bottom 1 percent lack good epistemic credentials, they should abstain. I have not said that people in the bottom 1 percent must abstain because they are in the bottom 1 percent. After all, we can imagine societies where even the bottom 1 percent has sufficiently good credentials to vote well. Also, I have not argued that you should always defer to someone who is better than you. Rather, I have argued that if you are going to vote badly, you should abstain. Someone might be a better voter than you but still be a bad voter. In that case, you should not defer to her. You should abstain. That is not the same thing as deferring to her. She should not vote either. If she does, she does something wrong. If you vote, you do something worse.

Despite these caveats, my main response to this objection is simply to grant it. Under certain conditions, you should defer to those who have better credentials.

Suppose Aubree is the wisest, most rational, most virtuous, and best informed among us. This would not imply we should all defer to her. Though she would make a better voter than any one of us, many of us together might do better than she would do by herself. (Similarly, a given professor might know more about philosophy than any of the third-year graduate students, but the third-year graduate students might collectively know more than the professor.) Sometimes, though not always, many weaker minds are better than one strong mind, though it is not yet well understood when this is the case and when not.[12]

So suppose instead not only that Aubree is wiser and more virtuous than each of us but that she is better than all of us collectively. If we ask Aubree how government should be structured, she is more likely to arrive at the correct answer than the rest of us would, regardless of what method (voting, deliberation, etc.) we use to arrive at a collective decision. Finally, suppose we all justifiedly believe that Aubree is this wise, well informed, and virtuous. (That Aubree is in fact wiser than we are is not enough; we need to be justified in believing this. Otherwise, if we deferred to her, it would be fortuitous.)[13]

In this case, we ought to ask Aubree what we should do and then do it.[14] After all, by hypothesis, the best decision method is to follow Aubree's advice. She, of course, does not have the right to rule just because she is more likely to be right, but because she is more likely to be right, we should take her advice. Ex hypothesi, her view on what we should do is the best view to be had. (Suppose she were omniscient and omnibenevolent. In that case, she has not only the best answer but the right answer. If we disagree with her, we are wrong.) So, if we can count on everyone to abstain rather than to vote against Aubree's view, then we should abstain and have her vote by herself. Or, alternatively, we should ask her how we ought to vote, and then voters should vote that way. Or perhaps we should just make her queen.

If we do not defer to Aubree—if we do not vote the way she says we should—then we substitute a less reliable decision procedure in place of a more reliable one. We increase the probability of arriving at harmful and unjust policies.

From a personal point of view, perhaps there are limits to how much deference is desirable. Suppose a daemon, via telepathy, constantly gives me correct advice about what I ought to do. It is at least arguable that developing independent thinking skills and other virtues of practical wisdom would be worthwhile for me, even though strictly speaking I do not need these virtues.[15] However, there is a difference between deferring to an expert on every aspect of one's life and deferring to experts on some aspects. So, if we collectively defer to Aubree on the issue of how to govern, we might still each be autonomous, independent thinkers in other, more important aspects of our lives.

Developing practical wisdom is a good thing. It takes practice and exercise to develop it. However, the voting booth is not a good place to get this exercise. When we exercise at a gymnasium, for the most part, we internalize the costs of poor weight-lifting technique. If you are out of shape, you don't make other people suffer. However, when we vote, other people bear the costs. We externalize our bad decision-making techniques onto innocent bystanders.

John Stuart Mill hypothesized that democratic participation has an educative function—it tends to make people smarter. He appears to be wrong about this—the empirical evidence suggests otherwise.[16] However, even if he were correct, that this is a good argument for participation is not obvious. If the rest of you impose bad governance on me, it is a poor excuse to say you were pursuing the educative function of democracy. How dare you make me suffer as a result of your attempt to become smarter? Why couldn't you play Sudoku and study economics instead?

In principle, if there were someone like Aubree and we all knew this, then I agree we ought to defer to her. Doing so is not objectionable.

The reason it might seem objectionable is that in practice it is a different story. In practice, we seldom have people like Aubree. In practice, there is rarely one person who is more reliable than any other set of people. That is not to say that, if you are seeking the truth, polling *everyone* is always better than asking an expert. For instance, if you want to know the truth about evolution or the effects of free trade, you would do a better job asking a random biologist or economist instead of polling the populace at large. However, there is probably no biologist (or economist) who is as an individual more reliable than the top 5 percent of biologists (or economists) together.

Part of the reason for this is that within some limits, there is value in cognitive diversity. By cognitive diversity, I mean diverse perspectives ("ways of representing situations and problems"), diverse interpretations ("ways of categorizing or partitioning perspectives"), diverse heuristics ("ways of generating solutions to problems") and diverse predictive models ("ways of inferring cause and effect").[17] Scott Page argues, using mathematical models, that when it comes to making accurate predictions, increasing the amount of cognitive diversity among decision makers is as important as increasing the predictive power of individuals within the group.[18] That is, sophistication and cognitive diversity are equally good.[19]

Page does not argue that having many diverse but stupid predictors always works better than having fewer less-diverse smart predictors. On Page's account, completely unsophisticated but diverse crowds do not make good predictions.[20] Systematically biased crowds do not make good predictions. Rather, Page modestly concludes that having many diverse good predictors tends to be more successful than having just a few excellent predictors.[21] Sometimes, two smart but different heads are better than one smarter head.

Objection: Do You Need a Ph.D. to Vote?

One might object that my theory implies that only people with Ph.D.s should vote. Only they will have the expertise enough to be able to claim that they are justified in their beliefs about politics, and so only they will be justified in voting.

This objection does not accuse me of believing that *all* Ph.D.s are justified in their views and that all Ph.D.s should vote. That would be implausible. Many Ph.D.s are silly ideologues. They accept various political views not because of evidence but because they want to fit in with their peers or maintain their self-image. They are mired in foolish idées fixes. The writings of many Ph.D.s are little more than pretentious, obscurantist twaddle.[22] Academics and other educated people often are caught up in intellectual fads. They accept doctrines because they are popular or seem intriguing, not because there is good evidence in support of them. For instance, many economists formulate views on the economy that are based on the sexiness of certain mathematical models. Bias and irrationality plague everyone, including scientists, social scientists, and philosophers. Perhaps highly educated people are especially prone to overestimating their own epistemic credentials, and so perhaps they vote badly in high numbers. Presumably this applies to me too. Perhaps I should not vote.

To be clear, my position is that people should vote only if they have good epistemic credentials. It might turn out that few people have good credentials (about politics), but it might not.

Social epistemology gives us some reason to think that the number of people with good epistemic credentials about politics is not vanishingly small. One can be justified in believing certain things by relying on the testimony of others, provided at least that one is justified in accepting their testimony. So, for instance, I am justified in believing that quarks exist even though I have not witnessed any of the experiments providing evidence of their existence. The reason I am justified is that I accept the testimony of physicists. Of course, I do not accept it blindly. Though I am not a good physicist, I am adept enough at distinguishing mainstream physics from quack physics and at distinguishing widely accepted physics from possibly correct but controversial physics. I am good at recognizing and remaining neutral when there is significant controversy among experts. Part of what helps me make such discriminations is that I had significant college and high school training in physics. However, I have nowhere near enough training to call myself a physicist.

Similarly, voters do not need to be experts on the issues they vote on, as long as they can reliably discover who the trustworthy experts are and vote with expert opinion. This requires significant knowledge and some critical thinking ability, but it does not require expertise. One needs to have a good enough sense of what the consensus views are in relevant fields. It helps to read contrary views as well, because knowing whether consensus and orthodoxy result from rationality or irrationality is important. Keeping up with current events will be important. It is best to read a wide variety of sources from different ideological backgrounds. Having an awareness and ability to detect different cognitive biases is an important asset to a voter. A good level of distrust of politicians and a strong ability to see through rhetoric is important as well. Being able to separate genuine experts from popular pseudo-experts is important. For example, one should be able to distinguish between Edmund Phelps and Naomi Klein on economics or between Ken Miller and Ben Stein on evolutionary biology. A good liberal education and a good, critical mind are the main assets of a good voter. Some people qualify as good voters out of high school. Some need college training. Many will not be good voters no matter how much education they obtain. Regardless, it is not obvious that my theory implies that only a small percentage of people will be justified in voting.

However, suppose I am wrong. Suppose that, on the correct theory of epistemic justification, only a few people are justified in their political beliefs, even once we count the people who justifiedly accept the testimony of others. If so, then my theory implies that only these people should vote.

What then? On one hand, this need not be a problem. If everyone behaved as my theory of voting ethics suggests they ought, then they would defer to better voters and find this deference unproblematic. It would not undermine democratic stability. Now, in practice, I do not expect this to happen. Instead, I expect bad voters to continue to vote badly.[23] But that does not show that the theory is wrong. It just shows that people are not likely to act well.

OBJECTION: THE MORAL DISENFRANCHISEMENT OF POOR MINORITIES

Another objection to my argument says that it suggests the moral disenfranchisement of the poor and of minorities.[24] Arguably, poor blacks are less likely than rich whites to possess the proper credentials to be good voters. So my theory seems to suggest that some already disadvantaged people have a (unenforceable) moral obligation to refrain from voting. On top of the mistreatment they have received from the social system, I am now claiming that their votes are a kind of pollution. How mean! Or so the objection goes.

Now, obviously my theory of voting ethics does not say anything as straightforward as "only rich white people should vote" or "poor blacks should never vote." Rather, the theory says that only people who meet certain epistemic criteria should vote. Yet it might turn out that in our world the people who have an obligation to abstain disproportionately are poor, underprivileged minorities. (See chapter 7 for some empirical evidence that this is so.) Note that I have not asserted that this is the case. Instead, I am simply considering whether the possibility poses a problem for my theory.

For the sake of argument, imagine that our society is divided into two races, the Blues and the Greens. All of the Blues are rich, well educated, and are good voters per my theory. All of the Greens are poor, badly educated, and are bad voters per my theory. Also, the Greens are this way because of a complex set of sociological, economic, and political factors, which in turn stem from their history of being oppressed by the Blues.[25]

In this society, the Greens are badly served. We should find ways of generating better education and opportunity for the Greens. The system is broken and needs to be fixed. There is a real failing of social inclusion in this society.

Still, the Greens should not vote, even if they ought to have the right to do so. By hypothesis, if the Greens vote, either they will vote harmfully or their votes will be fortuitous.[26] By hypothesis, having the Greens vote en masse is unlikely to solve any problems. The Greens' votes would help the Greens only if the Greens know enough to support policies that would help them. By hypothesis, the Greens do not know enough.

One might argue that if the Greens vote en masse, then the Blues will be forced to reckon with them and will be forced to improve the lot of the Greens. However, this is true only if the Greens are sufficiently well informed, well meaning, and adequately rational in how they vote. That is, this is true only if the Greens are pretty good voters. If the Greens are bad voters, then the Blues will only need to pretend to care about the Greens' problems but can get away with doing nothing to solve them.[27]

Similarly, suppose that many Greens are born with natural talents and abilities, such that if they had been born into the better socioeconomic circumstances of the Blues, they would have become surgeons, engineers, professors, and lawyers. Instead, these naturally talented Greens are born into broken families, into crime-ridden, economically depressed areas, and into places with low educational opportunities. As a result, imagine that these Greens, despite their natural talents, are so scarred by their childhood circumstances that, when they grow up, none of them retain the ability to work as surgeons, engineers, professors, or lawyers.

If so, this is a terrible thing. Justice cries out for the problem to be fixed. But it does not follow that any of the scarred Greens should be surgeons, engineers, professors, or lawyers. By hypothesis, they are not in a position to do these jobs adequately. The very fact that they are not in such a position gives them grounds for complaint, but that does not mean they should do any of these things.

In parallel, suppose my father beat me daily when I was a child. As a result, I can no longer hold my hand steady enough to perform surgery, no matter how hard I try. If so, then I should not be a surgeon. It is not my fault that I should not be a surgeon. It is unjust that I have been placed in such a position. My father should apologize and compensate me. Still, I should not be a surgeon. Were I to perform surgery, I would hurt innocent people. Similarly, were the Greens to vote, they would hurt innocent people, including themselves. Or it would be pure luck if they did not.

So, if it turns out that poor minorities overwhelmingly qualify as bad voters on my theory, this does not mean my theory is wrong. Rather, it probably means that there is something wrong with our society, and we should try to fix the problem as best we can.

Should We Restrict the *Right* to Vote?

In most democracies, universal and equal adult suffrage is the default. That is, every citizen, upon reaching a legally defined age of reason, is granted a right to vote, and a right to vote of equal weight as everyone else's. The wisest person has as much voting power as the fool, and the most virtuous person has as much voting power as the most wicked (except, in some countries, if the wicked person is a convicted felon). Is this a desirable or just way to distribute political power?

Suppose some voters fail to meet the standards of good voting. Does this imply that they should not be permitted to vote, or that they should be deprived of the right to vote? Should political power—including the right to vote—be made conditional on epistemic competence, political knowledge, and moral goodness? In this section, I want to explain briefly why even if we can show someone is bad voter, it does not automatically follow that she should not have a right to vote. So, in this section, my goal is just to show why if someone is incompetent or corrupt about politics, it does not automatically follow that she should thereby lack the right to vote. That is, I want to explain why the claim that some people should not vote does not straightforwardly imply that universal suffrage is unjust.

Some epistocrats hold that people should have the right to vote only if they demonstrate sufficient knowledge and rationality. The idea is that in order to register to vote, citizens must pass a competence exam showing sufficient knowledge of civics, economics, political science, and related knowledge. Bryan Caplan says, "A test of voter competence is no more objectionable than a driving test. Both bad driving and bad voting are dangerous . . . to innocent bystanders."[28] The idea is that voters do not just choose for themselves but for others. As a citizen, I should be able to demand that anyone who exercises political power over me be (at least minimally) competent to do so. It would be unjust if I had to submit to an incompetent or corrupt jury, judge, or police force. So too would it be unjust for me to have to submit to an incompetent or corrupt electorate.

In principle, a competence exam could be an effective instrument to improve voting outcomes in ways that benefit all, including those excluded from voting. If angels ran the exams, we would have more reason to consider them.

In practice, the competence exam is ripe for abuse and institutional capture. Competence exams would be likely be used to disenfranchise people who might vote against the party in power. Special interest groups would fight to control the agency overseeing the exams. Even if the exam were fair and just in principle, it is unlikely that the exam would be administered in a fair and just way in practice. If we are looking for a practical policy instrument to improve actual democratic decision making, then we need not examine whether competence exams are unjust in principle. We can expect them to be unjust in practice. I think Caplan's own public-choice economics speaks against the poll exam rather than for it, though he disagrees.[29] One of us is wrong, and it might well be me. Perhaps the poll exam would be abused to some degree, but we would get such good political outcomes that tolerating the abuse would be worthwhile. I will not try to settle this debate here. Instead, I just want to note that even if a competence exam were acceptable in principle, whether such an exam could be administered properly in practice is partly an empirical matter.

Even if the exam system were free of corruption, there might be no way to design an exam that could track the morally relevant qualifications. A voter votes well when she votes in ways she justifiedly believes will promote the common good. She votes badly otherwise. It is not clear how we could design a test that would track whether someone's beliefs about what will promote the common good are justified. How would we punish or reward people for making bad or good choices about civil rights? If we try to test knowledge, what should we test? A good voter does not need to know trivia, such as how many U.S. states there are, or how many voting members of Congress there are. Consider this relatively modest proposal: a good voter should know basic textbook economics (even if she disagrees with it) and should be able to identify one or two platforms of the candidates for which she votes. However, even this kind of knowledge is not necessary to be a good voter, on my theory. You might be completely ignorant about the candidates and about social science, but know that candidate A is supported by people who deserve your trust and deference, and thus be justified in voting for A on those grounds. We cannot design a written test to check for justified deference to experts. So, even if exams are acceptable in principle, it is not clear whether we can design an acceptable one.

However, whether such exams are acceptable even in principle is also not clear. In a recent book, Estlund argues that restrictions on who can hold power have to be made on grounds that all reasonable people (or, more precisely, people with "qualified points of view") can accept. Here is a summary of his position: Estlund argues that if we are going to have political power, the default position is that it should be equally distributed. If we give power to some but not others, then this means those with power get to rule over those without power.[30] We are required to justify unequal power on grounds that can be accepted by all reasonable points of view potentially subject to that power.

However, Estlund argues, there is no way to meet this requirement. There is too much reasonable disagreement about who qualifies as an expert and who does not, about which people are good and which are corrupt. Even if, for example, my own theory of voting ethics is correct, some reasonable people will reasonably reject this view. (Though, of course, that is not to say that everyone who disagrees with me is reasonable for doing so.) Thus, even if I am correct in holding that some people should not vote, that does not mean the government is permitted to exclude them from voting. The theory of voting ethics presented here—even if true—might not be the kind of thing we can *impose* upon everyone. To impose it upon everyone requires that there are no reasonable objections to it.

Now, perhaps Estlund is mistaken in his defense of equal voting rights. However, to defend unequal voting rights requires that one overcome his objections, and that is a complicated project. At the very least, we cannot straightforwardly infer that if some people are bad voters, they should therefore be excluded from having voting rights.

Philippe Van Parijs has argued that it might be just to remove the political rights of elderly citizens. People should have political power only to the extent that they are likely to bear the consequences of their decisions. Because the elderly are near death, they have an incentive (and ability) to seize many costly benefits for themselves and leave future generations to pay the tab. Depriving the elderly of the right to vote might be a necessary means of preventing the elderly from violating rules of intergenerational justice.[31] His proposal faces many of the same problems as Caplan's. For one, at least *some* elderly people will qualify as good voters, and so they have a legitimate complaint if they are excluded from voting. And Estlund's objection applies to Van Parijs's proposal as well.

The question of who should have the right to vote is an important one. In the past history of the United States, and of other democracies, many citizens were excluded on arbitrary grounds, such as on sex and race. We made moral progress by eliminating these arbitrary restrictions on voting rights. Still, we should not just assume that universal equal suffrage is justified, or even that democracy itself is justified. This book is not a defense of democracy or of universal equal suffrage. My theory of voting ethics is compatible with universal equal suffrage, but it does not imply it or require it. (In fact, even an anarchist might accept my view. He might hold that we should not have democracy at all, but if we do, then people should abide by the theory of voting ethics presented here.)

WHY NOT EDUCATE VOTERS INSTEAD?

Here is another objection: instead of recommending that bad voters abstain, I should advocate better education such that fewer people vote badly. The problem with this objection is the word "instead." The alternative political proposal (that people should receive better education) does not conflict with my moral claim (that bad voters should abstain).

No doubt one way to improve democratic decision making is to improve citizen's knowledge of relevant philosophical and social-scientific issues. If every citizen had a firm grasp of basic economics, basic political science, and basic sociology, they would vote better than they now do. Perhaps public high schools should spend more time teaching statistics and economics, even if this comes at the cost of learning trigonometry and some Shakespeare.[32] (In the United States, most high school students get their ideas about economics through history texts, but unfortunately, because of peculiarities in the discipline of history, historians often hold false beliefs about economics.) All things being equal, educational reforms that improve citizens' knowledge and make them better voters are a good thing, and I do not oppose them.

However, if people are not well educated and as a result are not in a position to vote well, then they should not vote. It might not be their fault that they cannot vote well. Perhaps citizens have a real complaint against their states for failing to provide them with the right kind of education in the K–12 system. If so, then good voters should take that into consideration when they vote. But bad voters should still abstain, rather than risk imposing bad governance on everyone.

CHAPTER FIVE

For the Common Good

THE ENDS OF VOTING

THE *EGOISTIC* VIEW of voting holds that citizens rightly may choose government policies maximally favorable to themselves, regardless of what cost these programs impose upon others.[1] On this view, citizens rightly regard government as a source of privileges and grants. Politics is a competition for prizes to be paid for by the losers. Citizens rightly seek to form majority coalitions so they can impose their will upon and exploit the minority. When voting, Peter tries to rob Paul and Paul tries to rob Peter.

Many people believe there is nothing wrong with egoistic voting. Few people would claim you *should* vote egoistically. However, many would say it is morally permissible to do so. I have met many laypeople, though not political philosophers, who think that democracy is just a system in which citizens attempt to exploit one another, and so long as citizens do not violate each other's basic rights, this is fine. On its face, this is a bizarre view, but it is quite common. A more plausible defense of egoistic voting holds that when voters pursue their self-interest, they will be led to promote the common good, as if by an invisible hand.

In contrast, the *public-spirited view* holds that citizens ought to vote for the common good. On this view, citizens ought not aim for purely private interests, especially when such interests come at the expense of the common good. Voters should look for policies good for all, rather than seeking to exploit their fellow citizens through government.

This public-spirited view does not say that citizens must be servile. They need not offer themselves as sacrificial lambs for the good of society. In fact, institutions that allow and encourage people to pursue their self-interest can help serve the common good, provided that the institutions at least tend to minimize negative externalities.[2]

In this chapter, I defend the public-spirited view. I argue that voters generally should vote for policies or candidates that promote the common good rather than for policies or candidates that benefit themselves at the expense of the common good.

This chapter is about how voters should vote, not what their motives should be. So I do not argue that voters must care about or be motivated by the common good. Rather, I am claiming that voters, whatever their motives, generally should vote for policies that promote the common good. Voters might do so for nonaltruistic reasons without acting wrongly. For instance, suppose that Alf votes for policies that promote the common good. However, Alf does this not because it is his duty but only because his girlfriend pledged on Votergasm.com to have sex with him if he voted well. If so, then Alf votes in a publicly beneficial way for selfish reasons. His motives are not noble, but his actions are not wrong. (In the same spirit, a physician might cure people out of a desire for money, or a politician might reform healthcare out of a desire for power. In these cases, they have not acted wrongly, though their motives are not noble.)

Can Liberals Believe in the Common Good?

Before turning to why voters should vote in a public-spirited way, I address some skeptical worries about the notion of the common good.

Skepticism about the Idea of the Common Good

The term "common good" suggests something that is good for the collective, for the people as a body. Collectivists and statists tend to think that the body politic is a real organism, with a (strongly irreducible) good of its own. For instance, Giovanni Gentile and Benito Mussolini describe the fascist state as having a will and personality of its own, apart from the personality of individuals who belong to it. They say individuals should subordinate their private interests to the state's interests. Individuals are nothing more than cells in the state's body.

This way of understanding the common good leads some liberals to balk at the very notion of the common good. Liberals typically deny that there are strongly irreducible social goods.[3] Recall that strongly irreducible social goods are things that are good for society irrespective of whether they are good for any individual members of that society. Liberals are skeptical whether any such strongly irreducible social goods exist. Many liberals believe that collectives and societies are not the kinds of things that can have a good of their own. However, even if strongly irreducible goods are shown to exist, liberals hold that these goods should not be used as basis for public policy.[4]

Instead, liberals usually believe that institutions and policies can be justified only by appeal to the interests of individuals. For the common good to serve as a basis for policy, it must be reducible to the various interests of private individuals.

Background Conditions of Individuals' Goods

Most liberals hold that there is such a thing as the common good. The common good is a function of individual interests. Policies and institutions can be understood to be in the common good provided that they in some way serve these various individual interests.

Different citizens hold different conceptions of the good life. Take any two random people in a liberal society. They are likely to have different ideas of what is the best form of life. In very specific terms, I might think being a philosopher is the best life for me, while you think being a soldier is best for you. In the abstract, it might be that I think developing and exercising mental capacities is the best form of life, while you think participating in a venerable tradition is best.

Still, we both need some amount of the same kinds of goods to achieve our different conceptions of the good life. We both need personal and physical integrity, mental and physical health, some wealth, some degree of education, opportunities for economic and social advancement, some ability to influence others. It would be unusual to find someone who did not need these things at all. So there are certain kinds of goods that are instrumentally valuable to each of us.

We cannot get these goods on our own. We need to cooperate with each other to generate them. Living in a social system that helps us produce these goods is in our common interest. Generally, choosing policies that increase rather than decrease our access to these goods is in our common interest.

There are certain background conditions and institutions needed for each of us to pursue and achieve our conceptions of the good. Linda Raeder claims that "the common good in a "great society" such as an advanced liberal society—one characterized by an extensive division of labor and knowledge and integrated by common economic, legal, and moral practices—consists on the fulfillment of the fundamental value implicitly held by all its members: the preservation of the social order as a whole, the abstract, enduring structure within which all individual and organizational activities must occur."[5]

A well-functioning social order is part of the good for everyone, because without it we cannot pursue and achieve our various ends. So the preservation of well-functioning social order can be said to be in the common good.

Having a sufficient degree of shared ethical and social norms is also in the common good.[6] We need to coordinate with one another to achieve our various ends. We need to know what to expect from each other. We need to count on being treated with respect, and we need to have a shared understanding of what it means to treat each other with respect.

Certain background institutions and policies tend to promote the private interests of all or at least most citizens. Some institutions, such as well-functioning markets, liberal democratic government, the rule of law, and a culture of tolerance and respect, tend to promote greater wealth, longer and healthier lives, and lives with more cultural, social, and economic opportunities. Other institutions tend to demote these things. It is in the common good to promote the first kind of institutions rather than the second. Institutions, policies, and practices that are generally to everyone's advantage can be said to be in the common good.[7]

WHAT IS THE COMMON GOOD?

The previous section was intended to show that talk of the common good does not commit one to believing that society is some sort of organism with a good of its own. One can intelligibly talk about the common good even if one is an individualist, that is, a person who believes that only individuals (but not collectives) can have a good of their own. We can sensibly talk of certain institutions, practices, and states of affairs being in everyone's interest. However, I left the notion of the common good underspecified.

I do not intend to give a full theory of the common good here. The theory of voting ethics presented here is a module that can be added to a number of background theories of justice and the common good. Though not compatible with every possible political philosophy, the theory is compatible with many of them. I have argued that citizens ought to vote only for things they justifiedly believe would promote the common good. Think of "the common good" as a variable to be filled in by the correct theory of the ends of government. I have my own view of the right way to fill in this variable and would be happy to argue for it elsewhere, but doing so goes beyond the scope of the book. The theory of voting ethics presented here does not depend upon my view of the proper ends of government.

So, instead of arguing for a particular notion of the common good, I will say something about why every plausible democratic theory needs to have some notion of the common good or, more broadly, some notion of the right ends of politics. That is, every plausible democratic theory needs to hold that democracy is justified *in part* because it tends to produce the morally right outcomes.

To see why, consider the alternative. *Pure proceduralist* defenses of democracy hold that democracy is justified because it is an intrinsically just or right *method* for making decisions, regardless of what outcomes it produces. (In contrast, *substantive* defenses of democracy hold that democracy is justified because it tends to produce good outcomes.) For instance, many people advocate democracy because they think it has inherently fair procedures. They think democracy (with universal, equal franchise) is the fairest way to make political decisions. Democracy gives everyone a vote and a say, and so everyone has some chance to have her way.

Suppose you care only that political decisions be made fairly. If so, there is no special reason to prefer democracy. Instead of voting under majority rule, we could flip a coin or roll dice.[8] We could decide leaders and policies by lottery. These methods would be fair, in fact, fairer than any real voting procedures. (Unlike voters and elections boards, coins are not sexist, racist, classist, ethnocentric, or swayed by money or glamour.) If you cared only about fairness, you would have no reason to prefer majoritarian democracy to lotteries.

Someone might object that lotteries are *unfair* because they would be unlikely to give proper weight to the interests of each citizen. But we can construct a weighted lottery procedure to deal with this issue. So, for example, suppose 10 percent of citizens advocate X, 20 percent advocate Y, and 70 percent advocate Z. We could have a weighted lottery with a 10 percent chance of selecting X, 20 percent chance of selecting Y, and 70 percent chance of selecting Z. Those who X and Y would probably prefer this lottery to majoritary rule. Under majority rule, they are bound to lose, but in the lottery, they have a chance of winning.

If someone objects that lotteries are unfair, she might mean that lotteries could lead to exploitative policies or policies under which certain individuals' or groups' interests are ignored. This might be a good objection to using lotteries. Yet this objection concerns the fairness of the *outcome* of the lottery, not the fairness of the lottery *procedure*. That is, this objection holds that lotteries are bad because they cannot be expected to produce the right outcomes, or because they run too much risk of producing the wrong outcomes. So, if you object to lotteries for this reason, you are not a pure proceduralist. Instead, you agree with me that part of what justifies democracy is that it has a sufficiently high tendency to produce the morally right outcomes. In your view, the morally right outcomes have to be fair in some way.

Consider another purported alternative: suppose someone objects that there is no coherent notion of the common good or "the right ends of politics." Instead, democracy is just about keeping the peace. However, notice that it is not a pure proceduralist justification, but a substantive justification. It holds that political institutions are justified because they promote the right end, and that the right end is peace. This is a deflated, perhaps too deflated, conception of the common good. Regardless, it is *a* conception of the common good or of the right ends of government, and so it is not a pure proceduralist defense of democracy.

Finally, consider another purported alternative: suppose you claim to be a pragmatist. You are not interested in moral principles. You just advocate whatever works, and you advocate democracy because it works. Well, what counts as *working*? When you answer that question, you are going to give a substantive defense of democracy. For instance, suppose you say, "I advocate democracy because it works. And it works because it allows for the stable transmission of power." That is a substantive defense of democracy. You advocate democracy because it tends to be stable and to avoid violence in the transmission of power, not simply because it is an inherently fair or just way of making decisions.

I am not arguing the fairness of democratic procedures is irrelevant to the justification of democracy. (Nor am I arguing that it is relevant.) Rather, I am just arguing that no defense of democracy can succeed unless it holds that democracy has a sufficiently high tendency to produce the morally right outcomes, whatever those are.

The Right Ends of Government

This theory of voting ethics presented in this book is a module that can be added to various conceptions of the right ends of government. Consider some examples:

1. Rawlsian liberals hold that the right end of political institutions is to promote justice. According to the Rawlsian conception of justice (called "justice as fairness") justice requires that all citizens have a fully adequate scheme of basic liberties, that there is fair equality in the opportunities available to citizens, and that inequalities in people's basic goods (such as wealth, income, leisure) are permissible provided they are to the maximal advantage of the representative member of the least advantaged group.

2. Those with more strongly egalitarian conception of justice, such as certain Marxists, hold that governments ought to promote equality among citizens to a greater degree than Rawls's theory requires.

3. Republicans, such as Philip Pettit, hold that the primary task of governments is to create conditions of "freedom as non-domination." A person possesses "freedom as non-domination" when others cannot arbitrarily and with impunity interfere with her decision making.

4. Many deontological libertarians hold that the right end of government is to secure and protect basic rights, including rights of free speech, bodily integrity, and the right to hold and use property.

5. Certain consequentialists think that the right end of government is to promote human welfare. For example, David Schmidtz (whose

political philosophy can roughly be described as a kind of sophisticated welfarism) argues that political institutions should be judged primarily by how well they promote the common good. On his view, something is presumed to be in common good when it makes most people better off, provided that it either does not make anyone worse off or, if it does make some worse off, does so without exploiting them.[9] This presumption can be overridden by further concerns.

6. Some communitarians hold that the right end of government is to promote community, to create conditions under which citizens have strong bonds with one another. Government is meant to foster shared social norms and a shared social identity that pervades people's lives.

7. Perfectionists hold that the right end of government is to promote human excellence. Different perfectionists have different views of what constitutes human excellence, but they often have in mind things such as moral virtue, scientific and artistic achievement, and intellectual virtue.

The theory of voting ethics presented in this book is compatible with many versions of these theories of the right ends of government. The theory of voting ethics is not compatible with all theories of the common good—for example, it is not compatible with certain civic humanist theories that hold there is a duty to vote—but is compatible with many different views.

Note, however, that the theory of voting ethics presented here might allow someone to vote on the basis of the wrong conception of the common good. Suppose justice as fairness is the correct theory of the ends of government. I have argued that a voter must be justified in thinking that what she votes for would promote the common good. This need not mean that she must justifiedly believe that what she votes for will help instantiate justice as fairness. Imagine that she *mistakenly* but justifiedly believes that a perfectionist conception of the common good is correct and votes accordingly. So long as she is *justified* in her beliefs about what the common good is, and *justified* in thinking that she is voting for something that would promote the common good, it is permissible for her to vote to promote the common good so conceived, even though she is wrong about what the common good is. If she has justified but false moral beliefs, she may vote on the basis of those beliefs. The argument presented in chapter 3 requires not that voters be *correct* but that they be *epistemically justified*. And, sometimes, one can be epistemically justified but incorrect about certain beliefs. I leave to moral epistemologists the question of whether it is possible to justifiedly hold false *moral* beliefs in particular; but if it is possible, then my theory implies that it is permissible to vote on those beliefs.

Why Should We Vote for the Common Good?

In this section, I discuss some positive reasons why people ought to vote for the common good rather than for narrow self-interest. In the next section, I respond to what I consider the best defense of self-interest voting, which holds that democracies take self-interested votes as inputs and produce the common good as an output.

Giving Everyone a Stake

Everyone who is subject to coercive rules and is expected to conform with and maintain social institutions should have a stake in those rules and institutions. To expect people to comply with social rules is unjust unless those rules are sufficiently to their benefit. To the extent that the rules tend to benefit some groups at the expense of others, these other groups lack reasons to comply. To force them to comply with such rules, when they lack sufficient reasons to do so, is to subjugate them. Subjugating reasonable, responsible people is unjust. To vote for self-interest at the expense of the common good is to vote in favor of subjugating others.

We might think of the ballot as the symbol of democracy. But a more appropriate symbol would be a ballot attached to a gun. Democratic decisions are enforced with violence and the threat of violence. The stakes are high. Justifying violence and the threat of violence are no light tasks, morally speaking.

Stuart White argues that in a good society, citizens exhibit democratic mutual regard. White describes a society of democratic mutual regard as follows:

> As citizens, coming together to determine their shared laws and other common institutions that will regulate their life together in a fundamental way, individuals do not seek merely to impose their preferred institutions on others. For the purpose of designing these institutions, they regard each other as equals, and as possessing certain shared basic interests that these institutions must respect and protect. As citizens, they form their preferences across institutions, and seek to justify their institutional preferences to other citizens by offering reasons that appeal to their status as equals and, relatedly, to their shared basic interests.[10]

White's idea is that in a good society, citizens see each other as having the same fundamental political status. Importantly, they regard this equal political status as a high status—every individual citizen is important.[11] Institutions have to be justifiable to each of us, because each of us is important.

A society that lacks democratic mutual regard is to that extent a society of mutual disrespect. Citizens do not see other people's interests as important. They believe they may rightly act in predatory or exploitative ways toward other citizens. There is little admirable about this kind of society.

Society as a Positive-Sum Game

Societies are cooperative ventures for mutual gain. Societies flourish when they are constructed as positive-sum games, that is, games where everyone can come out a winner. Good rules make it so that people work for mutual advantage. For instance, the way a baker in a well-functioning market improves his material welfare is by providing bread that other people want. When the rules encourage this kind of behavior, people generally become better off over time.

On the other hand, suppose instead of competing to sell bread on the market, I try to rig the rules such that no one can compete with me, or I try to get a subsidy from the government. If I obtain a monopoly privilege, people buy from me only because I have literally forced my competitors out of business. I prosper as a baker not because I best serve others' interests, but because the better bakers are not permitted to sell. These kinds of monopolies rarely serve the common good. Or suppose I win a subsidy to keep my bakery afloat; I would go out of business otherwise. For every dollar of resources I use in making bread, I produce less than a dollar's worth of bread. By baking, I destroy wealth. The subsidy transfers wealth to me from those who create it, thus allowing me to sustain my business. These kinds of subsidies rarely serve the common good.

The egoistic view of voting treats politics like a poker game. Poker games are classic zero-sum games. In a zero-sum game, one person can win only to the extent that others lose. In poker, if I win $100, this means others at the table lost a total of $100. No money is gained or destroyed; it is merely moved around.

Actually, this characterization of the egoistic view is too kind. It is unlikely that egoistic voting just transfers wealth from losers to winners without affecting the total amount of wealth. Instead, egoistic voting is probably a negative-sum game. In negative-sum games, it is possible for everyone to come out a loser, worse off than they were before playing. Imagine a poker game where every time someone wins $1 at the table, another $1 disappears from the pot. In any given transaction, the winner is made better off. However, over time, almost everyone will be made worse off than they would if the game had not been played. At the end, there is less money on the table than there was before the game was played. It is unlikely that many people will come out ahead.

According to David Friedman,

> Special interest politics is a simple game. A hundred people sit in a circle, each with his pocket full of pennies. A politician walks around outside the circle, taking a penny from each person. No one minds; who cares about a penny? When he has gotten all the way around the circle, the politician throws fifty cents down in front of one person, who is overjoyed at the unexpected windfall. The process is repeated, ending with a different person. After a hundred rounds, everyone is a hundred cents poorer, fifty cents richer, and happy.[12]

Why think egoistic voting is like this? One reason is that insofar as coalitions of voters obtain special monopoly powers or other restrictions in their favor, they will tend to create deadweight losses.[13] A second reason is that politicians, lobbyists, bureaucrats, and the others who facilitate games of mutual exploitation have to be paid. A third reason is that such behaviors distort the economy and lead to efficiency losses, as unproductive enterprises are subsidized or investors take a wait-and-see approach.[14] (These are relatively uncontroversial conclusions in economics. I do not explain them further here, though, in part because doing so would make this chapter unnecessarily technical. Interested readers can look at my citations for more information.)

Voters who vote for narrow self-interest at the expense of the common good contribute to turning society from a positive-sum game into a negative-sum game. In chapter 3, I argued that citizens have a moral duty to refrain from participating in collectively harmful activities when the cost of personal restraint is low. Voters who vote for special-interest politics violate this duty. After all, the personal cost of refraining from selfish voting is minimal. Individual votes have vanishingly small expected utility.

For instance, suppose in the next election, Obama enjoys the same lead that he enjoyed coming into the previous election. Imagine he makes a bizarre campaign promise: he will pay each professional philosopher $1 million if he is reelected. Suppose I know that these payments come at the expense of the common good. Suppose also that I know Obama would have had no other effects, positive or negative, on the common good. If so, to me, Obama's victory is worth $1 million. Despite that, the expected utility of my vote for him would be thousands of orders of magnitude below a penny. Thus, though I have a huge stake in Obama winning, I have no stake in voting for Obama. I bear no significant cost, including opportunity cost, if I refrain from voting for him. I should thus keep my hands clean and not vote for him.

Retaliatory and Preemptive Exploitation

If other people are trying to exploit me through voting, should I be permitted to exploit them back in turn? My response is that being exploited by others may sometimes excuse certain kinds of rent-seeking behavior, but it does not normally excuse bad voting.

Here is a case where it does work. Suppose you go to the king and ask him to give you five of my sheep. Suppose the king's men are careless, so they accidently kill one of my sheep as they seize five others. You get five sheep, but I am out six. After you have done this, it seems morally excusable for me to ask the king to take some of your goats and given them to me. After all, you should not have taken my sheep, and you owe me compensation. If I refrain from asking the king to exploit you back in turn, I suffer a major loss, and I had no moral reason to endure this loss. You, not I, started the pattern of exploitation. I am not trying to exploit you. I am just seeking rectification.

On the other hand, suppose that, instead of asking the king to take five goats from you, I ask him to take some cows from Henry, a previously uninvolved third party. Here it looks as if I am doing something wrong. I am preying on Henry just as you preyed on me. Henry is an innocent bystander.

Still, if everyone or nearly everyone engages in predatory or mutually destructive behavior, and if not participating would impose a serious cost on you, then it might be permissible for you to participate. For example, suppose we are in a tragic commons. (See chapter 3, appendix 2.) We are overusing a commonly held well, causing it to dry up. In this case, I need water to survive. Here it is less obvious that I do something wrong by taking water, even though this tends to destroy the well. It is not my fault that the resource is being exploited. I am incapable of doing any better. If I stop exploiting it, I die. I might regret how bad the system is, but if I cannot change things, you cannot blame me.

Or consider Hobbes's state of nature. In the state of nature, everyone continually makes war with each other. Even if participating in the system of mutual violence repulses me, I cannot afford not to participate. If I refrain from violence, I will be killed, and no one will be saved in the process.

Voting is not like that. Typically, if other people are voting for special interests and are attempting to exploit you, then *regardless of how you vote*, you will suffer the same consequences. After all, your vote has only a vanishingly small chance of making a difference. So it is cheap and easy to have clean hands. This holds for everybody. Each of us could refrain from exploitative voting at no significant personal cost to ourselves. For each of us, because our individual votes count for practically nothing, trying to exploit others through voting fails to benefit us and also fails to save us from being exploited. So we might as well have clean hands and vote in a public-spirited way. And, of course, if enough of us did this, we would end the system of mutual exploitation and replace it with one of mutual gain.

One objection to this argument is that people vote in coalitions. For instance, members of CCPOA (California's prison guard union) often vote as a bloc for their interests at the expense of the common good. California's prison system is poorly run and overly expensive. Most experts believe that California sends too many people to jail, uses poor enforcement and deterrence strategies, and has too many prisons. Still, the CCPOA advocates increasingly punitive enforcement procedures and building more prisons, because doing so benefits its members. When a candidate in California proposes reforming the system, the CCPOA destroys that candidate's career by running attack ads claiming the candidate is soft on crime.[15]

Note that the CCPOA's collective voting power is not the problem. It has 30,000 members spread across the state. As a voting bloc, for most elections, it makes little difference. However, its advertisements scare uninformed, irrational voters. They convince voters to favor CCPOA-sponsored candidates, even though it is not in most voters' interests to do so.[16] If everyone except CCPOA members abided by the ethics of voting, that is, voted only for policies they justifiedly believed would serve the common good, the CCPOA would see its power drastically reduced.

People probably will not abide by the ethics of voting. So does this excuse Californian voters? May Californian voters vote in mutually exploitative ways as a form of self-defense against powerful voting blocs?

The short answer to this question is that it depends. It depends on how many other groups like the CCPOA there are and how much damage they are doing. All democracies suffer from rent seeking and special-interest-group politics. Sometimes, the best choice in the face of injustice is to suck it up and live with it. Some people steal, but that does not mean we may all become thieves. Rather, we should stop thieves as best we can and to continue to cooperate and observe property rights, even though some people exploit us for doing so. Similarly, it is often more advantageous for most of us to vote in cooperative ways that promote the common good, even though this means some special interest groups will take advantage of us. Only when democratic politics have severely degenerated does it make more sense for us to turn to mutual exploitation over cooperation. When a society is at that point, the political system is probably doomed.

If others try to exploit you, it may be because they are worried that you are trying to exploit them. Compare the problem of competitive voting to the Hobbesian state of nature. In the state of nature, people attack each other preemptively. They are worried others will attack them. Almost everyone wants peace, but they are not sure what others want. To the extent this is so, then one way to exit the state of nature is to lay down your weapons. For the most part, other people are a threat to you only because they think you are a threat of them. When you make it clear you are not a threat, they will not be a threat to you either.

Perhaps something like this is true of politics. Perhaps some people are genuinely predatory and will act like predators under any system. The best we can do is try to stop them, perhaps by limiting the power of government to satisfy their demands or through some other means. However, it is not in our common interest for all of us to behave as predators, just because some of us do. If my coalition can credibly signal to yours that we are interested in promoting the common good rather than preying on you, this can give both of us reason to stop predatory activity. We will still suffer from the machinations of groups like the CCPOA. Yet, we are better off just accepting that as the cost of cooperation, much as city dwellers just accept that their cars will be broken into once or twice over their lifetimes.

THE INVISIBLE HAND OF POLITICS?

One way to defend purely self-interested voting against my complaints is to show that purely self-interest voting does not come at the expense of the common good. Better yet, show that self-interested voting actually promotes the common good.

For Richard Posner, "Another reason for not wanting to raise the political consciousness of the U.S. population is that even well-educated and well-informed people find it difficult to reason accurately about matters remote from their immediate concerns. People who vote on the basis of their self-interest are at least voting about something they know first-hand, their own needs and preferences. Beware the high-minded voter."[17] Posner needs to be cautious about overstating what voters know. A self-interested voter can easily determine that she needs better economic opportunities. But she cannot easily determine which politician would actually best promote economic opportunities. She needs the social sciences, not just firsthand knowledge, for that. Still, Posner is right that it is generally easier for me to know if a policy will help *me* than to know if it will help *us*. He believes that democracy can take self-interest votes as inputs and produce outputs that are (more or less) in the common good. Why think that? An analogy to markets might help here.

Economists believe that, in general, in a well-functioning market system, when individuals pursue their self-interest, they promote the common good as well. A properly regulated system of property rights and contract laws tends to cause predominantly self-interested individuals to act in mutually beneficial rather than mutually destructive ways. Adam Smith claims that "every individual . . . labours to render the annual revenue of society as great as he can. He generally, indeed, neither intends to promote the publick interest, nor knows how much he is promoting it. . . . he intends only his own security. . . . [But] by directing [his] industry in such a manner as its produce may be of greatest value, he intends only his own gain, and he is in this, as in many cases, led by an invisible hand to promote an end that was no part of his intention."[18]

The "invisible hand" metaphor refers to how good institutions make it so that people's best shot at promoting their own interest is to make products that other people want at prices they can afford to pay. To get bread from the baker, I must provide him with something he wants. So long as negative externalities are adequately eliminated and so long as people are free to walk away from bad deals, the individual pursuit of profit tends to help others rather than harm them. The desire for profit aligns the market and coordinates everyone's activities. Self-interested behavior leads to publicly beneficial outcomes.

I am interested in whether these kinds of claims hold true of politics. I assume for the sake of argument that economists are correct about markets. The question I am asking here is whether self-interested voting works in democracy the way self-interested behavior purportedly works in markets. If every person votes for what she perceives to be her self-interest, does democracy lead her also to promote the public interest, as if by an invisible hand?

We should not expect a complete disconnect between self-interested voting and publicly beneficial outcomes. However, there are reasons to think that self-interested voting will not promote the common good. It is helpful to examine certain disanalogies between politics and markets to see why.

Generally, market exchanges are voluntary but political processes are not. In a market, you can walk away from proposed deals. To sell, you must locate a willing buyer. To buy, you must locate a willing seller. Individual transactions occur only because each party has an ex ante profit from the transaction. All parties expect to benefit from market exchanges; otherwise these exchanges would not occur.

The cost of these exchanges is, for the most part, internalized. When I buy and eat a candy bar, it might make me fat, but it will not make you fat. In general, private exchanges do not harm innocent bystanders.

(There are, of course, important exceptions to this rule.) The fact that these costs are internalized also incentivizes buyers and sellers to be adequately rational and well informed about their choices. If they make mistakes, they bear the costs of their actions. If they make good choices, they enjoy the benefits. Markets discipline market agents.

In contrast, political decisions are neither voluntary nor internalized. If the majority chooses X, everyone has to live with X. In the market, if I dislike Barbara Streisand's music, then I am free not to buy it. People are not free to walk away from bad bargains in politics as they are free to walk away from bad bargains in the market. As John Simmons says, "For many citizens there are few acceptable options to remaining in their states and obeying (most) law, and for most persons active resistance to the state is in effect impossible. And for none of us is there any option to living in some state or other, all of which make (at least) the same core demands on us. These facts raise serious doubts about the voluntariness of any widely performed acts that might be alleged to be binding acts of political consent."[19]

Because market decisions require the voluntary participation of all parties, there is a tendency for decisions to be in everyone's interests. In contrast, in democracy, the majority may simply impose its will on the minority.[20] If the minority hates the majority's decision enough, it might rebel. This means that democratic decisions made solely on the basis of self-interest would tend not to be bad enough to inspire widespread rebellion. (I.e., the majority will not pass laws bad enough that the minority is willing to risk death to overthrow the system.) But that is a low bar. It is a stretch to infer that democratic decisions would thus be guided toward the common good as if by an invisible hand.

Another disanalogy between markets and politics concerns the ease of obtaining relevant information. Market prices work like signals sent to consumers and producers. Market prices provide information about the relative scarcity of a good in light of the demand for that good. When a price goes up, producers are signaled and incentivized to increase production, whereas consumers are signaled and incentivized to decrease consumption. One important finding in economics is that consumers and producers are able to act upon this information without knowing exactly what prices are. (People have reacted appropriately to prices forever, but economists did not quite understand prices until the 1870s.) Prices tend to change quickly in light of changing supply and demand. In contrast, there is no analog of prices in politics. The information needed to make good political decisions is costly and difficult to obtain. The feedback mechanisms in politics are slow and indirect. A small-business owner can tell her business plan is working by noting whether she is making a profit, but a voter cannot easily tell whether the officials she elected are doing a good or bad job.

Note that I am not arguing here that in democracies, majorities habitually exploit the minority. (On the contrary, most exploitation comes about through backdoor rent seeking rather than through elections. Various rent-seeking minorities, such as corn growers in the United States, exploit the majority more than majorities exploit minorities.) Rather, what I am arguing is that we should not expect self-interested voting to serve the common good.[21] Democracies serve the common good as well as they do in part because citizens do not always attempt to serve their self-interest through voting. As I discuss in chapter 7, the empirical evidence suggests that voters tend to vote in what they perceive to be the national common good rather than what they perceive to be in their self-interest.

Federalism and systems of checks and balances do some work to alleviate the dangers of purely self-interested voting. But we should not be overly optimistic about these. Representative democracy creates plenty of opportunities for socially destructive rent seeking. Special interest groups can and do get their way by forming voting coalitions with others. As James Madison said, we cannot count on institutions to generate good results regardless of how people vote:

> As there is a degree of depravity in mankind which requires a certain degree of circumspection and distrust, so there are other qualities in human nature which justify a certain portion of esteem and confidence. Republican government presupposes the existence of these qualities in a higher degree than any other form. Were the picture which some have drawn . . . faithful likenesses of the human character, the inference would be that there is not sufficient virtue among men for self-government; and that nothing less than the chains of despotism can restrain them from destroying and devouring each other.[22]

While Madison thinks federalism does some work to restrain the effects of self-interest, he also thinks that democratic government requires citizens' self-restraint.

I wish we could promote the common good just by having people vote for their narrow self-interest. People are more reliable judges of self-interest than of the common good. Thus, it would be preferable if people could serve the common good simply by voting for self-interest.[23] I think there is no real invisible hand of politics, but I want to be wrong. Things would be a lot easier if people could serve the common good just by voting for self-interest.

THE BEST OR GOOD ENOUGH?

So far I have been arguing that voters should vote for candidates or policies that will promote the common good. However, some policies or candidates promote the common good more than others. For instance, suppose we have an election between two candidates, Penny Pretty Good and Ava Awesome. Penny would implement policies that would boost everyone's income by 5 percent over the next four years. Ava would implement policies that would double everyone's income. They are otherwise identical. Suppose you know that Ava is awesome whereas Penny is just pretty good. Are you obligated to vote for Ava?

In general, it seems voters are obligated to choose the policy or candidate which, given the evidence, they justifiedly believe will best serve the common good. Merely picking a candidate or policy that is likely to make improvements is not enough. Rather, voters ought to pick the candidate who will make the biggest improvements. They should choose Ava Awesome over the Penny Pretty Good.

To see why, consider some analogies. Suppose the Federal Reserve can choose between two monetary policies. Policy A would lead to 1 percent growth, while policy B would lead to 5 percent growth. A and B are otherwise identical. Suppose that the Fed knows that A and B will have these effects or, at least, that they *ought* to believe this, given their evidence. The Fed would act irresponsibly were it to choose A over B. It owes citizens a duty of care and ought to pick the policy that, given the evidence, is expected best to promote citizens' interests.

Or suppose my physician can prescribe either of two medications for my illness. The first drug is 50 percent effective and has minor side effects. The second drug is 95 percent effective and has no side effects. The drugs cost the same and are widely available. In this case, the physician would serve my interests by prescribing either drug. However, he ought to prescribe the second drug. It is clearly the better drug. He owes me a duty of care to choose the best course, not merely a good course. Now, if the second drug were costly, in short supply, largely unknown, or risky, that would change things. Then he would have to weigh different values, and he might reasonably prescribe the first drug instead of the second. However, given that one drug is simply superior to the other, he should pick the better drug.

Finally, suppose that Congress can choose between two school funding initiatives. The initiatives are otherwise identical, but one initiative can be expected to be superior to the other. If so, then Congress should choose the better initiative.

As a citizen, you do not owe it to others to provide them with the best possible governance. But if you take on the office of voter, you acquire additional moral responsibilities, just as you would were you to become the Federal Reserve chairperson, a physician, or a congressperson. The electorate decides who governs. Sometimes they decide policy directly. They owe it the governed to provide what they justifiedly believe or ought to believe is the best governance, just as others with political power owe it to the governed to do the same.

All things being equal, anyone wielding political power ought to use that power in ways that she justifiedly believes (or ought to believe) maximally promote the common good. This obligation fits well with a number of background moral theories. A eudaimonist or virtue ethicist would claim that a virtuous political agent always chooses what he knows to be the best course of action. A rule consequentialist would claim that norms requiring political agents to choose the course of action known to be best would form part of the optimal set of moral rules. A Kantian would argue that the maxim "When I have political power and can choose between a good and an excellent policy, I will choose the inferior policy" would fail the contradiction-in-will test. Or the Kantian might argue that political agents have special obligations in virtue of being political agents.

Strategic Voting and the Common Good

I have argued that voters must be justified in believing that the candidate or policy they vote for will promote the common good; otherwise, they must abstain. However, so far, I have ignored the possibility of strategic voting.

Politics is complicated. Sometimes, generating good outcomes is not simply a matter of voting for the best candidate, the candidate who would produce the best outcomes if only she had her way. Sometimes, producing good outcomes requires voting for bad candidates or suboptimal candidates.

Voting is a strategic game, not a parametric one. Parametric games, such as solitaire, have one player. Strategic games, such as chess, have more than one player.[24] In parametric games, the outcome depends on one person's choices. In strategic games, it depends on many people's choices. In strategic games, a player must worry that an opponent will anticipate and counteract her moves. To win, players need to anticipate and counteract other players' moves.

Imagine I could appoint political officeholders by myself. That is, suppose politics were a parametric game. Economists and political scientists refer to the candidates or policies I would choose, if I could dictate the outcome of each race in the election, as my *sincere preferences*.

Of course, I cannot dictate outcomes by myself. I must attempt to generate my favored outcomes in light of how other voters are likely to vote. They have different preferences from mine. To generate good outcomes, I might need to vote for candidates that are not my sincere preference. I am said to vote *strategically* when I vote for candidates that are not my sincere preference, in an attempt to produce preferred outcomes, in light of how I expect other voters to vote.

One kind of strategic voting is sophisticated voting. A sophisticated voter tries to predict other voters' votes and then attempts to generate her most preferred outcome given how she expects others to vote.[25] For example, my father prefers candidates of party X to win the presidency. However, during primaries, he often registers as a member of party Y and votes for whom he regards as the least electable member of Y. In doing so, he hopes to facilitate X's victory in the general election. If Y runs an unelectable candidate, then X has a better chance of winning the election.

Another common kind of strategic voting is compromise. A voter compromises when she votes for a less-preferred candidate over a more-preferred candidate, because the less-preferred candidate has a higher chance of success. For instance, many libertarians voted for Reagan in 1984 or for Obama in 2008 instead of the Libertarian Party candidates. The libertarians would, in fact, have preferred the Libertarian Party candidates to win. However, they worried about "throwing their votes away" on unelectable candidates. Instead of voting for the candidate they truly preferred, they voted for the candidate they thought was best among those with a decent chance of winning.

Another example of strategic voting is voting in the attempt to produce gridlock. Milton Friedman took a dim view of government's ability and willingness to serve the common good. Taking a cue from James Madison, he said sometimes the best one could hope for was gridlock. He thought gridlock prevents parties from pushing their agendas and makes it so that only widely supported policies pass. (E.g., Republicans might note that Republicans behaved better, by Republican standards, in the 1990s than in the 2000s. In the 1990s, the Republicans faced a Democratic president with veto power. In the 2000s, the Republicans controlled the presidency.) Gridlock could be a good reason to vote for bad candidates. So suppose I know that Republicans and Democrats tend to produce bad legislation, but they are both worse when they control all branches of government. I might vote for whatever party has less power in an attempt to restrain the other party. This could be an effective way of maintaining the status quo against misguided changes.

The ethics of strategic voting is in one sense very complicated, and in another sense, very easy. It is complicated in the sense that strategic voting is complicated. Different voting rules and governmental systems make different kinds of strategic voting more or less effective. The kinds of strategic voting that work in the United States, which has first-past-the-post elections, might not work in Israel, which has proportional representation. Also, assessing whether (for example) compromise voting is an effective rather than counterproductive strategy for promoting the common good requires thorough forays into game theory and political science.[26] A thorough investigation of these issues would make this book excessively long, technical, and accessible to only a small number of readers.

On the other hand, the ethics of strategic voting is easy, in the abstract. When considering a given form of strategic voting, one can ask, how likely is it to work (if my vote were to carry the day), and does it impose an unacceptable amount of risk? Previously I had argued that voters have an obligation to vote on the basis of justified moral and political beliefs and attitudes. I argued that citizens should not vote for candidates who support harmful or unjust policies or who are likely to do so. However, to accommodate strategic voting, I would add a clause or qualification to these claims. According to what we might call the *strategic voting clause*, a voter may vote for a candidate who is known to support bad policies provided that she justifiedly expects that electing this candidate in that particular race would be an effective means of promoting the common good, provided that electing the candidate does not impose excessive risk, or if she justifiedly expects voting this way to help promote the common good.

Consider gridlock voting as an example. Suppose I am voting in a general election, for instance, for a senator, I might justifiedly vote for a senator who supports bad policies because I expect doing so will produce publicly beneficial gridlock. Here, I imagine that I alone get to choose this particular senator. Now, the candidate supports bad policies, so if he got his way, it would hurt the common good. However, I might still be justified in voting for him, because I justifiedly believe that the candidate, if elected, would not get his way. Instead, throwing him into the mix with all of the candidates selected by other voters in other races would promote the common good. So I may vote for him because electing him is a means of promoting the common good.

The strategic voting clause does not imply that strategic voting is a good idea. It might be that strategic voting normally backfires or leads to bad results. Consider compromise voting. Supporters of third-party candidates in the United States complain that the reason the Democrats and Republicans always win is because voters do not vote their sincere preferences. If they voted sincerely, perhaps a third-party candidate would win, and perhaps this would be better for the common good. If every voter acted on the maxim, "I will vote for the candidate who, if elected, will be most beneficial to the common good," this might benefit the common good far better than compromise voting. It may be that we live with suboptimal electoral results precisely because people are inclined to compromise. If we introduced a norm against compromise voting, this might lead to better results. The very fact that I am inclined to compromise in light of other people's compromises helps to feed and maintain the tendency to compromise, which can be suboptimal.

In tennis, chess, or a *Half Life 2* death match, strategic playing makes sense. The player who abstains from strategic game playing loses. At the polls, however, you can avoid compromise voting at little cost to yourself or the common good. After all, the expected utility of your individual vote is effectively zero. Regardless of how you will vote, whether your sincere preference wins or loses is determined by how others vote. So there are some grounds to think you might as well vote for your sincere preference.

However, if you can make a difference, then the ethics of compromise voting is more complicated. Suppose there are three candidates, aptly named Good, Okay, and Bad, and suppose voters *ought to know* that Good is good, Okay is okay, and Bad is bad.[27] However, suppose most voters are irresponsible. Right now, most voters favor Bad, some favor Okay, and only a few favor Good. The Bad and Okay voters will not budge, no matter how much evidence you present them that Good is best. Also, Good supporters are well coordinated. They can vote as a bloc. Finally, suppose that Good supporters are numerous enough that, if they vote as a bloc for Okay, Okay will win. Otherwise (if they abstain or vote for Good), Bad will win.

In this case, unless Bad is very bad indeed, Good supporters generally have no obligation to vote as opposed to abstain. (See chapters 1 and 2.) However, they might acquire an obligation to vote rather than abstain in virtue of having made promises to one another to vote as a bloc.[28]

So suppose we Good supporters plan to vote, and it is in our power to sway the election from Bad to Okay if we vote for Okay. Should we vote for Good or Okay? (Is it *obligatory* to vote one way or another? Is it *permissible* to vote either way?) Here we have to judge and weigh some complex issues. Voting for Okay now prevents Bad from winning, but it also encourages people to compromise in future elections. Voting for Okay today might help reinforce the tendency for our elections to be among okay and bad candidates rather than good candidates. On the other hand, the worse Bad is, the more reason Good supporters have to vote for Okay. Sometimes, we cannot produce good electoral outcomes. If we have already committed ourselves to trying to produce good electoral outcomes, but cannot, it seems we should at least try to prevent bad outcomes. So it might be permissible or even obligatory to vote for Okay, provided we are reasonably sure that doing so does not cost us good outcomes in future elections.

These are only some considerations about strategic voting. I do not intend these claims to be decisive. I discuss them only to illustrate how complicated the issue of strategic voting can be. I do not intend to give a theory of the most effective forms of strategic voting. Certain social scientists would do a far better job of that than I. Rather, my goal in this section is merely to explain why, on my theory of voting ethics, there is no objection in principle to strategic voting, so long as strategic voting does not impose too much risk and tends to produce better outcomes than one justifiedly believes otherwise would occur

Jürgen Habermas objects to strategic voting in principle. He complains that strategic voting is disrespectful to other citizens. On his view, citizens should vote only for what they sincerely regard as candidates likely to produce the most justified proposals. But Gerry Gaus responds, "This is to ignore the ways electoral systems work, and in general to ignore the possible impact of sincere statements and actions in helping to produce wrongful laws."[29] If Gaus's empirical presupposition (that strategic voting might be the most effective way to produce good outcomes) is correct, this seems to end the debate. Habermas's complaint would have more force under more ideal democratic conditions, where citizens were better informed, more rational, and had stronger moral motivations. However, in contemporary politics, one must react to uninformed, irrational, and immoral voters who attempt to impose bad policies on everyone.

CONCLUSION

Voters should vote for what they justifiedly believe will best promote the common good. This may allow them to vote strategically under certain circumstances. In general, they should not vote for narrow self-interest. There is no reason to expect that self-interest voting will promote the common good as if by an invisible hand.

I end with a puzzle. Consider the following kinds of voting:

A. Vote for what one justifiedly perceives to be in the common good.
B. Vote for what one *unjustifiedly* perceives to be the common good.
C. Vote for what one justifiedly perceives to be in one's self-interest, regardless of its impact on the common good.
D. Vote for what one *unjustifiedly* perceives to be in one's self-interest, regardless of its impact on the common good.

I have argued that A is morally better than B, C, and D. However, this leaves open how to rank B, C, and D.[30] A voter ought to A. Yet suppose a voter is not going to A. Is it better for her to B, C, or D?

Roderick Chisholm introduced the concept of the "contrary-to-duty imperative."[31] A contrary-to-duty imperative tells you how to act given that you have decided not to do what is right. For instance, "You shouldn't murder innocent children for fun, but if you are going to do so, at least make it painless" and "You ought to keep your appointments, but if you aren't going to do so, at least tell the people who are waiting on you" are both contrary-to-duty imperatives. There might be contrary-to-duty imperatives for voting ethics as well. If you vote, you should vote for what you justifiedly perceive to be in the common good, but if you do not do that, then you should at least ____ instead. I am not sure how to fill in the blank. A person who does B is better intentioned than a person who does C or D, but I am not sure where B is morally better than C or D. That will depend at least in part on what the expected consequences of B, C, and D are. I leave this open for further investigation.

CHAPTER SIX

Buying and Selling Votes

Is It Wrong to Buy or Sell Votes?

Suppose you agree to vote for some candidate because I pay you to do so.[1] Is it wrong for me to make the offer? Would it be wrong for you to take it?[2]

Most people think so. The folk theory of voting ethics holds it is wrong to buy or sell votes. People regard vote selling as corrupt, abhorrent, and distasteful. They take it not just to be wrong, but uncontroversially wrong.

In this chapter, I argue for some counterintuitive claims. I argue that under some conditions there is nothing morally wrong with buying and selling votes. Vote selling and buying are not inherently or intrinsically wrong. (Note: I use "inherently" and "intrinsically" as synonyms.) When they are wrong, what makes them wrong is that they lead to violations of the duties I have described in earlier chapters. So long as vote buying and selling do not lead to such violations, it is not wrong.

I do not expect my arguments to convince many readers. However, I am puzzled why readers will not be convinced. When I have discussed these issues with others, many of them are confident that vote selling is always wrong, but they cannot explain why it is wrong in the kinds of cases I present.[3] Perhaps they are right—vote selling is always wrong—but they just cannot explain why. Sometimes we know things that we cannot explain. Or perhaps they are mistaken.

So I present this chapter as a challenge. I want to shift the burden of justification onto those who think vote buying and selling are always wrong. I want them to provide me with an intuitively plausible, well-developed, and clear explanation of why vote buying and selling are wrong, even in the cases where I argue they are permissible.

On my view, for the most part, the ethics of vote buying and selling *reduces* to the ethics of voting already described in this book. I have argued for Principle 1:

1. People who choose to vote must vote for candidates or policies they justifiedly expect to promote the common good; otherwise, they must abstain.

My main theses for this chapter are: If a voter abides by Principle 1, then she does nothing wrong by selling her vote. If a buyer pays a voter to vote in accordance with Principle 1, then the buyer does nothing wrong by buying a vote.

Vote selling and buying are not in principle wrong. They have no inherent moral status. Vote selling cannot *transform* otherwise morally acceptable actions into wrongful actions. If it is morally permissible for you to vote a certain way for free, then it is permissible to vote that way for payment. If it is morally acceptable for someone to vote a certain way for free, then it is morally acceptable for you to pay her to vote that way. So, in this chapter, I argue for Principle 2:

> 2. It is morally permissible to buy or sell votes provided doing so is known to be unlikely to lead to violations of Principle 1.[4]

However, vote commodification is not morally neutral. While selling one's vote cannot transform a right action into a bad one, it can *amplify* the wrongness of a wrong action. It is wrong to vote without sufficient epistemic justification. It is normally wrong to vote against the common good. If you are paid to vote wrongly, this is often morally worse than doing so without payment. Similarly, it is wrong to kill an innocent person, but it is often worse to do so for money.

Normally, it is also morally wrong to pay someone to perform a wrong action. So it is tempting to conclude that if it is wrong to vote in certain ways, then it is wrong to pay people to vote those ways. One might think that a natural extension of my theory is Principle 3:

> 3. One should not pay someone to violate Principle 1, nor should one accept money to violate Principle 1.

However, there are some reasons to reject 3. Principle 3* appears to be closer to the truth.

> 3*. It is morally permissible to pay someone else to vote for a candidate or policy, provided the person making the payment would be voting rightly if she herself voted for the candidate or policy, and provided that one reasonably believes that the person receiving the payment will vote as directed. Otherwise, one should not pay someone to violate Principle 1. One should not accept money to violate Principle 1.

Principle 3* is a mouthful and will be explained at greater length.

For the purposes of this chapter, I assume that it is not illegal to buy or sell votes. That is, I am asking whether vote buying and selling would be wrong independently of their legal status. In places where they are against the law, it might always be wrong to buy or sell votes, not because these actions are wrong in themselves, but because it is wrong to break the law.

I am interested here in the ethics of vote selling rather than the politics of selling. Thus, I do not argue that vote selling should be legal. Perhaps it should not be.[5] Even though vote selling is sometimes morally permissible, perhaps if it were legally permitted, most vote selling would be done in socially destructive ways. Perhaps there is no feasible way to criminalize only the wrongful vote selling—we have to criminalize all of it or none of it. If so, then it might be good to make vote selling illegal.

In summary, this chapter has two main purposes. First, I want to cast doubt on the commonsense view that vote buying and selling are always wrong. However, in doing so, also I want to show that in those cases where vote buying and selling are wrong, part of what makes them wrong is that they lead to violations of Principle 1, which I have defended over the past three chapters.

VOTE SELLING AS PAID PERFORMANCE

Here is a common argument against vote selling: Your right to vote is inalienable, just as your rights to basic personal liberty or to free speech are inalienable. The right to vote is not like a property right to a guitar or house. You may sell a guitar or house, but you may not sell yourself into slavery. You may not sell away your right to free speech. Some kinds of rights cannot be sold. The right to vote is one of those rights.

This argument is fine, as far is it goes. I introduce this argument only to show that it is irrelevant to my thesis. I say that vote buying and selling are sometimes permissible, but I am not defending A or B:

A. *Forfeiture*: It is morally permissible to accept money to forfeit one's right to vote, such that this right to vote disappears. It is morally permissible to pay someone to forfeit her right to vote, such that her right to vote disappears.

B. *Transfer*: It is morally permissible to sell one's vote to another person, such that the seller acquires another vote. It is morally permissible to pay someone to sell her vote, such that the seller acquires another vote.

I say that vote selling is sometimes permissible. But this does not mean I believe it is permissible to pay someone to forfeit her right to vote or for you to acquire her right to vote. I do not regard the right to vote as being similar to a property rights in chattel. I do not argue that you may sell your vote because you *own* your vote and may do whatever you please with your property.

Instead, I am interested in vote buying as a kind of paid performance, as in C:

C. *Performance*: It is morally permissible, under some circumstances, to pay someone to vote rather than abstain, or to pay someone to vote for a particular candidate or policy, rather than abstain or vote for a different candidate or policy.

On my view, under some circumstances, a seller may accept payment to vote a certain way. She retains her right to vote, and the buyer does not gain an additional right to vote.

A parallel example can illustrate the differences among A, B, and C. Suppose you own a plot of land. I offer you some money. If, by accepting payment, you thereby revert your land back to the commons, that is an example of (A), forfeiture. If you accept payment, and as result I acquire the right to your land, that is an example of (B), transfer. (If I pay for a temporary right to stay on the land and use it in certain ways, that is a case of rental.) But suppose you had been planning to grow buckwheat on your land, but I pay you to grow corn instead. Suppose I do not acquire any right to come in contact with your land, nor do I acquire any right to the corn you produce. Our contract is just for you to grow corn instead of buckwheat. This is an example of (C), paid performance.

We might talk about vote buyers as acquiring additional votes or of vote sellers as losing their votes. We can imagine systems in which votes could actually be purchased as property is. But the kind of vote buying we see in the United States is not like that. It is strictly metaphorical to describe a vote buyer as acquiring an additional vote or to describe a vote seller as losing a vote. If I (illegally) "buy" your vote, I do not come to have two votes. Instead, all that has happened is that I have given you money on your promise to vote a certain way. The vote buyer pays the vote seller to perform an action. No rights to votes are lost, gained, or transferred in the process.

A good analogy to this is prostitution. If I pay a prostitute to have sex with me, I do not thereby acquire a right to her genitals. They remain *hers*. I do not come to own two sets of genitals, even for a short time. Instead, paying a prostitute for sex means paying her to perform certain actions. No rights to anyone's body are lost, gained, or transferred in the process. If someone were to criticize prostitution on the grounds that it involves buying another person's body, that person would miss the mark. Prostitution involves paying a prostitute to use her body in a certain way, but it does not involve actually buying her body (as in chattel slavery) or part of her body (as in organ sales). Nor is it equivalent to renting her body. Similarly, paying a voter to vote involves paying her to use her vote a certain way, but it does not involve buying her vote. The buyer does not get to cast two ballots.

SOME IRRELEVANT ARGUMENTS AGAINST VOTE SELLING

There may be good reasons to make vote buying and selling illegal. Perhaps permitting vote buying and selling would in practice lead to terrible outcomes. However, if this is true, it is only because in practice we can expect people who buy and sell votes to violate Principle 1. If people followed Principle 1, this kind of objection to vote sales would be undermined.

Richard Hasen reviews the literature on vote buying and concludes that people have offered three main arguments against it:

> Despite the almost universal condemnation of core vote buying, commentators disagree on the underlying rationales for its prohibition. Some offer an equality argument against vote buying: the poor are more likely to sell their votes than are the wealthy, leading to political outcomes favoring the wealthy. Others offer an efficiency argument against vote buying: vote buying allows buyers to engage in rent-seeking that diminishes overall social wealth. Finally, some commentators offer an inalienability argument against vote buying: votes belong to the community as a whole and should not be alienable by individual voters. This alienability argument may support an anti-commodification norm that causes voters to make public-regarding voting decisions.[6]

The main worry is that if vote buying were legal, this would undermine the common good. However, each argument that Hasen discusses assumes that voters will vote in self-interested ways when vote buying is allowed. (Hasen also mentions a worry that votes should not be alienated, but I have already addressed that.)

Perhaps these worries are well grounded. Perhaps, as a matter of fact, if vote buying were legally permitted, this would lead to inefficient outcomes or to the exploitation of the poor by the rich. If so, these may be excellent grounds for making vote buying illegal.

However, these points are irrelevant to the argument I am going to make. After all, I argue that vote buying and selling are permissible when they do not lead to violations of Principle 1. Principle 1 says that people who choose to vote must vote in ways they justifiedly expect to promote the common good; otherwise, they must abstain. If people were to follow Principle 1, then they would vote sociotropically. The rich would not buy votes in order to exploit the poor.[7] People would not engage in destructive rent seeking through voting. Paid voters would vote in ways that tend to benefit the common good. This said, I explore further some worries about vote commodification.

SOME CASES OF RIGHTFUL VOTE BUYING AND SELLING

In this section, I discuss some cases where vote buying and selling seem morally acceptable. In the first two cases, the sellers were planning to abstain, but the buyer pays them to vote according to the sellers' best judgment. In the third case, the buyer pays the seller to vote for the buyer's preferred particular candidate. I do not expect these examples to convince people, though I am puzzled by their response.

Paying the Unmotivated Hero

Suppose Alan is a political expert. He has exceptional civic virtue. In addition to working a socially useful job as a small-business owner, Alan coaches a little league team, volunteers many hours per week with Habitat for Humanity, gives blood regularly, and gives significant amounts to charity. He is also the former mayor of his town but has recently retired from public service. He is a World War II veteran and received many medals for his heroism.

Next Tuesday is an election. Alan has been working hard over the past few weeks. He plans to spend Tuesday watching *The Godfather* films rather than vote.

Bob knows Alan is planning not to vote. He knows that Alan is a political expert and a good person, so he knows that Alan would not violate Principle 1. Bob offers Alan $100 to vote. Bob says, "Alan, you've already done so much for others. I don't blame you for wanting to take a break rather than vote. But, I like to see good people vote, and I'm willing to pay you $100 to do it." Alan accepts the money and goes to the polls. When there, Alan uses his own excellent judgment to decide whom to vote for. He votes with the public good in mind, and he is epistemically justified in thinking that the candidate for whom he votes will do the best job promoting the common good.

In this case, I do not see how Alan or Bob has done anything wrong. By hypothesis, Alan has good judgment and votes for candidates he justifiedly expects to promote the common good. Alan has paid his debts to society. He probably has more civic virtue than any reader (and the writer) of this book. As I showed in chapters 1 and 2, Alan had no duty to vote, and so it was his prerogative to watch movies rather than vote. If he voted for free, he would do us a small favor, but he does not owe us any more favors. Why should he refuse payment in return for doing us even more good? If Alan voted for free, he would have done something supererogatory. What evil is introduced into the world by his accepting payment instead of voting for free?

If Bob had convinced Alan to vote by praising voting, this would not be wrong. What evil is introduced into the world by his offering to pay Alan instead? Bob prefers to see good people vote well, and he is willing to reimburse them for their trouble. Bob does us a public service, albeit a tiny one, by paying Alan.

Consider a similar case. Suppose, out of public spirit, Alan has been picking up litter in his town for the past thirty days. After thirty days, only a few streets are left dirty, so he has only one day of work left to make the town litter free. On the thirty-first day, he decides to watch *Godfather* films instead. The people who live on the dirty streets say to him, "Alan, we know you deserve a break. It makes sense that you'd take a day for yourself. You certainly don't owe it to us to clean our streets today rather than stay home. You don't owe it to us to clean our streets at all. However, we'd strongly prefer to have our streets cleaned, and so we're willing to pay you $250 to clean them now instead of watching movies." It would be generous—but supererogatory—if Alan declined the money and worked for free. But Alan would not be doing something wrong were he to accept the money.

When Alan takes money to vote or the clean the streets, no one is (likely to be) harmed. (This claim is controversial, and I discuss it further below.) All parties to the transaction are benefited. Innocent third parties are benefited or at least not harmed. Everyone is a winner or at least no worse off. The same goes for voting.

Given this, if you think Alan or Bob acted wrongly, you bear the philosophical burden of proof. You need to produce a coherent, defensible principle that explains what makes their actions wrong. (In the coming sections, I respond to a few arguments that attempt to show Alan is doing something wrong.) Until you produce such a good explanation of what makes Alan's and Bob's actions wrong, you should be skeptical of your belief that they are acting wrongly.

One might object that some acts are harmless in isolation but harmful when many people do then. Perhaps a "What-if-everyone-did-it?"–kind of argument could be made here. But this does not pose an objection to paying people like Alan to vote.[8] Suppose we scale up these kinds of actions. That is, suppose some philanthropist reliably identifies many virtuous political experts and pays them each a small sum to vote. At best, this means that we all enjoy better political outcomes than we otherwise would. At worst, it means that money is spent in an unsuccessful attempt to produce good political outcomes. Perhaps irrational, immoral, stupid, or ignorant voters would outvote the paid virtuous experts. If so, the philanthropist spent her money in vain, but that is not morally wrong. In parallel, sometimes money is committed to promising medical research but the research fails to discover any good therapies. This means the money was spent in vain, but it does not automatically make the spending wrong.

Paying the Unmotivated Average Person

I described Alan as being highly virtuous. However, it does not appear to be wrong to pay less virtuous people to vote or for less virtuous people to accept payment to vote.

Consider a case similar to that of Alan and Bob. Imagine that David pays Charlie $100 to vote on the basis of Charlie's best judgment. David knows that Charlie is an expert and will vote in ways that promote the common good. Unlike Alan, Charlie has average character. He has paid his debts to society and has done sufficient work to promote the common good, but he has not gone above and beyond the call of duty. In this case, it still seems that neither Charlie nor David does something wrong. Charlie had no duty to vote, though it would be nice of him to do so. When he votes, he votes in accordance with Principle 1. However, rather than doing it for free, he does it because David pays him to. Charlie deserves neither praise for his actions nor condemnation. On the other hand, thanks to David, one more good vote has been cast. If I have any complaint against David, it is that he overpaid for that one vote. If David wants to be public-spirited, he could have done more good giving the money to Oxfam. Still, he has not done something wrong.

Paying Someone to Vote for the Best Candidate

In the two preceding cases, vote sellers are paid to vote according to their own best judgment, rather than the judgment of the buyer. However, suppose instead that sellers vote according to the best judgment of the buyer. As long as the sellers abide by Principle 1, they do not do anything wrong in taking money to vote.

Suppose Ed is a political expert and well motivated. Fred is not an expert, but is honest and trustworthy. If Fred agrees to do something, he does it. Ed and Fred both know all of this about themselves and each other. Suppose Ed pays Fred to vote for a particular candidate C. Ed knows that C is best. When Ed votes, he will vote for C, and Ed should vote that way according to Principle 1. So Ed pays Fred to vote the same way that Ed will vote.

If Fred accepts the money and votes as Ed directs him, does he do something wrong? This will depend on whether Fred may use Ed's testimony as a basis for his vote.[9] Suppose (correctly, I think) that Fred would be justified in believing candidate C is best because Ed said C was best. If so, then it would be morally permissible for Fred to vote without payment for C, because Fred would be justified in believing that C is best on the basis of Ed's testimony. If Fred voted that way for free, he would not do anything wrong. Why would it be wrong to accept payment to do it?

When Fred takes money to vote, no one is likely to be harmed. (Again, this is perhaps a controversial claim, as I discuss later.) Everyone is a winner or at least no worse off. Given this, if you think Fred is acting wrongly, you bear the philosophical burden of proof. You need to produce a coherent, defensible principle that explains what makes his actions wrong.

If, however, the correct epistemological theory (whatever that is) indicates that Fred should not believe C is best in light of Ed's testimony, then Ed does something wrong in voting for C. However, he does something wrong because he violates Principle 1. Now, taking money to do something wrong may amplify the wrongness, but it does not transform a right action into a wrong one. Fred would be doing something wrong if he voted for C for free.

As for Ed, we should thank him for increasing the likelihood that a good candidate would be elected.

Does Good Voting Harm People?

A number of times, I have claimed that if voters abide by Principle 1— that is, if they vote only for those candidates or policies which they justifiedly believe will promote the common good—then this will tend to benefit people and hurt no one, regardless of whether the voters are paid to vote or not. This claim deserves further investigation.

Of course, even good voting can harm people. After all, to vote well is to vote in ways one justifiedly believes will promote the common good. However, sometimes one can be justified in believing something will promote the common good, but it will not in fact promote the common good. In chapter 3, we already discussed why this kind of voting is excused even when a policy turns out badly, so I do not dwell further on this issue. Strictly speaking, saying that good voting (whether paid or unpaid) does not harm people is a simplification of a more complex truth.

My assertion that good voting does not (tend to inexcusably) harm people also appears to depend on a moralized definition of "harm." After all, even good votes can *frustrate* the preferences of others. For instance, suppose Johnny Corruption wants to be president, but some philanthropist pays millions of people to vote against Johnny Corruption in favor of Gloria Good. As a result, Corruption loses the election to Good. This frustrates Corruption's preferences. He does not gain the political power he desired, and his supporters will be unhappy, at least in the short term. Should we thus say that good voting harms Corruption and his supporters?

Whether this counts as a *harming* them is up for philosophical debate, but I would like to avoid that debate.[10] We might decide to describe (paid or unpaid) good voting as harmful, because it frustrates people who support the wrong political goals. Still, the moral import is the same: taking money to vote well is permissible, because doing so tends to benefit others, and it does not tend either (on one account of "harm") to harm people or (on a less moralized account of "harm") to cause any morally objectionable harms.

Suppose we determine, on the best theory of *harm*, that frustrating a person's preferences always counts as a kind of harm. Even if so, this would imply that not all harms are morally objectionable. To illustrate this, suppose Fred loves Gina but Gina is indifferent to Fred. Her indifference frustrates Fred's desires and makes him miserable. Even if this means Gina harms Fred, this does not appear to be an objectionable harm. Gina is entitled to harm Fred that way.

So perhaps it is best to say that Corruption is indeed made worse off—because he loses the power he expected to gain—but this a legitimate harm. Corruption *should not* have power.

Similarly, if society stops tolerating racism, this could be said to harm KKK members. The KKK is now a marginalized, disreputable group. Marginalization makes many Klansmen unhappy. Still, even if marginalization harms Klansmen, it is not wrong to harm them this way. It is also not wrong to frustrate Johnny Corruption's political goals.

Nearly everything we do imposes some kind of externality on others, but not all externalities are morally equivalent. If I crank up my 90-watt high-gain guitar amplifier in the middle of the night, this imposes a cost on my neighbors. It makes them worse off, and it is wrong for me to make them worse off in this way. From a social perspective, allowing this kind of behavior tends in the long run to make everyone's life worse. On the other hand, suppose someone invents a less expensive mousetrap and, as a result, puts the old mousetrap manufacturer out of business; this also imposes a cost (a "pecuniary externality") upon the old manufacturer. It makes the old manufacturer worse off, but in this case it is not wrong to do so. From a social perspective, this kind of behavior tends in the long run to make almost everyone's life better. Even the old mousetrap manufacturer enjoys the high standard of living he has only because these kinds of externalities are allowed. (Had he been born into a world where people believed it wrong to compete on the market, he would have been born into dire poverty.) Both actions—cranking my amplifier at midnight and introducing a better mousetrap—harm some people, but one action is wrong and the other is not.

Frustrating people's political preferences through good voting is not an exploitative kind of harm. In his discussion of exploitation, Schmidtz notes that

> an exploitative institution makes some worse off as a method of making others better off. However, when an institution empowers us to disarm would-be muggers, its purpose is to make muggers worse off as a method of making others better off. Do we want to say disarming muggers is a form of exploitation? Presumably not. Thus, some refinement is in order. An exploitative institution uses its targets as a resource. More concretely, exploitation makes some people better off in virtue of the *existence* of the targets. In contrast, disarming muggers does not make people better off in virtue of the existence of muggers, and therefore is not a form of exploitation.[11]

Presumably, this analysis holds true not only for exploitative institutions but for exploitative actions. If I sell mousetraps at lower prices than my competitors, I take business from them, but I do not exploit them. Similarly, if I pay voters not to vote for Johnny Corruption, I frustrate his political ambitions, but I do not exploit them. I do not use Corruption as a means to further my own goals. I am not better off in virtue of the existence of Corruption. Quite the contrary. He is not a resource I am trying to exploit but a pest I am trying to remove.

Thus, instead of claiming that vote buying and selling are not (typically) harmful when everyone abides by Principle 1, I might instead claim that vote buying and selling do not tend to cause any morally objectionable harms when everyone abides by Principle 1. The moral import is the same, even if the description is not.

INDIFFERENT VOTERS

Paul Sheehy has argued that voters who are indifferent to the outcome of an election should not vote.[12] Sheehy himself has not considered vote buying and selling in particular. In this section, I consider whether his argument could be used in an attempt to show that vote selling and buying are wrong.

Sheehy suggests that, "to the extent that an electorate is divided between those who have a preferred outcome and those who do not, it seems fair that the outcome be settled by the majority view amongst the former group."[13] People who do not care about an outcome should not take actions that could spoil the results for people who do care. "Those who do care about the outcome have an investment of interest and hope to a particular outcome. By not voting the indifferent citizens are put at no obvious disadvantage, nor do they endure any loss."[14]

In the preceding cases, Alan, Charlie, or Fred was not described as indifferent to the outcome. Alan might have preferred that candidate X wins instead of Y, even though he was not motivated to vote for X without compensation. Similarly, I watched (under duress) the first season of *Dancing with the Stars*. I preferred that Kelly Monaco win, though I did not bother vote for her.

Still, we can imagine cases similar to A, B, and C in which the voters are indifferent to the outcome. Suppose Harry is a political expert and always keeps his word. Harry knows that candidate X will promote the common good while candidate Y will partly undermine it. But Harry is too indifferent to others to vote. He is a pure egoist. However, Bob knows all of this about Harry and offers Harry a small sum to induce him to vote. As a result, Harry votes for X.

Harry lacks virtue, but his action is not wrong. After all, people should vote for X. The people who prefer Y do so either because they are to some extent immoral, ignorant, or irrational or because they made an honest mistake. When Harry votes for X, he is voting the way the other voters should vote. (Or, more precisely, some voters might not be obligated to vote for X because they are justified in believing Y is the better candidate, even though Y is not in fact the better candidate.)

Sheehy's argument seems to assume that there is no underlying moral obligation to vote for particular candidates or policies. His argument treats voting as if it were merely a method for deciding among otherwise morally indifferent preferences. Some cases of voting are nothing more than that, so perhaps his argument works for those kinds of cases. Suppose whether we have a blue or red flag is a morally indifferent issue. If we decide that issue democratically and I have no interest in the outcome, then perhaps Sheehy is right that I should not vote.[15] However, politics is not generally about morally indifferent preferences. Instead, politics usually involves issues of prosperity and poverty, peace and war, and justice and injustice.

Suppose many voters prefer an empire-building, nationalist candidate. Suppose there are also many indifferent egoists. These egoists know the empire-building candidate harms the common good and know an alternative candidate is better. However, being egoists, they are indifferent to others' welfare. A philanthropist pays them to vote for the better candidate. As a result, the indifferent egoists spoil the election in favor of a peaceful, wealth-building candidate who promotes justice and freedom. The egoists lack good motivation, but they have not done anything wrong. Similarly, suppose an egoist agrees to protect your home from burglary for payment. When he stops a burglar, he does not do anything wrong, even though (aside from the monetary payment) he is otherwise indifferent to your security.

The empire-building candidate is a bad candidate. Some voters vote for this candidate because they violate Principle 1. That is, some of them knowingly vote against the common good, or they believe themselves to be voting for the common good but are unjustified in this belief. These voters vote wrongly, and having their votes defeated is morally preferable. On the other hand, some voters in the majority might be justified in believing that the bad candidate is a good one. In this case, they are excused—they are not voting wrongly—but they should be glad that their votes are defeated. After all, they want to promote the common good, but they mistakenly have taken a counterproductive strategy.

COMMODIFICATION AND BLOCKED TRADES

Someone might object to my argument by saying that some things should not be for sale. Of course, it would not be a good objection just to pound the table and declare that this is so. Suppose someone made the following argument:

1. Votes are non-commodities.
2. Something is a non-commodity if and only if it is impermissible to buy or sell it.
3. Therefore, it is morally impermissible to buy or sell votes.

This argument begs the question. To avoid begging the question, we need some noncircular explanation of why some things should never be for sale, period, even in those cases where selling those things hurts no one and helps some people.

The Corrupted Meaning Argument

One possibility is that introducing money into certain relationships devalues or corrupts the relationship. Money violates the shared meaning of the relationship and changes the kind of significance and value it holds for those within the relationship. For example, my partner and I sometimes exchange favors with each other, but one might claim that if we offered each other money for favors, this would corrupt our marriage. I am skeptical about whether this claim holds true even of marriages, but I am even more skeptical about whether this point could extend to voting.

Suppose I offered my partner $100 to have sex with me or to vacuum the house. She would justifiedly be offended.[16] My offer would violate our mutual understanding of the kind of relationship we want to have. We exchange favors sometimes, but we do not exchange cash. Still, such monetary offers are not inherently wrong. Rather, in this case, my partner and I have a mutual understanding that we do not wish to have this kind of relationship. There might be domestic partners with a different kind of understanding, where they happily and healthily accept such exchanges. Just because my partner and I choose not to conduct our marriage that way does not mean it is wrong for other couples to do so. Nor does it mean that all marriages involving monetary payments are corrupt.

Besides, even if such exchanges were wrong or unhealthy in marriages, the relationship of a citizen to her liberal democratic government or to her fellow citizens is not like her relationship with her spouse. (If it is, the citizen has a bad marriage.) Citizenship is (generally) involuntary, impersonal, and instrumental. Citizenship in contemporary liberal democracies is not much like friendship, romantic love, or family. For most of us, being a citizen of a given country just means we were born (not by choice) into a diverse society of strangers. We have basic human compassion and respect for others in our society, but most other citizens remain strangers, many of whom we have little in common with. What makes us a citizen of one place rather than another is determined by political boundaries. These boundaries are mostly the contingent results of morally arbitrary demarcations, wars, and conquest. For the most part, all we distinctively share with our fellow citizens are some public goods and social insurance. Some people have a more romantic view of citizenship, so this gives them reason to refrain from buying and selling votes. But it does not thereby give them a complaint against those of us with a less romantic view of citizenship.

The Erosion Argument

Still, there is a closely related argument that deserves further attention. It goes something like this:

The Erosion Argument:

1. If people are allowed to take money to vote (even if people abide by Principle 1), then this will (significantly) erode civic virtue and altruism.

2. Thus, it is wrong to buy and sell votes, even if people abide by Principle 1.

The erosion argument asserts that introducing money into voting will corrupt people's moral attitudes. As a result, they will come to have less civic virtue. They will be less concerned with promoting the common good and doing their part.

Premise 1 is an empirical claim. It requires empirical support through careful peer-reviewed studies. The person making this objection bears the burden of proof. Many philosophers and social theorists have asserted something like premise 1, but they rarely provide empirical evidence. Instead, they just expect the claims to seem plausible to readers. But that is not good enough. So, in the absence of actual empirical support for the objection, we should regard as a potential problem, but not yet a real problem.[17]

Also, just how vote selling is supposed to erode civic virtue is not clear. What is the mechanism? Here is a plausible variation of the Erosion Argument, which makes this clearer:

The Modified Erosion Argument:

1. People need to believe that voting is sacred (or has some other privileged moral status) and that money and voting must never mix. Otherwise, they will lose civic virtue and vote badly.
2. If people buy and sell votes (even if they abide by Principle 1), this will cause them or others to lose the belief that voting is sacred.
3. It is wrong to do something that causes others to lose civic virtue and vote badly.
4. Therefore, it is wrong to buy and sell votes.

This argument claims citizens will not behave well at the voting booth unless they believe that voting is a civic sacrament or has some other privileged moral status. If they see others taking money to vote—even if they are being paid to vote well—they will either stop voting or will vote badly.

Even if this were so, it would not mean that vote selling is wrong. It would at best show that people need to *believe* it is wrong. Suppose, in parallel, it turned out that unless most people believe Kantianism to be true, they would start killing each other. Would this show that Kantianism is the correct moral theory? Of course not. Instead, it would merely show that people need to believe in Kantianism to induce them to do the right thing. Utilitarianism might still be the correct moral theory. Similarly, vote buying and selling may sometimes be permissible, but we cannot tell people this, because they need to believe otherwise if they are to vote well. This would not show a problem with my argument; it would show that people cannot handle the truth. So, perhaps, for people to have adequate civic virtue, we need them to believe that money and voting must never mix. But that does not mean that in fact money and voting must never mix.

Premise 3 appears to be false. It is sometimes permissible for a person to do X, even if her doing X induces others to lose virtue or to perform wrong actions. For instance, suppose I buy food from a local grocery store. Many bystanders, upon seeing me buy food, come to believe that all human relationships are purely instrumental. As a result, they lose all moral motivation and become thieves. Now, that this happened is regrettable, but it neither makes my buying food wrong nor makes me responsible for their bad behavior. Instead, the thieves made a mistake—they are the ones who acted wrongly. They should not have concluded that all human relationships are instrumental nor should they have lost their moral motivations and become thieves. I am not responsible for their depraved reaction to my innocent actions. Similarly, suppose Bob pays Alan to vote well. Gordon witnesses this transaction, lose his sense of civic virtue, and starts voting badly. This does not automatically make Bob's or Alan's actions wrong. Here, Gordon is the wrongdoer. He should not have lost his sense of civic virtue, nor should he have started voting badly. That was a depraved response to seeing Bob paying Alan to vote, and that he had such a response is Gordon's fault (not Bob's or Alan's).

Who Would Vote Well for Free?

Another version of the preceding objection goes as follows:

1. If people are allowed to take money to vote well (i.e., vote according to Principle 1), then hardly anyone will vote well for free.
2. It is important that people vote well for free, so it is wrong to do something that would significantly reduce voting for free.
3. Therefore, it is wrong to buy and sell votes, even if people abide by Principle 1.

This argument also has significant problems.

It appears to confuse the legal question (should vote selling and buying be legal?) with the moral question (are vote selling and buying inherently wrong?). (Is the "allowed" in premise 1 supposed to mean *legally* allowed or *morally* allowed?) We are concerned here not with the legal question but with the moral question. As we discussed briefly, we might have good reasons to make vote selling illegal, not because vote selling is inherently wrong, but because if it were legal, we should expect lots of wrongful vote selling.

As with the Erosion Argument, premise 1 of this argument is an empirical claim. We need empirical evidence for this claim. Otherwise, we should regard it as possibly true, but not yet shown to be true.

Also, there are reasons to think premise 1 is not true. Richard Titmuss made a similar argument against blood selling. Titmuss argued that people should not be allowed to sell blood, because if they were permitted to do so, this would corrode their altruistic sensibilities, and few people would be willing to donate blood.[18] Yet, as Cécile Fabre says, the empirical evidence suggests Titmuss is wrong.[19] For instance, blood selling is legal in the United States but illegal in England. Despite that, more or less the same percentage of Americans and English donate blood (and they donate with the same regularity), though some Americans also sell blood.[20] So some kinds of activity remain voluntary even when it is possible to be paid to do them.

Perhaps the real complaint here is that voters should always be volunteers. Regardless of the effects of paid voting, people should choose to vote from public-spiritedness and never for money. My response is to ask why this should be so. Why would it be intrinsically wrong for people to be paid to vote, either as individuals or en masse? Many important activities, including policing, food production, and clothing production—which are all more important than voting—are paid. Little of such work is done voluntarily. Many stereotypical exercises of civic virtue, such as holding political office, serving in the military, performing jury duty, are paid. (Jury duty does not pay well but is enforced through penalties. So jurists are not volunteers either.) Physicians and teachers are paid for their work. Why is it important that voters volunteer, when these other people do not?[21] I would not advocate having governments pay voters to vote (I think this would encourage bad voting), but I fail to see how taking money to vote is intrinsically wrong.[22] Rather, it seems more plausible that what makes paid voting wrong, when it is wrong, is that it leads to bad voting.

The Analogy to Prostitution

One might complain that selling one's vote is like political prostitution. Buying someone's vote is like buying sex. Selling a vote is like selling sex. It is debasing.

This argument does not work. In real life, perhaps most sex trading has been morally wrong. However, if so, it is not because sex trading is inherently immoral. The problem with sex trading is that prostitutes are often beaten, exploited, and raped, that they are sometimes enslaved, and they often enter sex markets only because they are in dire economic circumstances. Many women would find selling themselves for sex psychologically traumatizing. But none of this implies prostitution is inherently wrong. Instead, it is wrong to beat, rape, enslave, exploit, and traumatize women. If buying and selling sex usually are wrong, they are wrong because of the presence of certain conditions that in principle could be absent.

Consider the character Belle in the TV series *Secret Diary of a Call Girl*. Belle is a college graduate. She chooses to be a (high-class) prostitute because it pays well and she enjoys sex. She is not desperate and could get another job. Belle has not been beaten, raped, enslaved, or exploited. She has not experienced mental illness, addiction, or childhood trauma. Selling sex does not traumatize her; rather, she enjoys it. Some people might find her behavior distasteful, repulsive, or undignified, but that does not make it wrong. Buying sex from someone like Belle is not inherently wrong. It is a mutually enjoyable, mutually beneficial exchange with an autonomous, consenting adult. Buying sex from Belle is roughly on par, morally speaking, with paying a luthier to build you a guitar.[23]

Now, perhaps no actual prostitutes have been like Belle.[24] If so, then perhaps all actual payments for sex have been wrong. (Perhaps not.) Still, that would not show that buying sex is inherently wrong. It would just show that the conditions under which it is not wrong to buy sex have not occurred. Similarly, perhaps all actual vote buying and selling have been wrong. If so, that is probably because actual vote buying and selling have almost always been attempts to secure private interests at the expense of the common good. It is not because vote buying and selling are wrong in themselves.

Sex is not sacred. Neither is voting. Some people have a deep emotional aversion to certain trades. They find certain trades repugnant. (Steven Levitt and Stephen Dubner remind us that in the past, people thought it was repugnant to charge interest on loans, to sell sperm, and to buy life insurance.[25] Nowadays, buying life insurance seems the mark of a responsible parent. In the past, it was seen as a vulgar attempt to profit from death.) People tend to moralize their disgust reactions. It takes training to learn that disgust is not a reliable guide to right and wrong.

Ideology and Diversity of Opinion regarding Commodification

Perhaps I fail to see vote selling as inherently evil because my moral intuition is corrupt. Perhaps it is a basic moral fact that some trades are immoral, regardless of their consequences, and I am too corrupt to realize this.

Consider, in parallel, issues about organ selling. Suppose our best empirical research shows that organ selling makes poor people richer and sick people healthier. On my view, that would decide the debate in favor of permitting organ sales. Yet many people believe it is inherently wrong to sell organs, even if it were demonstrated that properly regulated organ sales would have good consequences for all involved parties and prevent many deaths.[26] They regard such sales as debasing the intrinsic dignity of human beings. Perhaps these people have better-developed faculties of moral judgment than I do. I just cannot quite see the wrongness because my moral vision is weak.

Intuitions about the moral permissibility of different trades vary greatly and correlate strongly with ideology. This might be because people of better moral sense tend to adopt one ideology rather than another. However, it is more plausible that people first adopt an ideology and then, on the basis of that ideology, determine whether trades are morally permissible.

Philip Tetlock has studied how ideology affects people's beliefs about the morality of different trades.[27] Gaus summarizes Tetlock's findings as follows: "While not surprisingly, libertarians believe few transactions should be blocked, Tetlock finds that 'Marxist respondents were prototypical "censorious busybodies." Even routine market transactions . . . provoke [in them] a measure of moral condemnation.'" Gaus concludes, "So we should be wary of saying that a certain trade offends 'our' moral sensibilities, for 'we' have very different attitudes toward the morality of specific trades."[28]

Consider that Marxists accept some version of Marxist economics, while liberals usually accept some version of neoclassical economics. It is less likely that people become Marxists because they think most trades should be blocked than that they think most trades should be blocked because they accept Marxist economics. People's attitudes toward trades might be byproducts of their economic views. On the neoclassical economic view, voluntary trade is generally considered good, because it leads to Pareto-improvements. On the other hand, people who subscribe to Marxist economics tend to view most trades within a market setting as harmful in one way or another. So perhaps someone with a Marxist economic view will have a gut-level distaste for trades, even when such trades are shown to be harmless.

If attitudes toward trades are a byproduct of people's economic views, this should worry Marxists. (Of course, it won't, but it should.) Marxist economic theory is in deep disrepute, though it remains popular outside of economics departments. In contrast, liberals and libertarians tend to accept mainstream economic theory. Even when they accept more heterodox theories, they tend to accept theories that have genuine purchase within the economics discipline.

So, if liberals and Marxists differ on this issue, one tentative explanation is that Marxists' moral judgment is clouded by their heterodox economic views. On the other hand, some Marxists hold that markets are not the morally best way for human beings to relate to one another.[29] In an ideal world, everyone would help each other for free rather than for payment. Perhaps these Marxists are right. But if so, this does not give us grounds to lament vote buying and selling in particular.

Some people regard vote selling as wrong because they believe it is inherently undignified. They assert that a self-respecting, dignified person would not accept money to vote, and a person who respects others' dignity would not offer money.

These claims are not obviously false, but they are not obviously true. Intuitions about what is dignified and undignified vary widely and also seem to correlate with ideology. Views about what is necessary for self-respect and human dignity tend to be controversial. Some people think it is undignified to accept money to do anything, such as to teach and write philosophy. Some people think any consensual exchange is dignified and respectful. Some Catholics regard all extramarital sex as violating human dignity, while Immanuel Kant thought masturbation was undignified. John Tomasi points out that

> it is important to note that self-respect is an elusive, quasi-psychological notion. Along with wealth and income, a great range of goods might therefore plausibly be claimed to be [necessary for] the . . . dignity of citizens. For example, multiculturalists have argued that a secure cultural context of choice is a primary good—a precondition for the exercise of autonomy on which liberal self-respect depends. Feminists have argued that women can only achieve equal dignity and self-respect in a community free of certain kinds of erotic literature and imagery. Citizens of faith sometimes claim that their self-respect depends upon the public affirmation of divinity, consistent with separation of church and state. Socialists have argued that wage and salaried labor is intrinsically demeaning of human dignity: self-respect requires the public ownership of the means of production.[30]

Tomasi does not claim *everything* related to human dignity is controversial, but certainly a great deal of it is. What people regard as undignified is disputed. This makes appeals to human dignity problematic. Perhaps vote selling is inherently undignified, but we would need to hear good reasons why.[31] We should be skeptical of blank appeals to human dignity. As Peter Singer says, "Philosophers frequently introduce ideas of dignity, respect, and worth at the point at which other reasons appear to be lacking, but this is hardly good enough. Fine phrases are the last resource of those who have run out of arguments."[32]

So, if it is undignified to accept money to vote, what makes it so? It is not (usually) undignified to accept money to work construction, to give a guest lecture, to take orders from a military superior, to take orders from one's boss at the bakery, or to accept money to write an encyclopedia article one otherwise would not write. What would make voting different? I suspect the issue is that many people have a quasi-religious reverence for democracy. For someone such as I—who approves of democracy but does not *revere* it—vote selling does not seem inherently undignified. However, strong democrats and civic humanists would likely regard vote selling as inherently degrading and unworthy of a human being.

We could try to resolve this dispute by examining shared moral beliefs that do not appear to result from people's different political ideologies or from controversial attitudes about what makes for a complete and dignified human life. Here are two such shared moral beliefs: Presumptively, if something tends to harm people, it is wrong. Presumptively, if something tends to benefit people but does not tend to harm anyone, it is not wrong. Thus, presumptively, vote buying and selling are morally permissible when voters vote in ways that they justifiedly believe promote the common good. When the paid voters vote in ways they justifiedly believe will promote the common good, this will tend to benefit some people and tend not to hurt others.

TAKING STOCK

Many people think that vote buying and selling are wrong in themselves. I speculate that this belief stems from two sources.

One source is a nonrational, emotional aversion. Children of democratic societies have a kind of romantic enthusiasm for democracy drilled into them from a young age. Vote buying and selling seem sacrilegious.

The second source of this belief comes from overgeneralizing a reasonable worry. In real life, most acts of vote buying and selling are morally corrupt and socially destructive. One might be tempted to conclude that vote buying and selling are intrinsically wrong. But this overgeneralizes. A better explanation is that vote buying and selling in real life are wrong because they tend to lead to harmful outcomes and exploitation. They tend to do this because they tend to be violations of Principle 1 (which says people who choose to vote must vote in ways they justifiedly expect to promote the common good; otherwise, they must abstain). However, if people abided by Principle 1, then vote buying and selling would tend to be socially beneficial. So long as people abide by Principle 1, we should not expect vote buying and selling to increase the likelihood of bad political outcomes.

By default, an action is morally permissible until shown otherwise. The person who wants to declare an action wrong bears the burden of proof. If the action is shown not to be (illegitimately) harmful and to even be beneficial, then this burden grows heavier.

So, at this point, the burden of proof is on the person who thinks vote buying and selling are always wrong. That person needs to explain why it is wrong in the cases I described previously. Until a good explanation is forthcoming, then we should accept Principle 2, which says that vote buying and selling are not wrong provided they do not lead to violations of the duty described by Principle 1.

Paying Someone Not to Do Good

Suppose Alan plans to vote in the next election.[33] Gilbert knows Alan is a good voter—if Alan votes, he will vote well. Gilbert offers Alan $100 to stay home and watch *Godfather* films instead of voting. Does Gilbert do something wrong? Does his action show that he has bad or imperfect moral character?

In order to assess whether Gilbert's action is wrong or shows bad character, we need to fill in more details about the case. Gilbert could be doing something morally neutral. Suppose it turns out that Gilbert wants to pay Alan because Alan is a good film critic, Gilbert wants Alan's opinion of the films, Gilbert (for blameless reasons) needs the opinion by the end of the day tomorrow, and tomorrow just happens to be election day. Here Gilbert does not have bad motivations. Gilbert does not de dicto desire to stop Alan from voting. Rather, Gilbert intends to have Alan watch the *Godfather* films, though this has the foreseeable but unintended consequence that Alan will not vote.

Gilbert's action does not appear to be wrong. Because Alan's individual vote has vanishingly small expected utility, Alan's abstention does not have any major consequences. Had Alan voted, this would not have prevented any great evils nor produced any great goods. Gilbert is not paying Alan *not to vote* per se but, rather, paying him to watch some films, though this means Alan will not perform the supererogatory action of voting well. This is no worse than when my employer pays me to teach classes, even though this has the predictable, if unintended, consequence of lessening the amount of volunteer work I do. My university does not pay me *not to volunteer*. Rather, it pays me to teach, though this means I volunteer less than I otherwise might.

However, suppose Gilbert actually intends to prevent Alan from voting well. In the preceding case, we imagined that Gilbert wanted Alan to watch and critique the *Godfather* films. Imagine instead that Gilbert specifically wishes to prevent Alan from voting. He pays Alan *not to vote*. Suppose the reason Gilbert does this is simply because he does not want Alan to perform a superogatory action. In this case, it is easy to conclude that Gilbert exhibits deficient moral character. However, that his action is wrong is not clear. (Recall in chapter 1 we discussed how some actions, such as destroying the last redwood, might exhibit bad character even if the actions are not strictly speaking wrong.) After all, Gilbert's action does not hurt anyone. Alan's vote has vanishingly small expected utility, so it is no significant loss that he fails to vote.

Contrast this is to another case. Suppose Alan is on his way to donate blood. Gilbert says to Alan, "I'd prefer that you do not donate blood. So I'll give you $250 to stay home." Alan takes the money and, as a result, fails to do some good he had planned to do. No one is harmed, but some people in need might not be helped. However, it is unlikely that anyone will die who would have lived if only Alan had donated blood. Unless Gilbert had some exculpatory motivations (e.g., he somehow knew that Alan would die while giving blood, and his offer was the only way to stop Alan), Gilbert exhibits bad moral character. However, whether Gilbert does anything morally wrong is still unclear, even if his actions display bad character.

Contrast this case to yet another. Suppose Alan is planning to donate a kidney.[34] (He has not promised to do so, so no one is expecting his kidney, but simply plans to do so.) Because donating a kidney is super-erogatory, it is morally permissible for Alan not to donate the kidney. Gilbert says to Alan, "I'd prefer that you not donate that kidney. So I'll give you $250,000 to stay home." Alan takes the money. As a result, someone who would have been saved dies. Here, it seems Gilbert has done something wrong. The reason it is permissible for Alan not to donate the kidney is that donating a kidney is costly and painful for him. However, Gilbert has now intervened to ensure that a life will fail to be saved, at significant personal cost to himself, and for no good reason. Gilbert prevents a significant good from happening simply to satisfy a strange preference of his.

When Gilbert pays people not to vote, the deontic status of Gilbert's action depends in part on the consequences of the action. This in turn will normally depend on the number of voters he pays not to vote. If Gilbert paid all or a large number of good voters to stay home rather than vote, he would make it so that the election is decided by bad voters. As a result, we would all have to suffer from worse governance, or, if we did not, it would be fortuitous. So, if Gilbert paid many good voters to stay home, we would have a real complaint against him. He is using money to produce bad government.

In the preceding cases, for Alan to vote, donate blood, or donate a kidney was praiseworthy but morally optional. Thus, for him to *fail to perform* these actions, even for frivolous reasons, was morally permissible. If he accepts money in exchange for nonperformance, his act might display a bad or corrupt character but is not wrong.

However, whether Alan's taking money displays bad character itself depends on the circumstances of the cases. Suppose Gilbert just pays Alan not to donate blood *that day*. Suppose that Alan had not made an appointment to donate blood but was merely going to walk in. This way, we need not worry that he broke a promise or inconvenienced anyone. Suppose Alan takes the money and then donates blood the next day. That is no worse than times when I have postponed donating blood because I wanted to go to lunch with a colleague or because I wanted to finish writing an article. Suppose instead Gilbert pays Alan never to donate blood again. Alan takes the money but then volunteers at a soup kitchen instead of donating blood. Again, this choice does not appear to show bad character. He decided to promote the common good one way rather than another because of a monetary incentive. People frequently choose among different ways of making a contribution on the basis of personal incentives. People want to make a difference, but they also want to make a difference in a way they will enjoy. So suppose a graduating student can do equal good as a high school teacher or as a physician but chooses to become a physician because it pays better. She does not display bad character for making that choice. We could debate whether someone of *perfect* moral character would be indifferent to these monetary incentives, but a person does not display *bad* character just because she is motivated partly by monetary incentives.

PAYING FOR GOOD BEHAVIOR FROM BAD VOTERS

So far we have discussed paying good voters to vote well and paying good voters not to vote. What about paying bad voters to cast a good vote or to abstain?

In the earlier case C, Ed advises Fred of the right way to vote and then pays Fred to vote that way. Fred knows that Ed is an expert and has the right motivations, so Fred presumably is justified in acting on Fred's advice. I argued that the fact that Ed pays Fred to act on this advice introduces no wrongness into the world.

However, suppose Ed (the expert) pays Ted to vote for a particular candidate. Unlike Fred, Ted has no knowledge of Ed's trustworthiness. Ted is willing to sell his vote to the highest bidder, regardless of the bidder's moral or epistemic qualifications. Ted takes Ed's money and votes the way Ed paid him to do. As a result, Ted votes the way he would have voted had he been well informed, rational, and well motivated. Has Ted done something wrong? Has Ed?

Ted has violated Principle 1. Ted votes the right way for the wrong reasons. In fact, Ted's vote helps promote the common good, but Ted does not justifiedly believe this. Ted does not know what effect the candidate he supports is likely to have on the common good. Thus, Ted is a fortuitous voter. Recall that fortuitous voting occurs when citizens vote for what are in fact beneficial policies or candidates likely to enact beneficial policies, but they are unjustified in thinking that these policies or candidates are good. In chapter 3, I argued that this kind of voting was wrong. So I take it that Ted acted wrongly.

What if Ed knows Ted is acting wrongly? Suppose Ed knows that Ted is not justified in voting on Ed's advice. Thus, Ed knows that Ted is merely a fortuitous voter. So Ed has paid Ted to do something wrong. Does this mean Ed has done something wrong?

We should pause before saying yes. Perhaps the answer depends on the alternatives available to Ed. Suppose Ted planned to vote for Y, the bad candidate. Because Ted is unreasonable and irrational about politics, no amount of argument or evidence would convince Ted to vote for X, the good candidate. However, while rational argument cannot convince Ted to change his vote, money can. Suppose Ed knows that Ted is trustworthy—if Ed pays Ted to vote for X, then Ted will vote for X. In this case, Ed pays Ted to vote the way Ted ought to vote were Ted better informed and better motivated. Ted should regard himself as imposing unacceptable risk on us. But from Ed's perspective, Ed is not imposing unacceptable risk by paying Ted to vote for a good candidate. Ted does not understand exactly what he is doing or the reasons for voting for one person rather than another. But so long as Ted can reliably carry out instructions, then Ted's vote can be expected to contribute to political outcomes. In this case, it seems that Ed has done us a (very) small favor. He has transformed a bad vote into a good one.

Suppose you know that many voters are going to vote for a harmful candidate. They cannot be convinced by evidence and argument. If you pay them to vote for the beneficial candidate, you produce a good outcome for all of us. They should not take your money and they should not vote, but given that they are going to vote, it is not wrong for you to pay them to vote better.

For instance, suppose it were true that women could have won the right to vote in the United States thirty years earlier had some philanthropist bribed voters to vote in favor of women's suffrage. Or suppose this philanthropist could prevent racists from voting for racist outcomes by bribing them to vote for egalitarian outcomes. In either case, it is not obvious the philanthropist acts wrongly. Instead, he is using money to induce bad people to do what they should do.

Similar remarks apply to paying for abstention. Suppose Ed can get Ted to abstain from voting for $50. This is similar to a wealthy environmentalist trying to reduce pollution by paying car owners not to drive. It may be an ineffective strategy, but it is not obviously morally wrong.

These are some reasons to think it is not wrong to pay for good behavior from bad voters. However, I am unsure of how sound they are. There are contrary considerations as well. I am worried about what would happen if such payments became widespread. Suppose I announce that I will pay would-be air polluters not to pollute. Perhaps this will reduce air pollution. Or perhaps it will induce people to threaten to pollute in hope of receiving a payment for forbearance. Some of these people will make good on their threats if they do not receive payment. Similarly, suppose I announce that I will pay would-be bad voters not to pollute the polls with their votes. Perhaps people would then form coalitions of bad voters who will threaten to vote badly unless they are paid to abstain or vote for better candidates. Worries like these might provide good reasons to make the practice of paying for good behavior from bad voters illegal.

Conclusion

Vote buying and selling have no inherent moral status. When they are wrong, what makes them wrong is that they lead to violations of the ethics of voting. That is, they lead people to vote badly. When voters are paid to vote well, this tends to benefit others rather than harm them, or, at least, those who are harmed are legitimately harmed.

In the real world, when we see widespread vote buying, this is a sign of political corruption. In the real world, vote buying tends to be malicious and exploitative. However, in principle, it need not be. Paying someone to vote well or accepting money to vote well is not wrong. Instead, it is wrong to vote badly, and it is typically worse to vote badly for money.

CHAPTER SEVEN

How Well Do Voters Behave?

ACTUAL VOTERS

IN THIS BOOK, I argue for some standards about how voters ought to behave. My conclusions are:

1. Citizens do not have a duty to vote. At most, they have duties of beneficence and reciprocity that can be discharged any number of ways besides voting.
2. In general, voters should vote for things that tend to promote the common good rather than try to promote narrow self-interest at the expense of the common good.
3. Voters face epistemic requirements. They must be epistemically justified in believing that the candidate or policy they support is likely to promote the common good. Otherwise, they ought to abstain.
4. Vote buying and selling are sometimes morally permissible, provided these activities do not violate the duties listed here.

The original contribution of this book was to argue for these claims and to argue against contrary claims. So, as of now, I have completed my philosophical project.

In this chapter, I describe some social-scientific research on the behavior of actual citizens and voters. There is an extensive literature on this topic. I do not pretend to cover everything. I am being selective. I talk here about *some* of the worrisome findings. That said, I try not to mislead readers into thinking things are worse than they are.

The literature I review gives us grounds for thinking many or perhaps most voters are bad voters. It appears that many voters consistently violate the standards articulated in this book. It also appears that nonvoters would violate the standards if they were to vote.

Almost nothing in the previous chapters depends upon the research described in this chapter. If the work I describe turns out to be wrong, this leaves my theory of voting ethics intact. The research says that citizens are often ignorant, misinformed, and irrational about political issues. My theory of voting ethics says that if a citizen is ignorant, unjustifiedly misinformed, or irrational, then she should not vote. However, if the research is wrong, and citizens are in fact well informed and rational, then my theory of voting ethics says that they may vote (provided they vote to promote the common good).

(Nationalist) Sociotropic Voting

First, we start with some (sort of) good news. Commonsense tells us that voters vote for their self-interest. Commonsense is mistaken.[1]

Political scientists (or, at least those political scientists who do empirical studies of voting behavior rather than rely upon a priori models) generally agree that voters tend not to vote for what they perceive to be in their narrow self-interest. For example, the elderly are not significantly more likely to support social security programs than younger workers. Rather, voters tend to vote for what they perceive to be in the *national* interest.[2] Voters at least *want* to promote the (national) common good.

However, though voters tend to vote for what they *believe* serves the nation's interests, this does not imply that they are justified in these beliefs or that their beliefs are true. Voters intend to promote the national interest, but that does not imply that they in fact promote the national interest. Good intentions are not enough to make good policy. Voters might not know what they are doing. It may turn out that some or many of them are mistaken about what promotes the national interest. If so, then their altruistic intentions do not benefit us.

Imagine that Betty Benevolence desires to help others. However, Betty has irrational beliefs about what helps others. When she sees a hungry child, she steals his remaining food. When she sees a sick man, she injects him with smallpox. When she sees someone in pain, she kicks his shins. Betty may intend to do good, but she does harm. Some research purports to show that voters are much like Betty Benevolence. They intend to make things better, but they make things worse. They are misinformed or irrational about what promotes the common good and thus choose counterproductive strategies.

Sociotropic voting is surprising. People are not pure egoists, but they tend to be more selfish than altruistic, and most of their altruism is directed at close families and friends. Why, then, do we find so much sociotropic rather than egoistic voting?

One leading hypothesis claims that voting is cheap altruism. The expected utility of my vote is vanishingly small regardless of whether I vote for narrow self-interest or for the common good. So suppose I have some moral motivation, and I would like to think of myself as a good person, but I do not want to incur any major expense in acting on others' behalf.

I might recognize there is nothing to be gained from voting for narrow self-interest and thus instead vote for what I perceive to be the common good. If you want to indulge altruistic motives and believe that you have done your part, voting sociotropically is cheaper and easier than volunteering at a soup kitchen or giving money to Oxfam.

A recent paper provides some empirical evidence in favor of this explanation.[3] Timothy Feddersen, Sean Gailmard, and Alvaro Sandroni conducted a series of economic experiments in which subjects could choose to vote in self-interested or public-spirited ways. In experimental economics, players know the rules of the game they are playing and are paid large enough sums of money (based on how they play) to motivate them to play in realistic ways. Fedderson, Gailmard, and Sandroni wanted to see how voters would respond to changes in the expected utility of their votes. They had subjects play a series of games that varied the probability that an individual subject's vote would be decisive. In games where subjects' individual votes had a low probability of being decisive, and thus individual votes were of low expected utility, subjects voted in an unselfish, public-spirited way. In games where subjects' individual votes had high probabilities of being decisive, and thus individual votes had high expected utility, the subjects voted for narrow self-interest at the expense of the common good.

Fedderson, Gailmard, and Sandroni's work suggests that if you want voters to vote sociotropically, you should ensure that they have little to gain from voting egoistically. In real elections, we ensure this by making it so that individual votes have vanishingly small expected utility.

However, this reduces the incentives for voters to know what they are doing. Because individual votes count so little, voters vote for what they believe to be in the common good. But, because individual voters count so little, voters do not work hard to learn what is in the common good. Russell Hardin points out that, "in general, we make the effort to know something in large part *because we think it will serve our interest to know it.*"[4] Yet, regardless of whether you have altruistic or selfish interests, it is not unusually in your interest to know much about politics.

RATIONAL IGNORANCE

Around the late 1950s, researchers began trying to measure citizens' political knowledge. Study after study confirmed that most citizens are ignorant about politics. Overall levels of political knowledge are low. For example, 79 percent of Americans cannot identify their state senators. During election years, most citizens cannot identify any congressional candidates in their district.[5] Immediately before the 2004 presidential election, almost 70 percent of American citizens were unaware that Congress had added a prescription drug benefit to Medicare, though this was a giant increase to the federal budget and was the largest new entitlement program in decades.[6] Generally, citizens in other democracies are no better informed than Americans, though political knowledge seems to be somewhat higher in smaller, more homogeneous countries.

Political knowledge is distributed unevenly. Most people know little, but some people know a lot, and some people know nothing. After we survey citizens, suppose we divide them into four groups, putting the 25 percent most knowledgeable citizens into the top quartile and the 25 percent least knowledgeable into the bottom quartile. We can then ask, How much more knowledgeable is the top quartile compared to the bottom quartile? Scott Althaus finds, using data from the 1992 American National Election Studies (a survey of voter knowledge), the top quartile knows much, but the bottom quartiles knows hardly anything. For instance, 93.4 percent of people in the top quartile, but only 13.1 percent of people in the bottom quartile, know that the Republicans tend to be more conservative than the Democrats.[7] Among people in the lowest knowledge quartile, only 12.2 percent and 9.7 percent knew which party controlled the House of Representatives and Senate, respectively. The bottom 25 percent of citizens does worse than a coin flip when it comes to political knowledge—they are systematically in error.

Political knowledge also correlates with different demographic factors, sometimes strongly, sometimes weakly. For instance, Althaus finds that political knowledge in the United States is positively correlated with having a college degree, being rich, working an executive or professional job, being a member of the Republican Party, being middle-aged rather than young or old, being male, living in the West or East, being married, owning a home, and living in an urban or suburban area. It is negatively correlated with being black, being a union member, and living in the South or Midwest.[8] (Recall that in chapter 4, one worry about my theory of voting ethics was that it would characterize many poor minorities as bad voters or potential bad voters. Here is some evidence that this worry was correct.)

Surveys of political knowledge generally study easily settled or quantifiable sources of knowledge, such as who occupies various offices, what ideologies different politicians claim to espouse, or what powers different branches of government have. In the introduction, I argued that having this kind of information is not sufficient to make a person well informed about politics. It is one thing to know which policies different politicians favor and are likely to promote. However, it is another matter to have the relevant background in social science needed to evaluate these positions. For example, it is one thing to know whether candidates favor high tariffs, but it takes specialized knowledge to know what effects high tariffs tend to have on the economy. Surveys of voter belief rarely attempt to measure whether citizens have this second, harder-to-acquire kind of knowledge. However, because this second kind of knowledge is more difficult to acquire than the first (e.g., it is easier to learn which candidate is friendlier to free trade than to learn whether free trade is a good thing), we can expect citizens to be even less knowledgeable about these issues.

Why do citizens know so little about politics? The standard answer is that citizens are *rationally ignorant*. Individual citizens have almost no power over government, and individual votes have almost zero expected utility. Thus, political knowledge does voters little good. Acquiring knowledge is costly and difficult. If you knew that your vote were likely to be decisive, then you would invest time and effort into acquiring political knowledge. However, when you realize that your vote makes no difference, you probably decide not to bother. (This is true regardless of whether you have altruistic or selfish motivations.) For many citizens, the cost of acquiring political knowledge outweighs the expected benefit of having this knowledge.

People will sometimes cite evidence of voter ignorance and then complain, "Americans are stupid!"[9] Well, yes, some Americans are stupid, but most are quite intelligent and skilled, despite being ignorant about politics (and some other issues, such as world geography).[10] They do not invest in political knowledge because the investment does not pay. They have their own lives to lead. They have other valuable things to contribute to society. The political class often lampoons citizens' lack of knowledge, but citizens often have better things to do (for themselves and for each other) than invest in knowledge that is of no special use to them or to others.

That most people are ignorant about politics is not surprising. What is surprising is that some people know so much. Why? Some people find politics interesting and entertaining. Others feel obligated to be knowledgeable. Others wish to cultivate an informed, rational self-image or public-image. Others are knowledgeable because they are expected to be knowledgeable. Others are misinformed about the instrumental values of their votes—they take the time to be well informed because they mistakenly believe their votes make a difference.

DOES KNOWLEDGE CHANGE WHAT VOTERS CHOOSE?

Political ignorance matters only if it makes a difference in how people vote. Conceivably, it might not. Suppose Bob is ignorant and votes for policies P. Now suppose we educate Bob, but he continues to vote for policies P. It is at least possible that most voters are like Bob—acquiring knowledge does not change how they vote. It is also possible that they are not. We would need to check to be sure. If voters are like Bob, then political ignorance should not worry us. Alas, it is not so. Knowledge does make a difference.

Heuristics and Information Shortcuts

Here is an optimistic hypothesis: perhaps ignorant voters use heuristics and shortcuts that enable them to select the right answer despite their ignorance.

Richard Lau and David Redlawsk studied voter decision making at length, trying to determine how well voters choose despite their informational shortcomings. Lau and Redlawsk say a voter "votes correctly" when she votes the way she would vote were she fully informed.[11] Lau and Redlawsk ran experimental mock elections designed to determine what kinds of information voters seek and to determine how well they tend to vote. In some of their experiments, they made voters decide quickly, then had the voters acquire more information, and then examined whether voters would revise their votes after acquiring new information.

At first glance, Lau and Redlawsk's finding seems hopeful. It appears that voters somehow vote correctly despite their ignorance. Lau and Redlawsk conclude that around 70 percent of voters tend to vote correctly in experimental two-person presidential elections. That is, around 70 percent of voters would not change their votes were they to acquire more information. However, voters do much worse when there are more than two candidates. When there are four candidates, the percentage that votes correctly drops to 31 percent.

If we extrapolate these findings, we can ask what they imply about real presidential elections. Because primaries tend to have many candidates, Lau and Redlawsk's work suggests that voters tend to choose the wrong candidates during presidential primaries. However, during the general presidential election, perhaps as many as 70 percent of voters make the better choice between the two major party candidates whom they wrongly selected during the primaries.

Of course, to make even this rather pessimistic extrapolation, we have to ignore third parties. In fact, in U.S. presidential elections, voters typically have at least five or six choices. For example, the 2008 Massachusetts ballot listed six candidates for president. Nothing in Lau and Redlawsk's experimental design suggests that we may ignore the presence of third parties when estimating how well real voters do. Lau and Redlawsk say a person votes correctly when she votes for the candidate she would have selected were she well informed. If voters were well informed, they might select third parties.

Lau and Redlawsk also find that so-called incorrect voters tend to favor one side rather than another. They do not vote randomly. Thus, even in the best-case scenario, when 70 percent of voters vote correctly, incorrect voters might alter the election results. Lau and Redlawsk suspect that voters do far better on presidential elections than other elections. This is worrisome, they say, because "our federal system ensures that much of what is important in politics happens at lower levels of government."[12] So they believe their experimental results overstate how well real voters do.

Note that Lau and Redlawsk's definition of "correct voting" does not match what I call good voting. Many of the people they would describe as voting correctly violate the ethics of voting. Lau and Redlawsk's notion of "correct voting" does not require that voters vote to produce good results. For example, suppose a German voter in 1932 voted for the Nazis because he hoped they would exterminate Jews. This voter would count as voting correctly according to Lau and Redlawsk's definition of "correct voting." However, this voter counts as a bad voter on my theory of voting ethics.

Also, Lau and Redlawsk use a deflated notion of what it means to be fully informed. For them, a fully informed voter knows who the candidates are and knows which policies the candidates prefer. But Lau and Redlawsk's definition of "fully informed" does not require that voters be well informed about the likely consequences of those policies. So suppose voter Jane cares only about promoting the U.S. economy. She incorrectly believes that protectionism tends to be more effective than free trade at achieving this goal, despite the overwhelming evidence that this is not so. She correctly identifies and votes for the most protectionist candidate. On Lau and Redlawsk's definitions of "fully informed" and "voting correctly," Jane qualifies as fully informed and a correct voter. In contrast, I would describe her as a misinformed, bad voter.

Lau and Redlawsk present their findings in a more positive light than I have. Partly, this is because, as I have noted, they have permissive conceptions of what it means to be fully informed and to vote correctly.[13] Partly it is because they focus on the best-case scenario—how well ignorant voters do in two-candidate presidential elections. However, their experiment findings suggest that uninformed voters do not, in general, manage to make the best choices despite their lack of knowledge.

Enlightened Preferences

Imagine you took the American populace, with its current demographics, but magically boosted everyone's political knowledge. Would Americans' policy preferences change or stay the same?[14] If preferences would change, would there be a general trend in how their preferences change?

The answers to these questions tell us something about how knowledge affects voter behavior and also something about how knowledge correlates with ideology.

Your *enlightened policy preferences* are the policies you would prefer if you had maximal political knowledge. Suppose right now you prefer policy set P. Imagine we keep almost everything about you the same but boosted your political knowledge. You now know all there is to know about politics. Suppose adding knowledge changes your preferences— you now prefer policy set Q instead of P. These policies are your *enlightened preferences*. Your enlightened preferences are what you would prefer if you were fully informed. (If acquiring full information would not change any of your current preferences, then your current preferences are also your enlightened preferences.)

Scott Althaus has tried to estimate what voters' enlightened preferences are. Bryan Caplan summarizes Althaus's methods as follows:

1. Administer a survey of policy preferences *combined with* a test of objective political knowledge. [Althaus's data sets are the 1988, 1992, and 1994 American National Election Studies.]
2. Statistically estimate individual's policy preferences as a function of their objective political knowledge and their demographics—such as income, race, and gender.
3. Simulate what policy preferences *would* look like if all members of all demographic groups had the *maximum* level of objective political knowledge.[15]

So Althaus's method was to determine, statistically, how policy preferences correlate both with objective political knowledge and with various demographic factors. Because he had a massive data set, he could determine what effect knowledge has on people's policy preferences while controlling for biases and attitudes caused by their demographic factors. For instance, he could determine how knowledge affects one's attitudes about trade policy while controlling for income. Althaus wanted to estimate what an *enlightened public*—a society that exactly mirrors ours demographically, but in which everyone has complete political knowledge—would prefer.

Althaus concluded that not only do policy preferences change as people acquire more knowledge but their preferences change in systematic ways. On social issues, the enlightened public is more tolerant and open. People are less likely to support school prayer and more likely to support equal rights for homosexuals. They are more likely to support abortion on demand. As the public becomes enlightened, they become more in favor of free markets and less in favor of strong government control of the economy. (This effect is strongest among those in the bottom economic quartile.) They tend to favor tax increases to reduce the government deficit.[16] They favor less punitive measures on crime and less hawkish military policy.[17]

Note that Althaus's conception of full political knowledge has some of the problems facing Lau and Redlawsk's conception. When Althaus simulates full knowledge, he is simulating people as if they had extensive information about what candidates prefer, how political parties behave, what powers different government branches have, and other facts. He does not directly simulate what would happen if, in addition to knowing these things, everyone had full social-scientific knowledge. His "fully informed" public might still be uninformed about the natural and social sciences.

However, this is less problematic for Althaus than for Lau and Redlawsk. The people who are most knowledgeable about the topics Althaus studies tend also to be most knowledgeable about the natural and social sciences. So, when Althaus statistically simulates what would happen if the voting public were fully informed, he in effect uses a broader notion of full information than Lau or Redlawsk do.

Althaus's work, like Lau and Redlawsk's, indicates that knowledge makes a difference. If citizens knew more, they would prefer different policies.

The Miracle of Aggregation?

Increasing people's political knowledge seems to change their policy preferences in a systematic way. By itself, this does not yet show us that we should be worried about ignorant voters.[18]

Althaus's work suggests that informed voters tend to converge on certain policy preferences.[19] However, suppose uninformed voters are all over the board. Suppose the ignorant are so ignorant that they vote randomly. If so, then their votes would be unproblematic.

Imagine that our society is made up of 100 million voters. Two percent of the voters are well informed. The well-informed voters all prefer candidate A over candidate B. The other 98 percent are completely ignorant. When the ignorant voters vote, they have no information to help them decide how to cast their votes. Thus, for them, choosing between A and B is like a coin flip. They cast their votes randomly. If you flip a coin 100 million times, you're going to get very close to 50 percent heads and 50 percent tails. Thus, among the ignorant voters, 50 percent will vote for A and 50 percent will vote for B. The uninformed voters cancel each other out, leaving the informed voters to decide the election. The informed voters all vote for candidate A. Thus, A will end up with 51 percent of the total vote and B will get 49 percent. A will win the election.

This is called "the miracle of aggregation." The idea of the miracle of aggregation is that large democracies with only a tiny percentage of informed voters can perform as well as democracies made up entirely of informed voters. It seems miraculous indeed. It would be wonderful if 98 million uninformed voters canceled each other out, leaving the election to be decided by the 2 million informed voters.

However, the miracle of aggregation can occur only if uninformed voters vote randomly. If they do not vote randomly, there is no miracle.

Alas, there are reasons to think ignorant voters do not vote randomly. For instance, there have been many studies confirming *position bias*—where early answers in multiple-choice tests tend to be favored over later answers. Ballots approximate such multiple-choice tests, and we can expect position bias to influence ignorant voters' votes away from random selection. Random orderings in ballots may overcome this, but then there are other similar biases that could prevent ignorant voters from voting in random and therefore harmless ways. For example, ignorant voters often make a choice based on the attractiveness of the candidates' names.

The miracle of aggregation assumes a model of democracy in which many voters are completely ignorant. However, if voters are only *mostly* ignorant, they might not vote randomly. Of course, in real life, uninformed voters are not completely ignorant. Sometimes a little knowledge is a bad thing.

For example, even largely ignorant voters are often able to recognize incumbents on the ballot box. Voters tend to favor incumbents. If voters believe (correctly or incorrectly) that times are good, they tend to reward incumbents, and if they believe times are bad, they tend to punish incumbents, regardless of whether the incumbents are responsible for how things are and regardless of whether there's reason to think challengers would be better.[20] In real life, ignorant voters are often not ignorant enough to vote randomly—they choose familiar names, and familiar names are not necessarily good ones.

Many voters react in bizarre ways to incumbents. For example, Andrew Healy has a series of papers showing that voters in the United States and elsewhere punish incumbent candidates for bad weather.[21] If you are a congressperson, and your district has an unusual number of tornadoes during your term, you are less likely to be reelected. This suggests that voters have difficulty distinguishing between bad luck and incompetence when they evaluate an incumbent's performance. (Surely, voters do not believe their representatives are to blame for the weather. However, bad weather makes voters feel unhappy, and they take it out on their representatives.)

The main worry about the miracle of aggregation is that it assumes uninformed voters are not systematically in error. But they often are systematically in error. For instance, most Americans would prefer to see foreign aid reduced. Most of them think that foreign aid is one of the largest items on the federal budget, when in fact it is one of the smaller items. (The average American thinks that 18 percent of the federal budget is devoted to foreign aid, but in fact it's about 1 percent.)[22]

It might turn out that ignorant people have systematic biases and bents toward certain policies. If so, then they will not vote randomly, and there will be no miracle of aggregation. If the majority of people are ignorant and if ignorant people systematically favor certain kinds of policies, there is a good chance they will get their way. That could be bad for all of us.

SYSTEMATIC ERRORS AND RATIONAL IRRATIONALITY

Bryan Caplan contends that citizens have systematically erroneous views on economic policy.[23] They are not merely ignorant know-nothings; they are misinformed and know *less* than nothing. For a great many issues, we would get better government performance by deciding questions on the basis of coin flips than by asking voters.

Caplan argues that voters underestimate to what degree self-interested behavior can lead to publicly beneficial results. They thus call for government intervention in the economy far more than they would if they better understood how markets work. They tend to regard foreign trade in zero-sum terms (e.g., to see foreigners' gains as domestic losses), to be distrustful and resentful of immigrants, to misunderstand balance of trade issues, and support subsidizing inefficient enterprises in a misguided attempt to boost exports. They do not understand the market's power of creative destruction and choose policies that spread work or subsidize inefficient and obsolete industries at a loss to most people's welfare. Finally, they have a pessimistic bias—they tend "to overestimate the severity of economic problems and underestimate the (recent) past, present, and future performance of the economy."[24]

One partial explanation for this pessimistic bias might simply be that people are bad at making certain kinds of calculations. Fabian Christandl and Detlef Fetchenhauer wanted to know how well people understand compounding economic growth. They ran experiments in which they asked subjects to estimate how much national income would grow over the next 25 years, if the annual growth rates were 1%, 3%, or 5 percent.[25] Subjects made wildly inaccurate estimates. In fact, if the economy grows at 5 percent per year for the next 25 years, national income will increase by 238 percent. However, subjects' mean estimate was 82 percent, about one-third of the correct answer. More than 90 percent of subjects *under*estimated the correct amount of growth; less than 10 percent estimated correctly or overestimated. The most plausible explanation why subjects give such low estimates is that they have difficulty understanding exponential growth.[26] Perhaps this partly explains why people systematically underestimate the future performance of the economy.

Caplan notes that many surveys show systematic divergence between the economic beliefs of economists and of laypeople. For example, while the overwhelming majority of economists believe government should *not* use price controls to curb inflation, the overwhelming majority of non-economists think government *should* use such controls. Most economists think tariffs and other restrictions of trade usually reduce the general welfare, but the public favors tariffs in order to promote welfare.[27]

One survey showing this divergence is the Survey of Americans and Economists on the Economy (SAEE), conducted in 1996 by the Washington Post, Kaiser Family Foundation, and Harvard University Survey Project. When asked why the economy was not doing better, the public thought "there are too many immigrants" was between a minor and a major reason, while economists thought it was not a reason at all. The public thought "technology is displacing workers," "business profits are too high," "companies are sending jobs overseas," and "companies are downsizing" are reasons why the economy was not doing better, while economists did not.[28] The public thought spikes in oil prices resulted from corporate greed, while economists overwhelmingly believed these changes resulted from normal supply and demand.[29] The SAEE and other surveys provide evidence that the public has a tenuous grasp of basic economics and continues to make the errors Adam Smith was trying to correct back in 1776.[30]

If laypeople and economists have systematically different views of the economy, this suggests that laypeople are in systematic error. However, it is possible that economists are biased. They are, after all, disproportionately white, upper-middle class, and male. Perhaps this leads economists to favor policies that benefit white, upper-middle class males.

To correct for this possible source of bias among economists, Caplan borrows Althaus's statistical methods. He simulates what the economic policy preferences of an enlightened public would be, using survey date from the SAEE. That is, imagine we made it so that everyone in the United States has the knowledge needed to hold a Ph.D. in economics. Caplan concludes that people would change their economic policy preferences in a systematic way. In an enlightened public, people would systematically have more pro-market views than those who make up the real, unenlightened public. (Note that while Althaus and Caplan come to similar conclusions using a similar statistical method, they used different sets of data.)

Of course, it might still be that economists, not laypeople, are systematically in error. After all, economists might be in the grip of false economic theories, while laypeople's commonsense views on the economy might be correct. However, absent positive evidence that this is so, it is more plausible that economists know more about the economy than laypeople.

Suppose Caplan is right that laypeople have systematically false beliefs about economics. One reason this might be so is simply that much of economic theory is counterintuitive. The labor theory of value holds that the price of a good is determined by the socially useful labor that produced the object. This seems commonsensical, but it is wrong. The objective input theory of value holds that the price of a good is determined by the price of its components. This also seems commonsensical, but it is also wrong. The theory of comparative advantage says that even if A is much better at producing everything that B produces, A and B can still engage in mutually beneficial trade. Intuitively this seems false—why would A want to buy widgets from B when A is better than B at making widgets?—but it is true. Mercantilist economic theory says that wealth comes from maximizing exports while minimizing imports so as to maintain a net intake of gold bullion. Intuitively, this seems true, but it is false. Or suppose you toured all the General Motors plants in 2008 and watched the workers make cars. It would be counterintuitive, but nevertheless correct, to conclude that you are witnessing the mass destruction of wealth.

Laypeople and economists tend to have systematically different policy preferences and views on the economy. Caplan argues that this is not merely because laypeople are ignorant, but because they are irrational. He says that if laypeople were merely ignorant of economics, we would expect erroneous beliefs, but not systematically erroneous beliefs. However, laypeople tend to converge on the same false beliefs rather than holding a wide array of false beliefs. In addition, people have emotional attachments to their false beliefs and the beliefs are resistant to change in the face of countervailing evidence. This suggests irrationality and bias rather than mere ignorance.

To explain why economic biases persist, and why people's beliefs about economics resist change even in the face of countervailing evidence, Caplan argues that people exhibit "rational irrationality."[31] A person is said to exhibit rational irrationality when it is *instrumentally* rational for him to be *epistemically* irrational. An *instrumentally* rational person chooses the best strategies to achieve his goals. An *epistemically* irrational person ignores and evades evidence against his beliefs, holds his beliefs without evidence or with only weak evidence, has contradictions in his thinking, employs logical fallacies in belief formation, and exhibits characteristic epistemic vices such as close-mindedness.

Epistemically irrational political beliefs can reinforce one's self-image; boost one's self-esteem; make one feel noble, smart, superior, safe, or comfortable; and can help achieve conformity with the group and thus facilitate social acceptance. Thus, epistemic irrationality can be instrumentally rational.

If I falsely believe the road I am crossing is free of cars, I might die. So I have a strong incentive to form beliefs about the road in a rational way. However, if I falsely believe that import quotas are good for the economy, this has no directly harmful effects. (On the contrary, the belief can have significant instrumental value. It might make me feel patriotic; serve my xenophobia; serve as an outlet to rationalize, sublimate, or redirect racist attitudes; or help me pretend to have solidarity with union workers.) For each of us, our individual votes are of little consequence in determining electoral outcomes. When we discussed rational ignorance, we noted that for any given voter, no matter how altruistic or selfish her motives, the expected cost of being well informed is greater than the expected benefit. Similarly, for any given voter, the expected cost of maintaining her epistemic rationality in the sphere of politics is greater than the expected benefit. Epistemic rationality is hard and takes self-discipline.

When it comes to politics, individuals have every incentive to indulge their irrational impulses. Demand for irrational beliefs is like demand for most other goods. The lower the cost, the more will be demanded. The cost to the typical voter of voting in epistemically irrational ways is nearly zero. The cost of overcoming bias and epistemic irrationality is high. The psychological benefit of this irrationality is significant. Thus, voters demand a high amount of epistemic irrationality. Most voters have the incentive to remain irrational about economic policy.

Western democracies' policy decisions mostly concern economic issues. Yet it seems unlikely that voters form irrational beliefs *only* about economic issues. Given their incentives, they probably exhibit similar irrational belief patterns about international relations, sociological issues, the efficacy of war, the teaching of evolution in public schools, the justice of affirmative action, the efficacy and sociological effects of harsh prison sentences, and more. We can expect many voters to be irrational about the wide range of policies democracies enact.[32]

Perhaps Caplan is right that people tend to have systematic bents toward certain false beliefs about economics. Yet, should we agree with him that the best explanation for this is that people are rationally irrational? There might be some other explanation other than rational irrationality. Caplan has identified systematic errors, but he has not ruled out contrary explanations for those systematic errors.

Still, the existence of rational irrationality is supported by at least one recent psychological study. Drew Westen published an experiment on *motivated reasoning*, the theory that the brain tries to converge on beliefs that produce maximum positive feelings and minimize negative feelings.[33]

Westen's subjects were loyal Republicans and Democrats. Subjects were shown a statement by a celebrity, followed by information potentially making the celebrity seem hypocritical. Then, subjects were presented with an "exculpatory statement." (A test run had a quote by Walter Cronkite saying he would never do TV work again after retiring, followed by footage showing he did work again after retiring, followed by an explanation saying it was a special favor.) In the experiment, the celebrities were identifiable as Republicans or Democrats. Democrat subjects strongly agreed that the famous Republicans contradicted themselves but only weakly agreed that the Democrats contradicted themselves. Republican subjects likewise readily accepted exculpatory statements from their favored party, but not the other party. Functional magnetic resonance imaging (fMRI) showed that subject's pleasure centers were activated when condemning members of the other party, and activated again when subjects denied evidence against members of their own party.

WHO HEARS THE OTHER SIDE?

In *On Liberty*, John Stuart Mill argued that people are not in a good position to hold their own views until they have charitably confronted contrary views. Part of what it takes to be justified in believing X is to understand why people might believe ~X. Partly for these reasons, contemporary deliberative democrats think that citizens have an obligation to consider and respond to contrary views when forming their own preferences. It is important that citizens understand other citizens' reasons for their different views. Citizens who fail to do so are likely to vote without a good sense of others' concerns and of merits and demerits of their own views. Deliberative democrats wish to see citizens come together to discuss political issues in a serious, dispassionate, and open way.

Let's describe two kinds of democratic citizens.

1. *Deliberative* citizens have frequent significant crosscutting political discussion. That is, they frequently consider and respond to contrary views. They are careful in forming their own political preferences. They are able to articulate good reasons on behalf of contrary views. They have high levels of political knowledge.

2. *Participatory* citizens engage heavily with politics. They run for office, run campaigns, vote, give money to campaigns, attend town hall meetings, engage in protests, write letters to the editor, etc.

In principle, a good deliberative citizen can also be a good participatory citizen. These are not logically exclusive categories. Most democratic theorists wish citizens to be deliberative and participatory.

However, Diana Mutz's empirical work shows that deliberation and participation do not come together. Deliberative citizens do not participate much, and participatory citizens do not deliberate much. The people who are most active in politics tend to be (in my words, not Mutz's) cartoon ideologues.[34] The people who are most careful in formulating their own political views and who spend the most time considering contrary views tend not to participate in politics.

Being exposed to contrary points of view tends to lessen one's enthusiasm for one's own political views. Deliberation with others who hold contrary views tends to make one ambivalent and apathetic about politics.[35] True believers make better activists than cautious, self-skeptical thinkers. (Imagine a street evangelist saying, "Hear ye! My religion *might* be the one true path, but, you know, there are some good grounds for doubt!") Crosscutting political exposure decreases the likelihood that a person will vote, reduces the number of political activities a person engages in, and makes people take longer to decide how to vote.[36]

In contrast, active, participatory citizens tend not to engage in much deliberation and tend not to have much crosscutting political discussion.[37] Instead, they seek out and interact only with others with whom they already agree. When asked why other people hold contrary points of view, participatory citizens tend to respond that others must be stupid or corrupt. Participatory citizens are often unable to give charitable explanations of why people might hold contrary views. (This is worrisome, because people who tend to demonize all contrary views tend to be unjustified in their own views.) In contrast, citizens who exhibit high degrees of the deliberative virtues are able to give charitable accounts of contrary viewpoints.

Many deliberative democratic political theorists hold that the government should provide more meaningful opportunities for political participation. Mutz argues that if we created these opportunities, the people most likely to take advantage of them are extremists and partisans. The empirical evidence suggests that the people most willing to bear the personal costs (in terms of time and effort) of participation are those with the most extreme views.[38] Extremists are interested in politics and tend to be the most dissatisfied with the status quo, and thus tend to be the most highly participatory citizens.

Mutz's empirical findings give us reason to worry. Politically active citizens wield more influence than the inactive citizens do. Yet the deliberative citizens (who tend to be inactive) will tend to have better grounds for their views than the participatory citizens. So Mutz's work suggests that politics tends to be run by people with poor epistemic credentials.[39] Politically active citizens tend to lack the deliberative virtues, to be extremists, and to think that anyone who disagrees with them is corrupt and stupid.

Conclusion: Making Voters Better

Suppose, for the sake of argument, that every argument I have made is sound. Suppose I am correct about what it takes to vote well, and suppose I have adequately refuted all reasonable objections to my arguments. Even if that were so, this book probably would not make people better voters. In part, this is because the people who are most likely to be bad voters are also least likely to read this book. In part, it is because actual human beings are not perfectly rational. The more irrational someone is, the less likely she is to be swayed by rational argument. So, even if my arguments are sound, they will convince people only to the extent that they are rational.

So someone might complain that the book is *impractical*. In one sense, it is not impractical: everything I have argued that people should do is easy for them to do. In another sense, it is impractical: people will not do what they should, even though they easily could. This book is not likely to change that. More simply: this book is a piece of moral philosophy, not a manual for civic education.

Thus, the purpose of this book is to argue for certain positions on voting ethics. My goal has been to defend certain normative claims. If this book induces better behavior among voters, great, but I do not expect that. My purpose has been proof, not persuasion or behavior modification. If voters behave badly, we will need more than a philosophy book to fix that.

Notes

INTRODUCTION: VOTING AS AN ETHICAL ISSUE

1. Elster (1997, 10–11) says that there is
   a confusion between the kind of behavior that is appropriate in the market place and that which is appropriate in the forum. The notion of consumer sovereignty [in the market] is acceptable because, and to the extent that, the consumer chooses between courses of action that differ only in the way it affects him. In political choice situations, however, the citizen is asked to express his preference over states that also differ in the way they affect other people.

2. Political outcomes also tend to reflect the policy preferences of the median voter. For more on the median voter theorem, including a summary of empirical testing of the theorem, see Mueller 2003, 243–46. For more on "the supply side of politics," and how voter behavior influences political outcomes, see Caplan 2007, 166–81.

3. Caplan 2007, 186–90, calls this "democratic fundamentalism."

4. In the 1990 American Citizen Participation Study, 78 percent of respondents said that doing one's duty as a citizen was a very important reason to vote, while 18 percent said it was somewhat important. Only 4 percent said it was not important. Also, 86 percent said that voting was very or somewhat important as a way of doing their share. See http://www.icpsr.umich.edu/icpsrweb/ICPSR/studies/06635.

5. For an overview of why some political theorists reject standards for good voting, see Dovi 2007, 2.

6. There is another possible position, popular among some anarchists: it is wrong to vote, period. See, for example, Smith 1982a, 1982b, 1983.

7. Some countries, such as Australia and Belgium, have compulsory voting. Or, more precisely, they compel citizens to submit a ballot, though citizens remain free to leave the ballot blank or to spoil it. When such laws are in place, perhaps citizens acquire a duty to vote that is derived from a duty to follow the laws of a reasonably just country. (Perhaps not, though.) So I assert that citizens have no duty to vote on the assumption that they are not legally required to do so. If they are legally required to do so, the ethics of voting becomes more complicated.

8. According to Thomas Christiano (2006),
   It is hard to see how citizens can satisfy even moderate standards for beliefs about out how best to achieve their political aims. Knowledge of means requires an immense amount of social science and knowledge of particular facts. For citizens to have this kind of knowledge generally would require that we abandon the division of labor in society. On the other hand, citizens do have first hand and daily experience with thinking about the values

and aims they pursue. This gives them a chance to satisfy standards of belief regarding what the best aims are.

Christiano suggests a division of labor for democracy. The people choose the aims of government action, while experts determine how to achieve those aims. I find this proposal attractive, were it feasible.

9. For some discussion of irrationality about politics, see Schmidtz and Brennan 2010, chap. 6.

10. In general, the political right to X does not imply that X-ing is right. See Waldron 1981; Melden 1959.

11. For one interesting recent discussion of this, see Fabre 2006, 23–27.

12. Of course, what goes into the right to free speech is itself a complicated matter, and I do not intend to gloss over that. Obviously, it is important to note that the right to free speech does not necessarily mean one has a right to yell "fire" in a crowded theater, to spout one's political views in other people's living rooms at 3 a.m., or to threaten to kill people.

13. Feinberg 1970.

14. See Estlund 2007, 20; Arneson 2003.

15. Indeed, the theory of voting ethics I give here does not even commit me to holding that democracy is a good form of government. An anarchist might read this book and agree that it properly describes what people should do given that they have a legal right to vote, but then also maintain that no one should have a legal right to vote (because all states, including democratic states, are unjust).

16. See Schmidtz and Brennan 2010, 20.

17. For example, apparently many people support minimum-wage laws not because they think these laws will improve the welfare of the poor but because they want to express concern for the poor. (Even economists sometimes take this view. See Klein and Dompe 2007.) I find this position perverse. If you want to create something to symbolize your concern for some great cause, carve a statue or write a poem. Don't have it come at the expense of the common good. Support the minimum wage only if it works; otherwise, don't support it. (See Pincione and Tesón 2006, chap. 5, for a sustained critique of symbolic politics.)

18. Some theorists use the word "democracy" in a value-loaded sense, where a society does not count as *really* democratic unless it is just, is committed to specific liberal rights, has limits on majority power, has lots of deliberation and participation, and so on. I do not use the term that way. I use "democracy" to refer to all of the political arrangements a normal layperson thinks of as democracies, such as the U.S. or U.K. governments. For my purposes, a system is democratic to the extent that ultimate political power belongs to the people subject to that power. Corrupt, oppressive, illiberal democracies count as democracies, as I use the term "democracy" in this book.

19. See Schmidtz and Brennan 2010, chap. 6, for empirical support of these claims.

20. http://www.publicpolicypolling.com/pdf/PPP_Release_NJ_916.pdf> (last accessed September 22, 2009).

21. Caplan 2007, 166–81; Less, Moretti, and Butler 2004.

22. Davis and Figgins's (2009, 200) survey of more than 300 professional economists indicates that most economists (despite differences in ideology) agree

that elected officials do not understand the economic issues about which they pass policy. Only 10 percent of economists surveyed believe that the "the typical bill passed by the United States Congress and signed into law generates a positive net social benefit for society."

23. Because this book is about the ethics of voting rather than the (prudential) rationality of voting, I do not try to establish that voting is rational or irrational. If someone asked me whether voting is prudentially rational, here is my quick response: if you don't enjoy voting, it's not prudent to vote. However, it is generally prudent to be the kind of person who does not care that much about whether it is prudent to vote. Individual acts might be irrational, but it might be rational to be the kind of person that does not care much about the rationality of individual acts.

CHAPTER ONE: ARGUMENTS FOR A DUTY TO VOTE

1. This premise is not obviously true. Actions of this sort might be supererogatory rather than obligatory.

2. One might argue that individual votes matter, even if they do not tip the balance, because if a candidate obtains a large majority, she will be seen as "having a mandate" and this gives her greater ability to pass legislation. However, this simply relocates the problem. The person making this argument needs to find some way to measure how much individual votes contribute to creating a mandate. The logic is in many respects the same as before. For any individual vote, the likelihood that her vote makes a difference in pushing her candidate from simply winning to being seen as having a mandate is vanishingly small. Even if there is a continuum between merely winning and having a mandate, the marginal impact of an individual vote is vanishingly small.

3. Cf. Hardin 2009, 70–71.

4. Talking of expected utility does not commit us to utilitarianism or to hedonism. "Utility" just refers to the value of different outcomes. It does not have to mean pleasure or happiness.

5. Barry 1978a, 39.

6. See Lomasky and Brennan 2000, 66. See also G. Brennan and Lomasky 1993, 56–57, 119. In *Democracy and Decision*, Brennan and Lomasky outline what is now considered the best way of calculating the value of individual votes (though their formulae are not without controversy). Suppose there are two candidates, D and E. We can calculate the utility of my vote as $U = p[V(D) - V(E)]$, where U is the utility of my vote for D, p is the probability of my vote being decisive, and $[V(D) - V(E)]$ represents the difference in the value of the two candidates. The probability of my vote being decisive is a function of two other variables: the number of people voting in the election, and the anticipated proportional majority enjoyed by one of the candidates. A candidate has an anticipated proportional majority when, going into the election, she is already a favorite and is leading in the polls. Technically speaking, the anticipated proportionally majority is the probability that a random voter will vote for the leading candidate. For some criticism of this method of calculating expected utilities, see Fischer 1999.

7. Steven Landsburg (2004) uses similar formulae and arrives at similar numbers. He argues that the likelihood of being decisive is the same as the likelihood of winning Powerball 128 times in a row.

8. Somin 2006 and Edlin, Gelman, and Kaplan 2007 both argue that voting is rational if one has altruistic motives, because at least in some elections, the expected utility of a vote in terms of its ability to promote the common good is high. However, Somin uses an obsolete formula (from Riker and Ordeshook 1968) for calculating the probability of being decisive and does not respond to G. Brennan and Lomasky's 1993 critique of this formula. Edlin et al. use a different formula that also appears to overstate the probability of being decisive. However, I do not critique their formula here.

9. Edlin and Karaca-Mandic 2006.

10. For the 2008 U.S. presidential election, Steven Spielberg produced a short propaganda film attempting to induce more voting. A number of celebrities on the film said that they did not understand how someone could think that individual votes don't matter, especially in light of how close the Florida election was in 2000. Nonetheless, the expected utility of a Floridian's vote coming into the 2000 presidential election was, in fact, many thousands of orders of magnitude below a penny. However, now that the election has passed, we are not stuck having to use expected utility as a measure of voting. We can instead estimate actual utility. And, given how the other voters voted, the actual utility (in terms of affect on the outcome of an election) of any one Floridian's vote in 2000 was exactly $0. Cf. Hardin 2009, 71.

11. This is (what I intend to be) a friendly reconstruction of the argument made in Downs 1956, 257.

12. Downs 1956, 257.

13. For further criticism of Downs, see Gaus 2008, 186–90.

14. Cf. Barry 1978b, 20.

15. Tuck 2008, chap. 3, argues that even in cases where there are no such determinate thresholds, we should deliberate as if there were such thresholds.

16. If we were to print (in 12-point Times New Roman font) the expected utility of this vote in the form $0.000.......33, on a single piece of paper, the paper would be about 20 miles long.

17. Hardin 2009, 77, says that Downs made this argument because even he did not yet grasp the logic of collective action. Hardin says that many critics of Downs see the argument as Downs admitting that voting is rational, but Hardin regards it as a "casual error."

18. For instance, when I worked briefly at GEICO, I was told that the company expected to pay 93 cents in claims for every dollar in premiums. However, other companies, such as Allstate, pay more in claims than they receive in premiums, but make a profit by investing money before paying claims.

19. This point comes from Lomasky and Brennan 2000, 78.

20. Gerry Mackie argues that "voting for the sake of advancing democratic accountability is probably a continuous public good." However, he is careful to note that votes probably have diminishing returns, though he does not explain at length what impact this point has upon his theory of rational voting. See Mackie 2008, 21.

21. Many defenders of democracy used to use the Condorcet Jury Theorem to argue that democracies tend to make good decisions. Most now acknowledge that actual democracies are not well modeled by the theorem and so the theorem cannot be used to defend democracy. (See Estlund 2007, chap. 12, for a sustained account of why this is so.) However, note that even if democracies were adequately modeled by the theorem, adding additional reliable voters would show diminishing marginal returns. Suppose voters are 51 percent reliable and that a supermajority of 51 percent of the electorate is needed to pass a proposal. If so, then the first 100 voters have a collective reliability of 51.99 percent, the first 500 have a collective reliability of 59.86 percent, the first 10,000 have a collective reliability of 99.97 percent, etc. See Gaus 2003b, 159–160. So, if democracy were adequately modeled by the Condorcet Jury Theorem, having millions of people vote is wasteful.

22. Suppose fig. 2 represented a logarithmic function, such as $Q = \log_{10}(N)$. The logarithmic function of 10 million voters is 7, while the logarithmic function of 100 billion is 11. So, on this interpretation of fig. 2, the first 10 million voters do more to improve the quality of government than the next 100 billion voters. Suppose instead that fig. 2 showed $Q = \sqrt[3]{N}$. In this case, the first 10 million voters produce a $Q \approx 215$, while the first 50 million produce a $Q \approx 368$. The first vote is worth six orders of magnitude more than the 50 millionth. (Note that these equations are used just to illustrate the idea of diminishing returns.)

23. One might admit that in general it makes sense to evaluate activities by their marginal rather average contribution; however, in the case of simultaneous activities, such as voting, perhaps people should evaluate actions by their average consequences. However, this would lead to overvoting and wasted time. Rather than having everyone vote, an even better convention might be to determine what percentage of voters is needed (by asking when the worth of the marginal vote drops below, say, $1), and then have potential voters decide to vote based on rolling a 100-sided die. This would lead to nearly as high-quality governance as if everyone voted, but would have lower opportunity costs. See Tuck 2008, 45.

24. See the discussion in Lomasky and Brennan 2000, 78–79. See also Paten 1996, 30.

25. See Evans 2004, chap. 6, for a summary of explanations of voter turnout, some of which suggest that higher-quality governance produces higher turnout, rather than vice versa. Evans (p. 163) suggests that lower voting runs great risks but produces no empirical evidence to this effect. Lijphart 1999, 284–86, has some evidence that better governance causes higher participation rather than vice versa. See also Cox 2003; Levi and Stocker 2000. Timothy Besley (2006, 17–20) suggests that poor democratic health is correlated with low turnout, but also says that it is hard to show what consequences that has for welfare of citizens. The data he provides more strongly suggest that perceived low-quality governance causes decreased turnout rather than that increased turnout causes higher-quality governance. Mark Franklin (2004, 91–118) attributes low voter turnout in the United States in part to the separation of powers and to the perceived strong influence of special interests on government policy.

Fullinwinder 1988, 276, suggests off hand that high levels of turnout might reflect voter selfishness, as voters believe that they can capture advantages through voting.

26. Mackie 2008 argues that individual votes have instrumental value because they change the margin of victory or loss. However, the marginal value of each vote, in terms of its ability to produce good consequences by changing the margin of victory or loss, is probably vanishingly small. Mackie does not provide any grounds for thinking otherwise. He simply argues that if voters care about margins of victory, this can give them additional reason to vote.

27. This section incorporates and expands upon J. Brennan 2009.

28. Olson 1965.

29. Even granting Tuck's views on causation, his argument is bizarre. First, it seems at best metaphorical to think of my vote as having a probability of being in the efficacious set. If you and I are both voters for A, there is no real difference between my vote and yours. There is no real way to determine whose vote was efficacious and whose was not. For instance, I cannot roll a 100-sided die and conclude that my vote for A was efficacious provided the die rolls a 40 or less. All of the votes are the same. Note that the problem is not just merely that we lack a way of determining whose vote was efficacious and whose was not. The information is not available in principle because, metaphysically speaking, the votes are all the same. The 10,000 votes for A overdetermine the election of A. See Lewis 1983, 199–200.

30. One might try to argue that it has some objective value as follows: if the causally efficacious set has N members, then each vote in that set has 1/Nth the utility of the outcome the set causes. This could imply that individual votes potentially have high expected and actual utility. (Suppose Obama were worth $10 trillion more to the public good than McCain. If so, then an Obama vote in 2008 would be worth almost $150,000 by equation 1.) However, Tuck rejects this possibility. See Tuck 2008, 40–43.

31. Also, it is possible that there are other ways of being efficacious besides voting, and perhaps some of these other ways deliver more causal bang-for-the-buck. For instance, Stephen Colbert exerts more causal influence over electoral outcomes by making a snide remark than by casting a vote.

32. Cf. Amadae 2008.

33. Tuck 2008, 54; see also 32.

34. Gaus 2008, 8.

35. See Tuck 2008, 101.

36. Gaus 2008, 11.

37. Steve Kuhn, in his review of *Free Riding*, reaches similar conclusions using different arguments. See Kuhn 2010.

38. This paraphrases Tuck's (2008, 56) summary of Goodin (1998, 157).

39. A similar problem occurs for Goldman 1999. Goldman argues that even eligible voters who abstain bear a kind of causal responsibility for the outcome of an election, because they had the capacity to influence the outcome one way or another. Goldman hesitates to put much moral spin on his theory of causal responsibility. Here I note merely that someone who attempted to use his theory to prove there is a duty to vote would likely beg the question. Normally, when I

abstain from doing something, and some event occurs as a result, I am morally responsible for that event only if I have a preexisting duty to bring about some outcome. See Nozick 1974, 192.

40. Lomasky and Brennan 2000, 75.

41. Lomasky and Brennan 2000, 76.

42. Even Caplan, an anarchist, agrees to this point. See Caplan 2007, esp. 14.

43. See Nozick 1974, 93–95, for an examination of when it is not unfair to free-ride on public goods.

44. Waldron 2003, 318, makes this kind of argument.

45. Lomasky and Brennan 2000, 77–78.

46. Lomasky and Brennan 2000, 77–78.

47. At the very least, my fellow well-informed, rational, reasonable citizens could have a complaint against me. Perhaps even the ignorant, irrational, and unreasonable citizens do as well. It would be hypocritical for them to say that my failing to vote is bad because it increases their electoral effectiveness ("Hey, you abstainers make it more likely that we bad voters will carry the day!"), but nonetheless, they may be right.

48. Routley [Sylvan] 1973.

49. Hill, 1983.

Chapter Two: Civic Virtue without Politics

1. I will not try to advance necessary and sufficient conditions for what counts as political. I use the distinction as republicans use it. They regard some activities as political and others as private and nonpolitical. My goal is to argue that these latter activities can also be exercises of civic virtue. If republicans are mistaken in what counts as political, this means my thesis should be restated as follows: activities that republicans regard as nonpolitical can be exercises of civic virtue, and it is not necessary to engage in what republicans call political activity in order to have exceptional civic virtue.

2. "Republicanism," as used here, refers to a body of related political theories that hold that heavy political participation and political virtue are required from citizens in order to maintain a political order in which no one is dominated. (A related but distinct view, civic humanism, holds that such participation is constitutive of a good, fully human life.) Some republican theories can be regarded as alternatives to liberalism, while others are a variety of liberalism. I focus only on the republican idea of civic virtue, taking no stance on the uniqueness of republicanism as a theory of social order. For a critique from one liberal author of republican theories he views as antiliberal, see Gaus 2003a.

3. For example, Philip Pettit (1997) says "a regime of civic virtue" is "one under which people are disposed to serve, and serve honestly, in public office."

4. Oldfield 1990, 181.

5. The Latin word *civitas* and the Greek word *polis* may have been almost identical in meaning, but in contemporary English, the concept of the *civic* is broader than the concept of the *political*.

6. Rawls 1971, 5–6.

7. Schmidtz 2006, 7–9.

8. Cf. Archard 2001, 221.

9. Burtt 1990, 24.

10. Dagger 1997, 14.

11. Galston 2007, 630.

12. Crittendon 2007.

13. G. Brennan and Hamlin 1995.

14. Cf. also Pauer-Studer 2001, 188, and Honohan 2002, 147. Here are two other definitions: Lawrence Blum (2007, 534) says, "Civic virtues can then be understood as qualities that engage in the appropriate way with [the] civic order and its norms." This is as close as he comes to a definitional statement. Using this definition in lieu of the others would not harm my argument, for I can then claim to be giving an account of all the possible ways to engage appropriately with the civic order and its norms. Also, Andrew Buchwalter (1992, 551) says that Hegel defines "civic virtue" as something like the free willing of communal ends by the individual.

15. Sean Aas (in conversation) notes that there is a gap between saying that civic virtue makes you a good citizen and saying that civic virtue is the disposition to promote the common good. Sharon Krause (in conversation) notes that we sometimes use the term "civic virtue" in a way where it is an open question whether being a good citizen is compatible with being a good person.

16. Dagger 1997, 15.

17. Dagger 1997, 99 (emphasis in original).

18. Dagger later advances something of an argument that civic virtue is closely related to political participation. He argues that it is part of the common good that all citizens be free, that freedom is autonomy and self-government, and that therefore freedom is participation in government. (See Dagger 1997, 17.)

19. Crittenden 2007, citing Gutmann 1987, 287 (emphasis added).

20. Note that republicans and others do have arguments to the effect that citizens should engage in politics. However, it is one thing to argue that citizens should participate in politics (say, because that is what is required to protect liberties), and another to say that the concept of civic virtue is tightly linked to political participation.

21. See Schmidtz, 1995, 158–66, for a broadly consequentialist liberal argument for this conception. See also Gaus 1996, 172–75, for a justificatory liberal argument for a similar kind of conception. See also Rawls 1971, 233, 246, for a similar conception.

22. Richard Dagger, though a republican, accepts something like this conception of the common good.

23. See, for instance, G. Brennan and Lomasky 2006, 223–29.

24. My working hypothesis is that the more power (especially political power) and influence a person has, the more important it is that she has civic virtue.

25. Becker 1980, 37. For a recent work on whether citizens ought to do productive work, see White 2003.

26. Rawls 1971, 4.

27. Schmidtz 2006, 91.

28. Read 1958.

29. One obvious reason for this could simply be that they make bad contributions to politics. Hitler's, Stalin's, and Mao Zedong's contributions were obviously terrible on net. But even the average citizen can make harmful contributions.

30. Suppose, all things considered, we want 50 percent of citizens to vote well. What rule do citizens follow to decide whether they should vote rather than contribute to the common good in other ways? If the rule is "vote only if doing so has significant positive expected utility for the common good," no one will vote. If the rule is "vote, period," then everyone will vote. Neither of these is, by hypothesis, the best option. Another rule is, "If you are reasonably well-informed and will vote on the basis of good reasons, then unless voting is a real burden to you or to the common good, vote." This rule is not perfect either, but it is better than the other two at getting us to our target. Thanks to David Estlund for raising this issue.

31. G. Brennan and Lomasky 2006, 223.

32. This point should prompt us to ask whether civic virtue is always or even generally desirable, all things considered. Artists who pursue art for its own sake, regardless of its impact on the common good, probably produce better art and thus promote the common good more than artists who are strongly motivated to promote the common good. Perhaps this holds true of bakers, farmers, businesspersons, and many others. If so, then perhaps civic virtue is not very desirable.

33. Does this require that one actually succeed, rather than merely try, in making a positive difference? This is an important question, but need not be pursued here, because the answer does not help decide between the extrapolitical view of civic virtue and the republican view.

34. For an interesting survey about philosophers' attitudes, see http://experi mentalphilosophy.typepad.com/experimental_philosophy/2009/07/professors -on-the-morality-of-voting.html.

35. On one reading, Plato advocates rule by philosophers. (This seems to be a misreading, but it is common.) He might be right, but still, there are some grounds for suspicion, given that Plato is a philosopher. On one reading, Aristotle says that philosophizing is the highest, most human form of life. Perhaps he is right, but it is suspicious, because this comes from a philosopher. Similarly, when one sees contemporary political philosophers saying that it would be wonderful if the average citizen acted more like a political philosopher (by frequently debating issues of justice and politics with others), one has to be suspicious.

36. G. Brennan and Lomasky 2006, 232.

37. G. Brennan and Lomasky (2006, 231–32) make this point as well.

38. Oldfield 1990, 186.

39. This is not to say that liberal citizenship is always easy. As Gerry Gaus says, liberalism demands that people not be moral busybodies and mind their own business. Most people find this hard—they want to regulate or repress, not tolerate, the practices they find repugnant. See Gaus 1997.

40. Pocock 2003, 80.

41. See, for instance, Schmidtz and Brennan 2010, chaps. 1–5.

42. Walzer 1989, 212.

43. Walzer 1989, 218.

44. One might object to my argument by invoking the taxes-voting analogy again. Even if we agree that there are all sorts of ways to pay debts to society,

perhaps there are some ways of paying debts that everyone must engage in. For example, you cannot opt out of paying taxes just because you cured cancer. In response, I would say that if tax paying were legally optional, I find it plausible that a person who makes sufficiently high contributions to society might be relieved of any obligation to pay taxes. If you save the world from an asteroid strike, perhaps you should not have to pay income taxes ever again. (This does not mean that citizens should be permitted to decide for themselves whether to pay taxes. Rather, it just means that some of them might not actually owe taxes.) Despite that, my main response is that even if the point about taxes holds, the person making the Public Goods Argument needs to show that voting is like that. She has not done so, and I have presented a significant challenge to her claims.

CHAPTER THREE: WRONGFUL VOTING

1. I will not settle on a particular account of harmfulness or injustice in this chapter. The argument made here is compatible with a wide range of views on what constitutes harm.

2. Certain defenders of epistemic democracy use Condorcet's Jury Theorem to argue that democracies will tend to make good policy choices. Such defenders might claim that one is justified in voting provided one is more likely than not to be right. For critiques of this misuse of Condorcet, see Estlund 2007, chap. 12; Gaus 2003b, 158–65; Estlund 1997, 185–86.

3. I discuss the miracle of aggregation defense of ignorant voting in chapter 7.

4. If I did define the term that way, I would run into familiar problems with Kantian generalization arguments.

5. Caplan 2007, 166–81; Less, Moretti, and Butler 2004.

6. Thanks to David Estlund for recommending I use this analogy.

7. Hooker 2000, 32.

8. Hooker 2000, 159–74.

9. See Timmons 2002, 169–70.

10. Hurthouse 1998, 28.

11. Manning 1984, 217.

12. Thanks to Julia Driver for noting this distinction.

13. Note that I have just been asking whether voting for Bowles is wrong. If we change the question and ask instead whether someone who votes for Bowles is likely to be morally vicious, the answer is more obviously affirmative.

14. G. Brennan and Lomasky 1993, 186.

15. I got this example from Dick Arneson, in his online course notes, available at http://philosophyfaculty.ucsd.edu/faculty/rarneson/167ExamplesNozick-1.pdf/.

16. Nozick 1974, 74.

17. Hansson 2003, 305. See also Hansson 2007; Schmidtz 2006, 207.

18. What counts as exploitation? Exploitative institutions and rules make some people worse off *as a method* of making others better off. More specifically, they make some people better off in virtue of the existence of the targets of exploitation. So a rule disallowing rape or mugging does not exploit rapists or

muggers, because it does not improve people's lives in virtue of the existence of muggers and rapists. However, a rule allowing slavery does exploit the enslaved. It makes the enslaved worse off as a method of making the slave owners better off, and the owners are better off in virtue of the existence of the targets of exploitation. See Schmidtz 1995, 169–70.

19. For example, see Gaus 2010; Eberle 2002; Greenawalt 1995.

20. Some justificatory liberals argue that even Charles may not vote on the basis of religious reasons, unless those religious reasons can be publicly justified. They may be right. If so, then we may take this as an additional requirement on top of the requirements for good voting I have articulated here.

21. Still, I would expect that the overwhelming majority of religious voters are like Betty, many are like Edward, some are like David, and few are like Chris. However, if I am wrong about this, it is probably because I am mistaken about what evidence theists possess.

22. Cf. Hardin 2004, 80; Manin 1997, 218–32.

23. Gaus 2010. Cf. Rawls 1999, 135–36.

24. Gaus 2010.

25. Gaus 2010.

26. See Caplan 2007, 166–81; Less, Moretti, and Butler 2004.

27. Here, I quote from Jeremy Waldron's summary of John Elster's criticism of expressive voting. Waldron 2003, 317.

28. Someone might object that poetry writing can lead, indirectly, to legislative outcomes as well. Voting is already one step removed from legislation. Poetry (or philosophy) is just another step removed. Voting chooses legislators, and legislators choose laws. But poetry helps sway public opinion and helps to determine whom voters vote for. So, does this mean that I am committed to saying that writing poetry advocating bad laws is morally bad as well? Perhaps not—the effect of voting on legislation is much stronger than the effect of writing on legislation. There is a big difference between expressing a preference or attitude through poetry and *handing someone the reins of government*. On the other hand, I am comfortable saying that it can be wrong to write certain things because of their effect on electoral outcomes, though I will not explore this issue at length here.

29. Thanks to Geoff Brennan for suggesting this case.

30. Brink 1986.

31. J. Brennan 2008 argues that moral theory's primary task is not to produce a method of making decisions but to identify criteria of right as well as answer other theoretical questions about morality.

32. Thanks to Corey Brettschneider for asking the question that led to this paragraph.

33. Christiano 2004; Brettschneider 2007.

34. G. Hardin 1968.

CHAPTER FOUR: DEFERENCE AND ABSTENTION

1. Estlund 2007, 212.

2. Estlund 2007, 40.

3. Estlund 2007, 40.

4. Christiano 1996, 6.

5. Driver 2006, 635.

6. Cf. G. Brennan and Lomasky 2006, 246.

7. See Christman 2003; Gutmann 1993.

8. Nozick 1974, 290–92.

9. Perhaps people who lived their whole lives this way would develop false consciousness and begin to regard the situation as empowering and free.

10. Barber 2008, 141.

11. Walzer 1984, 305.

12. See Surowiecki 2005; Page 2007.

13. Suppose you decide, "I'd like to know what Locke's argument was for the justification of government authority. Rather than reading Locke, I will simply ask the next person I see and take his or her word for it." You happen to run into A. John Simmons, having no idea who he is, ask him, and take his word for it. In this case, you have fortuitously deferred to the best possible person, but you have done it for dumb reasons, and are not justified in doing so.

14. I assume in this argument that the goal is to use the decision method that has the greatest chance of being correct. However, this is not obviously the best way to judge the reliability of the system. Gerry Gaus points out (without necessarily endorsing) an alternative: rather than select the method with the best chance of being right, select the method that tends to have the minimal average deviation from being correct. One decision method that is a likely candidate for having the minimal average deviation from the truth is "median with a vengeance." In median with a vengeance, all positions on a given issue are scaled from 0 to 10, and the option corresponding to 5 is always selected. If (as is likely) the correct answers for various issues are randomly distributed, then median with a vengeance will have an average divergence from correctness of less than 3. See Gaus 2003b, 168–69. So, in order to avoid this objection (that we should look for minimal deviation rather than greatest likelihood of being correct), we could suppose not only that Aubree is most likely to be correct but that she also has the minimal deviation. Or we could just suppose that Aubree is always right.

15. On the other hand, relying on the daemon arguably does count as relying on one's own (extended) mind. See Clark and Chalmers 1998.

16. See Mutz 2006. For a contrary view, see also Ackerman and Fishkin 2004.

17. This paraphrases and partially quotes from Page 2007, 7.

18. However, even Page's work shows that increasing diversity can be a bad thing when people's perspectives are quite poor. He also notes that crowds can make bad, even mad, decisions, either when there are systematic biases or when conformist tendencies in deliberation lead to less accuracy and diversity. If individuals are unduly influenced by others who are charismatic but inaccurate, then group accuracy will suffer. See Page 2007, 212–14, 391–91; Page and Lamberson 2009. So, for example, Page's work does not refute Bryan Caplan's or vice versa. Rather, Page shows how crowds can be wise when certain conditions hold, and Caplan shows how these conditions do not hold when it

comes to people's views on economics. A further point: one problem with Page's work is that he tends to treat experts as nondiverse, as if they all have the same models of the world. But perhaps Page's work makes a better argument for having many diverse experts make decisions rather than for having many diverse nonexperts make decisions.

19. Note that Page's models work best for cases where issues are easily quantified or where qualitative answers to questions can be easily separated into distinct categories. It is not as clear how they apply other kinds of issues. Note also that Page does not mean, for example, that including more people from different vocations or different races tends to lead to group wisdom. Rather, what he means is that having many people with diverse sophisticated models of the world tends to lead to group wisdom. Also, insofar as uneducated people tend to have simplistic, unsophisticated models of the world, their input into collective decision making tends to lead to less accuracy. Page seems to recognize this at times, but then often appears to overreach in how well his models of diversity apply to actual democratic decision making. See Tetlock 2007 for a quick but sharp criticism of Page on this point.

20. Page 2008.

21. Page 2007, 346–47. At 147, Page says, "The best problem solvers tend to be similar; therefore, a collection of the best problem solvers performs little better than any one of them individually. A collection of random, but intelligent, problem solvers tends to be diverse. This diversity allows them to be collectively better. Or to put it more provocatively, *diversity trumps ability*."

22. See Sokal and Bricmont 1999; Frankfurt 2005.

23. This gives us good grounds for considering various reforms designed to insulate political policy from bad voters.

24. Thanks to Aaron Maltais for a version of this objection.

25. See Patterson 1999.

26. Caplan 2007, 157, says, "Good intentions are ubiquitous to politics; what is scarce is accurate beliefs. . . . Though it sounds naïve to count on the affluent to look out for the interests of the needy, that is roughly what the data advise. All kinds of voters hope to make society better off, but the well educated are more likely to get the job done."

27. Arguably this describes much of the behavior of the Democratic Party toward some of its constituents.

28. Caplan 2007, 197.

29. Another proposal is to have plural voting. Every citizen receives at least one vote, but can obtain extra votes by completing college or doing some other activity that demonstrates higher levels of political wisdom. For an extended but sympathetic criticism of this proposal, see Estlund 2007, chap. 11.

30. Estlund 2003, 37, 219.

31. Van Parijs 1993, 305.

32. For example, beginning in 2012, Arizonan high school students must pass one class in economics to graduate from high school. The Arizona Council on Economic Education spearheads efforts to improve economic literacy among Arizonan students.

CHAPTER FIVE: FOR THE COMMON GOOD

1. Cf. Dagger 1997, 104–5.

2. See Schmidtz and Brennan 2010, chaps. 2 and 4.

3. G. Brennan and Lomasky 2006, 223.

4. It is unclear whether even Gentile and Mussolini believe in strongly irreducible common goods. They argue that true freedom for individuals consists in belonging to the right kind of collective, and so liberalism takes away individuals' true liberty. See Mussolini and Gentile 1963.

5. Raeder 1998, 525.

6. See Bicchieri 2006 and 1993.

7. Cf. Gaus 1990, 51.

8. This objection to fairness-based pure proceduralist arguments comes from David Estlund. See Estlund 2007, 6, and my chapter 4.

9. Schmidtz 1995, 159. Why not say something must benefit literally everyone in order to be part of the common good? Schmidtz worries that this seems like too high a standard, at least if we want to talk of the common good as something to be promoted. For instance, would this mean that we should not pursue organ transplantation techniques until we can show that they literally benefit everyone? Because this definition is too strong, why not say it must benefit *most* (but not all) people, and leave it at that? Schmidtz says this sets too low a standard. We need some account of what the institution or policy does to those whom it does not benefit. One suggestion is that something is in the common good if it helps most people without making anyone worse off. Schmidtz worries that this account is too strong. It does not differentiate between how, for example, slavery and technological innovation might make some people worse off. Technological innovation might put some people out of business, but it does not make them worse off as a means of making others better off. In contrast, slavery makes some people worse off as a means of making others better off.

10. White 2003, 27.

11. In contrast, one could have an egalitarian conception of citizenship that all citizens are equally unimportant.

12. Friedman 1989, 107.

13. In economics, deadweight losses are said to occur when the market equilibrates at a non-Pareto-optimal spot, that is, when certain gains from trade are not realized. Price controls, subsidies, and monopolies often cause deadweight losses.

14. For a good overview of these issues, see Mueller 2003, 333–59.

15. Martin and Podger 2004.

16. As Hardin 2009, esp. 67, 74, argues, it is costly to learn which policies are in one's real interests. So voters often vote for what they perceive to be in their interests rather than what is in fact in their interests.

17. Posner 2003, 113.

18. Smith 1776, 456.

19. Wellman and Simmons 2006, 118.

20. For my self-interest to be realized through politics, I need to form some sort of winning coalition. I need to be part of a majority. So this means that demo-

cratic decisions will tend to promote the interests of the majority. But, again, this is compatible with these decisions coming at the expense of the losing coalition. The majority can exploit the minority and get away with it, because the minority is not free to walk away. Also, because democratic politics is subject to cycles, as coalitions change, it is not clear that in the long run the majority's interest will be served by such behaviors. In the long run, the systems approximate David Friedman's penny-redistribution thought experiment.

21. One final reason to be skeptical about self-interested voting leading to the common good has to do with Arrow's Impossibility Theorem. Because the theorem, its proof, and its interpretation are quite technical, rather than discussing it at length here, I direct readers to Gaus 2008, 151–74. Note that Arrow's Theorem does not apply merely to self-interested voting; it also applies to public-spirited voting when there are diverse opinions about what's in the common good. However, see Estlund 2007, chaps. 4 and 5, for an argument that Arrow's Theorem is irrelevant to evaluating the *authority* of democracy.

22. Madison, Hamilton, and Jay 1961, 322.

23. That is, they know their self-interest in the sense that they know they need more money or more opportunity. And we can find this out by polling them, perhaps. But that does not mean they know what social policies are in their interests. Voters are reliable guides to their own ends, but they are not necessarily reliable in knowing what policies are instrumental to those ends.

24. Schmidtz 1995, 167.

25. Mueller 2003, 119–20.

26. For one argument that compromise voting is irrational, see Behn and Vaupel 1984. For an argument in favor of compromise voting, see Geisz 2006.

27. I borrow these names and situation from Geisz 2006.

28. See Geisz 2006.

29. Gaus 2010, 32.

30. Thanks to Julia Driver for raising this issue.

31. Chisholm 1963.

CHAPTER SIX: BUYING AND SELLING VOTES

1. Walzer 1984, 23, talks about trading one's vote for a hat.

2. What if we offered sex instead, as Votergasm.com suggests we do? Votergasm asks citizens to at minimum withhold sex from nonvoters for a week following a presidential election. It describes those who pledge to have sex with at least one voter on election night as "patriots" and those who pledge to have sex with at least one voter plus withhold sex from nonvoters for four years as "American Heroes." Is Votergasm any worse or better than bribing with cash? Why?

3. For instance, one political theorist told me that vote selling is undemocratic. I pointed out that "democratic" does not reliably track *good*. It is more democratic to have elections every two weeks, but that does not make things morally better. I asked for the deeper explanation of why it is wrong, but my interlocutor said she is not sure. Another political theorist told me that voting should always be voluntary. I asked her why this is so—there are many other activities that are

sometimes voluntary and sometimes paid. She said that activities in the public sphere must always be voluntary. However, political officeholders, such as the president, are paid, and many people, such as columnists or editorialists, are paid to make political arguments in the public sphere. Ackerman and Fishkin (2004) advocate paying citizens to deliberate before voting. At certain times in ancient Athens, citizens were paid for going to the assembly.

4. Note that this chapter assumes that my account of voting ethics from earlier chapters of the book is correct. In particular, I assume that citizens generally have no duty to vote. So, for instance, Margaret Radin (1987, 1854) asserts that vote selling is wrong in part because voters have a duty to vote, and people should not be paid for things they have a duty to do. However, I am assuming that my argument in chapters 1 and 2 was sound and that in fact citizens have no duty to vote. (Radin believes we have a duty to vote but offers no argument to this effect.)

5. Economists and others have written at length about whether buying and selling votes leads to efficiency gains or losses, and whether there is a good case for government intervention. For example, see Hasen 2000; Kochin and Kochin 1998; Buchanan and Less 1986; Epstein 1985; Weiss 1988. Many of these authors think vote selling should be illegal, but their analyses are based on the assumption that voters, buyers, and sellers, are motivated by narrow self-interest. They do not analyze what would happen in voting markets where voters, buyers, and sellers abide by the ethics of voting described in this book.

6. Hasen 2000, 1325. Hasen argues that people inconsistently apply these arguments. There are five legally permitted practices, including, for example, allowing candidates to make campaign promises, which should be prohibited by these rationales. So either vote buying should be legalized or a number of practices people find unobjectionable should be criminalized.

7. Someone might complain that even if the rich would not buy votes to exploit the poor, it is still unacceptable that they would have disproportionate influence over policy. However, note that many people have disproportionate influence for other reasons. John Rawls has more influence than I do because he is a more famous philosopher. Stephen Colbert, Oprah Winfrey, and Karl Marx have more influence than either of us. If Oprah says she approves of X and this induces 100 people to vote X, is this less wrong than if I pay people to vote for X (assuming we all justifiedly believe that X promotes the common good)?

8. The closest thing that I can find to a paper that discusses wide-scale vote buying when voters vote ethically is Neeman and Orosel 2006. They conclude that vote buying when voters share interests normally leads to efficiency gains.

9. For an overview of some of the epistemological problems with testimony, see Adler 2006.

10. Some philosophers regard all frustrated desires as harmful, whereas others think only certain desires (such as those that would remain were the desirous agent fully informed and rational) count as harms when frustrated.

11. Schmidtz 1995, 160.

12. Sheehy 2002, 46–57.

13. Sheehy 2002, 48.

14. Sheehy 2002, 50.

15. On the other hand, suppose I have no preference between blue and red, but I do prefer having a red flag and an extra $100 to having a blue flag. It is not clear whether I count as an indifferent voter in Sheehy's case. It is also not clear whether it would be wrong for me to take money to vote for red from a willing red-preferring voter.

16. Cf. Sunstein 1997, 75. Sunstein says that offering to pay people to do certain things is insulting, and thus wrong. However, this depends in part on whether the person will be insulted, and also whether she *should* be insulted. Suppose you have no intention to insult anyone, but you just prefer that some people vote. Suppose you offer to pay Sunstein to vote. Apparently, he will be insulted. So perhaps you should be cautious in making the offer, and perhaps you would be wrong to make the offer to him. However, suppose you offer to pay me to vote. If I believe you are not trying to insult me but are just trying to motivate me, I will not be insulted. So it is not wrong for you to make me an offer.

17. This problem plagues Margaret Jane Radin's *Contested Commodities* (1996). Radin claims that if things are offered for sale, and if economists regard certain items as having potential market value, then this will degrade our moral attitudes. Yet, though this is an empirical claim, she provides no empirical evidence that this degradation would in fact occur. See Radzik and Schmidtz (1997), 612–15, for more on this problem.

18. Titmuss 1997.

19. See also K. Healey 2006, chap. 5.

20. Fabre 2006, 137.

21. One possibility is that these other activities take significant time, whereas voting does not. However, people probably will not be paid a doctor's salary to vote. Also, voting well does take a lot of time, because it requires investments in knowledge and rationality, though voting badly does not.

22. Saunders 2009 argues that states paying citizens to vote is preferable to states compelling citizens to vote.

23. Someone might claim that by selling sex, Belle debases herself, even though she does not regard it as debasing. But if Belle does not see herself as debased and you do, who is right? (Because I do not resent selling my labor, does that mean selling my labor does not debase me, but perhaps it does debase an orthodox Marxist?) The answers to these questions are not obvious.

24. The show is based on a real person, Brooke Magnanti, who is now a research scientist at the University of Bristol. See also Levitt and Dubner's (2009, 49–56) description of Allie.

25. Levitt and Dubner 2009, 201.

26. Cf. Gaus 2003a, 90. For a left-liberal argument in favor of allowing kidney sales, see Gill and Sade 2002. For a right-liberal argument in favor of allowing kidney sales, see Taylor 2005. For what it's worth, if it could be shown that organ selling would cure sick people and help poor people, I would regard that as a decisive argument in favor of legalizing vote selling.

27. Tetlock 2000.

28. Gaus 2003a, 89. Cf. Walzer 1984, 23, 110, 116.

29. See Cohen 2009.

30. Tomasi forthcoming, chap. 7.

31. In writing this chapter, I realized that someone might try to make an objection based on the concept of human dignity. I read numerous dignity-based arguments against, for example, organ sales, trying to find some argument I could use as a potential objection and which I could attempt to respond to. However, the arguments I found either were too weak to include here, or, when they had some force, applied only to the topics at hand (such as organ sales) and could not be applied to vote selling.

32. Singer 1974, 25.

33. Thanks to Brian Berkey, Dale Dorsey, Dale Miller, Douglas Portmore, Andrew Schroeder, Neil Sinhabubu, and others blogging at PEA Soup for helpful discussion of these issues. I owe quite a bit of this analysis to them. http://peasoup.typepad.com/peasoup/2009/06/paying-people-not-to-do-good-a-puzzle-about-superogation.html.

34. Thanks to Douglas Portmore for this case.

CHAPTER SEVEN: HOW WELL DO VOTERS BEHAVE?

1. Certain schools of political science, such as rational choice theory, assume that voters are self-interested and construct mathematical models based on this assumption. Many rational choice theorists confuse *self-interest* (those things which benefit a person) with *interests held by a self* (those things a person cares about, whether they benefit her or not). Green and Shapiro 1994 claim the empirical, predictive power of rational choice theory has been weak.

2. For example, see Funk and Garcia-Monet 1997; Funk 2000; Miller 1999, 1053–60; Mutz and Mondak 1997. Caplan (2007, 229) lists twelve other references for this claim. See also G. Brennan and Lomasky 1993, 108–14. They discuss at length the empirical evidence for and against the self-interested voter hypothesis.

3. Feddersen, Gailmard, and Sandroni 2009.

4. Hardin 2004, 79.

5. Hardin 2009, 60.

6. Somin 2004, 3–4.

7. Althaus 2003, 11.

8. Althaus 2003, 16.

9. For example, see this column by comedian Bill Maher. http://www.huffingtonpost.com/bill-maher/new-rule-smart-president_b_253996.html.

10. Similarly, Americans tend not to learn foreign languages either. They have little incentive to do so. If you grow up in Sweden, it is likely in your self-interest to learn English. If you grow up in an English-speaking country, it is not likely to be in your self-interest to learn a foreign language. English is the dominant language of academia, commerce, and politics. English is also a popular second language. So a native English speaker has little incentive to learn a second language.

11. Lau and Redlawsk 2006, 75.

12. Lau and Redlawsk 2006, 88–89.

13. Lau and Redlawsk (2006, 74–75) defend their permissive notion of "correct voting" by saying that it is illicit for researchers to assess voters by the

researcher's personal values. Lau and Redlawsk seem to suggest there are only two alternatives for a definition of "correct voting": define "correct voting" in terms of voters' subjective attitudes, or define it in terms of the researcher's subjective attitudes. However, there is another alternative: define it correctly, in terms of correct normative standards. This is an alternative I attempt to take in this book.

14. See Gelman 2008 for an extensive investigation of how demographic factors affect voting behavior.

15. Caplan 2007, 25.

16. Althaus 2003, 109–15, 129.

17. Althaus 2003, 129.

18. Note that Althaus 2003, chap. 2, has a technical critique of the miracle of aggregation showing statistically that errors are unlikely to be random and that they are more likely to compound than cancel out.

19. Mutz 2006, 32, reaches this conclusion too. For a possibly contrary view, see Baldassarri and Gelman 2008. Baldassarri and Gelman argue that education tends to polarize people. Educated Democrats are more partisan than uneducated Democrats, and educated Republicans are more partisan than uneducated Republicans.

20. Somin 2004, 14.

21. Healy 2007; Healy and Malhotra 2010.

22. Hardin 2009, 60; Alvarez 1997; Holbrook and Thomas 1996; Mutz 1993.

23. For a series of critical articles on Caplan and Caplan's response, see *Critical Review* 20:3 (2008).

24. Caplan 2007, 44 (emphasis deleted).

25. Christandl and Fetchenhauer 2009.

26. Suppose you have $100 in your savings account. It grows at 5 percent per year, with interest paid yearly. How long does it take for your account to double and to triple? The average person will respond, "I get $5 in interest per year, so it will take 20 years to double and 40 years to triple." In fact, you get $5 in interest the first year, $5.25 the second year, $5.50 the third year, etc. So it takes only 15 years to double your principle and 23 years to triple it.

27. Caplan 2007, 51. See also Alston, Kearl, and Vaughan 1992; Kearl et al., 1979.

28. Caplan 2007, 61–66. See also *Washington Post*, Kaiser Family Foundation, and Harvard University Survey Project, "Survey of Americans and Economists on the Economy," #1199, October 16, 2006. http://www.kff.org/kaiserpolls/1199-index.cfm.

29. Caplan 2007, 72.

30. See also Blinder 1989; Schumpeter 1950, esp. 154; Schumpeter 1954, esp. 234.

31. See Caplan 2001.

32. For a survey of twentieth-century findings on irrationality, see Schmidtz and Brennan 2010, chap. 6.

33. Westen et al., 2007. See also Westen 2008.

34. See Mutz 2006, 128.

35. Mutz 2006, 120.

36. Mutz 2006, 92, 110, 112–13.

37. Mutz 2006, 30. The more people join voluntary associations, the less they engage in crosscutting discussions. What demographic factors best predict that one will engage in crosscutting political discussion? Apparently, being nonwhite, poor, and uneducated. The reason for this is that white, rich, educated people have more control over the kinds of interactions they have with others. People generally do not enjoy having crosscutting political discussions. They enjoy agreement. So those with the most control over their lives choose not to engage in crosscutting discussions. See Mutz 2006, 27, 31, 46–47.

38. Mutz 2006, 135–36.

39. I do not want to overstate these worries. Caplan (2007, 198) argues not only that the well educated tend to have sounder economic beliefs than the uneducated but that the educated are more likely to vote than the uneducated. The median voter has greater economic literacy than the median nonvoter. So Mutz's findings give us reason to worry about who participates in politics, but some other findings give us contrary reasons.

References

Ackerman, Bruce, and James Fishkin. 2004. *Deliberation Day*. New Haven: Yale University Press.

Adler, Jonathan. 2006. "Epistemological Problems of Testimony." In *Stanford Encyclopedia of Philosophy*, ed. Edward Zalta. http://plato.stanford.edu/entries/testimony-episprob/.

Alston, Richard M., J. R. Kearl, and Michael B. Vaughan. 1992. "Is There a Consensus among Economists in the 1990's?" *American Economic Review* 82: 203–9.

Althaus, Scott. 2003. *Collective Preferences in Democratic Politics: Opinion Surveys and the Will of the People*. New York: Cambridge University Press.

Alvarez, R. Michael. 1997. *Information and Elections*. Ann Arbor: University of Michigan Press.

Amadae, S. M. 2008. "Richard Tuck's *Free Riding*." *Ethics* 119: 211–16.

Archard, David. 2001. "Political Disagreement, Legitimacy, and Civility." *Philosophical Explorations* 4: 207–22.

Arneson, Richard. 2003. "Debate: Defending the Purely Instrumental Account of Democratic Authority." *Journal of Political Philosophy* 11: 122–32.

Baldassarri, Delia, and Andrew Gelman. 2008. "Partisans without Restraint: Political Polarization and Trends in American Political Opinion." *American Journal of Sociology* 114: 408–46.

Barber, Benjamin. 2008. *Consumed*. New York: Norton.

Barry, Brian. 1978a. "Comment." In *Political Participation*, ed. Stanley Bern, 39. Canberra: Australian National University Press.

———. 1978b. *Sociologists, Economists, and Democracy*. Chicago: University of Chicago Press.

Becker, Gary. 1980. "The Obligation to Work." *Ethics* 91: 35–49.

Behn, Robert D., and James W. Vaupel. 1984. "The Wasted Vote Fallacy." *Journal of Policy Analysis and Management* 3: 607–12.

Besley, Timothy. 2006. *Principled Agents?* New York: Oxford University Press.

Bicchieri, Cristiana. 1993. *Rationality and Coordination*. New York: Cambridge University Press.

———. 2006. *The Grammar of Society: The Nature and Dynamics of Social Norms*. New York: Cambridge University Press.

Blinder, Alan. 1989. *Hard Heads, Soft Hearts: Tough-Minded Economics for a Just Society*. New York: Basic Books.

Blum, Lawrence. 2007. "Race, National Ideals, and Civic Virtue." *Social Theory and Practice* 33: 533–56.

Bosanquet, Bernard. 1895. *Aspects of the Social Problem*. New York: Macmillan.

Brennan, Geoffrey, and Alan Hamlin. 1995. "Economizing on Virtue." *Constitutional Political Economy* 6: 35–60.

Brennan, Geoffrey, and Loren Lomasky. 1993. *Democracy and Decision*. New York: Cambridge University Press.

———. 2006. "Against Reviving Republicanism." *Politics, Philosophy, and Economics* 5: 221–52.

Brennan, Jason. 2008. "Beyond the Bottom Line: The Theoretical Goals of Moral Theorizing." *Oxford Journal of Legal Studies* 28: 277–96.

———. 2009. "Tuck on the Rationality of Voting: A Critical Note." *Journal of Ethics and Social Philosophy* 3: 1–5. http://www.jesp.org/articles/download/ TuckontheRationalityofVoting.pdf.

Brettschneider, Corey. 2007. *Democratic Rights*. Princeton: Princeton University Press.

Brink, David O. 1986. "Utilitarian Morality and the Personal Point of View." *Journal of Philosophy* 83: 417–38.

Buchanan, James M., and David Lee. 1986. "Vote Buying in a Stylized Setting." *Public Choice* 49: 3–15.

Buchwalter, Andrew. 1992. "Hegel's Concept of Virtue." *Political Theory* 20: 548–83.

Burtt, Shelley. 1990. "The Good Citizen's Psyche: On the Psychology of Civic Virtue." *Polity* 23: 23–38.

Caplan, Bryan. 2001. "Rational Irrationality." *Kyklos* 54: 3–26.

———. 2007. *The Myth of the Rational Voter: Why Democracies Choose Bad Policies*. Princeton: Princeton University Press.

Chisholm, Roderick. 1963. "Contrary-to-Duty Imperatives and Deontic Logic." *Analysis* 24: 33–36.

Christandl, Fabian, and Detlef Fetchenhauer. 2009. "How Laypeople and Experts Misperceive the Effect of Economic Growth." *Journal of Economic Psychology* 30: 381–92.

Christiano, Thomas. 1996. *The Rule of the Many*. Boulder: Westview Press.

———. 2004. "The Authority of Democracy." *Journal of Political Philosophy* 12: 266–90.

———. 2006. "Democracy." In *Stanford Encyclopedia of Philosophy*, ed. Edward N. Zalta. http://plato.stanford.edu/entries/democracy/.

Christman, John. 2003. "Autonomy in Moral and Political Philosophy." In *Stanford Encyclopedia of Philosophy*, ed. Edward M. Zalta. http://plato.stanford .edu/entries/autonomy-moral/.

Clark, Andy, and David J. Chalmers. 1998. "The Extended Mind." *Analysis* 58: 10–23.

Cohen, G. A. 2009. *Why Not Socialism?* Princeton: Princeton University Press.

Cox, Michaelane. 2003. "When Trust Matters: Explaining Differences in Voter Turnout." *Journal of Common Market Studies* 41: 757–70.

Crittenden, Jack. 2007. "Civic Education." *Stanford Encyclopedia of Philosophy*. http://plato.stanford.edu/entries/civic-education/.

Dagger, Richard. 1997. *Civic Virtues: Rights, Citizenship, and Republican Liberalism*. New York: Oxford University Press.

Davis, William L., and Bog Figgins. 2009. "Do Economists Believe American Democracy Is Working?" *Econ Journal Watch* 6: 195–202.

Dovi, Suzanne. 2007. *The Good Representative*. Boston: Blackwell.

Downs, Anthony. 1956. *An Economic Theory of Democracy*. New York: Harper Collins.

Driver, Julia. 2006. "Autonomy and the Asymmetry Problem." *Philosophical Studies* 128: 619–44.

Eberle, Christopher. 2002. *Religious Conviction in Liberal Politics*. New York: Cambridge University Press.

Edlin, Aaron, Andrew Gelman, and Noah Kaplan. 2007. "Voting as a Rational Choice: Why and How People Vote to Improve the Well-Being of Others." *Rationality and Society* 19: 219–314.

Edlin, Aaron, and Pinar Karaca-Mandic. 2006. "The Accident Externality of Driving." *Journal of Political Economy* 114: 931–55.

Elster, Jon. 1997. "The Market and the Forum." In *Deliberative Democracy*, ed. James Bohman and William Rehg, 3–34. Cambridge, MA: MIT Press.

Epstein, Richard. 1985. "Why Restrain Alienation?" *Columbia Law Review* 85: 970–90.

Estlund, David. 1997. "Beyond Fairness and Deliberation: The Epistemic Dimension of Democratic Authority." In *Deliberative Democracy: Essays on Reason and Policies*, ed. James Bowman and William Rehg, 173–204. Cambridge, MA: MIT Press.

———. 2007. *Democratic Authority*. Princeton: Princeton University Press.

Evans, Jocelyn. 2004. *Voting and Voters*. Thousand Oaks: Sage.

Fabre, Cécile. 2006. *Whose Body Is It Anyway?* New York: Oxford University Press.

Feddersen, Timothy, Sean Gailmard, and Alvaro Sandroni. 2009. "A Bias toward Unselfishness in Large Elections: Theory and Experimental Evidence." *American Political Science Review* 103: 175–92.

Feinberg, Joel. 1970. "The Nature and Value of Rights." *Journal of Value Inquiry* 4: 243–60.

Fischer, A. J. 1999. "The Probability of Being Decisive." *Public Choice* 101: 263–67.

Frankfurt, Harry. 2005. *On Bullshit*. Princeton: Princeton University Press.

Franklin, Mark. 2004. *Voter Turnout and the Dynamics of Electoral Competition in Established Democracies since 1945*. New York: Cambridge University Press.

Friedman, David. 1989. *The Machinery of Freedom*. New York: Open Court.

Fullinwinder, Robert K. 1988. "Citizenship and Welfare." In *Democracy and the Welfare State*, ed. Amy Gutmann, 261–78. Princeton: Princeton University Press.

Funk, Carolyn. 2000. "The Dual Influence of Self-Interest and Societal Interest in Public Opinion." *Political Research Quarterly* 53: 37–62.

Funk, Carolyn, and Patricia Garcia-Monet. 1997. "The Relationship between Personal and National Concerns in Public Perceptions of the Economy." *Political Research Quarterly* 50: 317–42.

Galston, William. 2007. "Pluralism and Civic Virtue." *Social Theory and Practice* 33: 625–35.

Gaus, Gerald F. 1990. "The Commitment to the Common Good." In *On Political Obligation*, ed. Paul Harris, 24–64. New York: Routledge.

———. 1996. *Justificatory Liberalism*. New York: Oxford University Press.

———. 1997. "On the Difficult Virtue of Minding One's Own Business: Towards the Political Rehabilitation of Ebenezer Scrooge." *Philosopher* 5: 24–28.

———. 2003a. "Backwards into the Future: Neo-Republicanism as a Post-Socialist Critique of Market Society." *Social Philosophy and Policy* 20: 59–91.

———. 2003b. *Contemporary Theories of Liberalism*. Thousand Oaks: Sage.

———. 2008. *On Politics, Philosophy, and Economics*. Belmont: Wadsworth.

———. 2010. "The Place of Religious Belief in Public Reason Liberalism." In *Multiculturalism and Moral Conflict*, ed. Maria Dimova-Crookson and Peter Stirk, 19–37. New York: Routledge.

Geisz, Steven F. 2006. "An Indirect Argument for Strategic Voting." *Journal of Applied Philosophy* 23: 433–44.

Gelman, Andrew. 2008. *Red State, Blue State, Rich State, Poor State*. Princeton: Princeton University Press.

Gill, Michael B., and Robert M. Sade. 2002. "Paying for Kidneys: The Case against Prohibition." *Kennedy Institute of Ethics Journal* 12: 17–45.

Goldman, Alvin. 1999. "Why Citizens Should Vote: A Causal Responsibility Approach." *Social Philosophy and Policy* 16: 201–7.

Goodin, Robert E. 1988. *Reasons for Welfare*. Princeton: Princeton University Press.

Green, Donald, and Ian Shapiro. 1994. *Pathologies of Rational Choice Theory*. New Haven: Yale University Press.

Greenawalt, Kenneth. 1995. *Private Consciousnesses and Public Reasons*. New York: Oxford University Press.

Gutmann, Amy. 1987. *Democratic Education*. Princeton: Princeton University Press.

———. 1993. "Democracy." In *A Companion to Contemporary Political Philosophy*, ed. Robert Goodin and Philip Pettit, 411–21. Oxford: Blackwell.

Hansson, Sven Ove. 2003. "Ethical Criteria of Risk Acceptance." *Erkenntnis* 59: 291–309.

———. 2007. "Risk." In *Stanford Encyclopedia of Philosophy*, ed. Edward Zalta. http://plato.stanford.edu/entries/risk/.

Hardin, Garrett. 1968. "The Tragedy of the Commons." *Science* 162: 1243–48.

Hardin, Russell. 2004. "Representing Ignorance." *Social Philosophy and Policy* 21: 76–99.

———. 2009. *How Do You Know? The Economics of Ordinary Knowledge*. Princeton: Princeton University Press.

Hasen, Richard L. 2000. "Vote Buying." *California Law Review* 88: 1323–71.

Healy, Andrew. 2007. "Are Voters Irrational? The Uneducated and Partisan Ones Are." Unpublished manuscript, Loyola Marymount University.

Healy, Andrew, and Neil Malhotra. 2010. "Random Events, Economic Losses, and Retrospective Voting: Implications for Democratic Competence." Unpublished manuscript, Loyola Marymount University.

Healy, Kieran. 2006. *Last Best Gifts: Altruism and the Market for Human Blood and Organs*. Chicago: University of Chicago Press.

Hill, Thomas E., Jr. 1983. "Ideals of Human Excellence and Preserving Natural Environments." *Environmental Ethics* 5: 211–24.

Holbrook, Thomas, and James Garand. 1996. "Homo Economicus? Economic Information and Economic Voting." *Political Research Quarterly* 49: 351–75.

Honohan, Iseult. 2002. *Civic Republicanism*. New York: Routledge.

Hooker, Brad. 2000. *Ideal Code, Real World*. New York: Oxford University Press.

Hursthouse, Rosalind. 1998. *On Virtue Ethics*. New York: Oxford University Press.

Kearl, J. R., Clayne Pope, Gordon Whiting, and Larry Wimmer. 1979. "A Confusion of Economists." *American Economic Review* 69: 28–37.

Klein, Daniel B., and Steward Dompe. 2007. "Reasons for Supporting the Minimum Wage: Asking Signatories of the 'Raising the Minimum Wage' Statement." *Econ Journal Watch* 4: 125–67.

Kochin, Michael S., and Levis A. Kochin. 1998. "When Is Buying Votes Wrong?" *Public Choice* 9: 645–62.

Kuhn, Steven. 2010. Review of Richard Tuck, *Free Riding*. *Philosophical Review* 1: 112–14.

Landsburg, Steven E. 2004. "Don't Vote. It Makes More Sense to Play the Lottery." *Slate*. http://www.slate.com/id/2107240/.

Lau, Richard R., and David P. Redlawsk. 2006. *How Voters Decide: Information Processing during Election Campaigns*. New York: Cambridge University Press.

Less, David, Enrico Moretti, and Matthew Butler. 2004. "Do Voters Affect or Elect Policies? Evidence from the U.S. House." *Quarterly Journal of Economics* 119: 807–59.

Levi, Margaret, and Laura Stocker. 2000. "Political Trust and Trustworthiness." *Annual Review of Political Science* 3: 475–507.

Levitt, Steven D., and Stephen J. Dubner. 2009. *SuperFreakonomics*. New York: William Morrow.

Lewis, David. 1983. *Philosophical Papers II*. New York: Oxford University Press.

Lijphart, Arend. 1999. *Patterns of Democracy*. New Haven: Yale University Press.

Lomasky, Loren, and Geoffrey Brennan. 2000. "Is There a Duty to Vote?" *Social Philosophy and Policy* 17: 62–86.

Mackie, Gerry. 2008. "Why It's Rational to Vote." Unpublished manuscript, University of California, San Diego.

Madison, James, Alexander Hamilton, and John Jay. 1961. *The Federalist Papers*. Ed. Clinton Rossiter. New York: New American Library, 1961.

Manin, Bernard. 1997. *The Principles of Representative Government*. New York: Cambridge University Press.

Manning, Rita C. 1984. "Air Pollution: Group and Individual Obligations." *Environmental Ethics* 6: 211–25.

Martin, Mark, and Pamela J. Podger. 2004. "Prison Guards' Clout Difficult to Challenge." *San Francisco Chronicle*, February 2. http://www.sfgate.com/cgi-bin/article.cgi?file=/c/a/2004/02/02/MNGBC4MU911.DTL.

Melden, A. I. 1959. *Rights and Right Conduct*. New York: Oxford University Press.

Miller, Dale. 1999. "The Norm of Self-Interest." *American Psychologist* 54: 1053–60.

Mueller, Dennis C. 2003. *Public Choice III*. New York: Cambridge University Press.

Mussolini, Benito, and Giovanni Gentile. 1963. "The Doctrine of Fascism." In *Social and Political Philosophy*, ed. John Somerville and Ronald E. Santoni, 424–40. New York: Anchor Books.

Mutz, Diana. 1993. "Direct and Indirect Routes to Politicizing Personal Experience: Does Knowledge Make a Difference?" *Public Opinion Quarterly* 57: 483–502.

———. 2006. *Hearing the Other Side: Deliberative versus Participatory Democracy*. New York: Cambridge University Press.

Mutz, Diana, and Jeffrey Mondak. 1997. "Dimensions of Sociotropic Behavior: Group-Based Judgments of Fairness and Well-Being." *American Journal of Political Science* 41: 284–308.

Neeman, Zvika, and Gerhard O. Orosel. 2006. "On the Efficiency of Vote Buying When Voters Have Common Interests." *International Review of Law and Economics* 26: 536–56.

Nozick, Robert. 1974. *Anarchy, State, and Utopia*. New York: Basic Books.

Oldfield, Adrian. 1990. "Citizenship: An Unnatural Practice." *Political Quarterly* 61: 177–87.

Olson, Mancur. 1965. *The Logic of Collective Action*. Cambridge, MA: Harvard University Press.

Page, Scott. 2007. *The Difference*. Princeton: Princeton University Press.

———. 2008. "Microfoundations of Collective Wisdom." Paper presented at the conference on "Collective Wisdom: Principles and Mechanisms," College of France, Paris, May 22. http://download.sfrs.fr/media-1/sfrs/Mpg4/CDF/CdF1_7.mp4.

Page, Scott, and P. J. Lamberson. 2009. "Increasing Returns, Lock-Ins, and Early Mover Advantage." Unpublished manuscript, University of Michigan, Ann Arbor.

Paten, Alan. 1996. "The Republican Critique of Liberalism." *British Journal of Political Science* 26: 25–44.

Patterson, Orlando. 1999. *Rituals of Blood: Consequences of Slavery in Two American Centuries*. New York: Harper Collins.

Pauer-Studer, Herlinde. 2001. "Liberalism, Perfectionism, and Civic Virtue." *Philosophical Explorations* 4: 174–92.

Pettit, Philip. 1997. *Republicanism*. New York: Oxford University Press.

Pincione, Guido, and Fernando R. Tesón. 2006. *Rational Choice and Democratic Deliberation*. New York: Cambridge University Press.

Pocock, J. G. A. 2003. *The Machiavellian Moment*. Princeton: Princeton University Press.

Posner, Richard. 2003. *Law, Pragmatism, and Democracy*. Cambridge, MA: Harvard University Press.

Radin, Margaret Jane. 1987. "Market-Inalienability." *Harvard Law Review* 100: 1849–1937.

———. 1996. *Contested Commodities*. Cambridge, MA: Harvard University Press.

Radzik, Linda, and David Schmidtz. 1997. "Book Review: Contested Commodities." *Law and Philosophy* 16: 603–16.

Raeder, Linda C. 1998. "Liberalism and the Common Good: A Hayekian Perspective on Communitarianism." *Independent Review* 2: 519–35.

Rawls, John. 1971. *A Theory of Justice*. Cambridge, MA: Harvard University Press.

———. 1999. *The Law of Peoples*. Cambridge, MA: Harvard University Press.

Read, Leonard E. 1958. "I, Pencil." *The Freeman* 8: 7–18.

Riker, William H., and Peter Ordeshook. 1968. "A Theory of the Calculus of Voting." *American Political Science Review* 62: 25–42.

Routley, Richard. 1973. "Is There a Need for a New, an Environmental Ethic?" In *Proceedings of the XVth World Congress of Philosophy*, 1:205–10. New York: Sophia Press.

Saunders, Ben. 2009. "Making Voting Pay." *Politics* 29: 130–36.

Schmidtz, David. 1995. *Rational Choice and Moral Agency*. Princeton: Princeton University Press.

———. 2006. *Elements of Justice*. New York: Cambridge University Press.

Schmidtz, David, and Jason Brennan. 2010. *A Brief History of Liberty*. Boston: Blackwell.

Schmidtz, David, and Elizabeth Willott. 2002. *Environmental Ethics: What Really Matters, What Really Works*. New York: Oxford University Press.

Schumpeter, Joseph. 1950. *Capitalism, Socialism, and Democracy*. New York: Oxford University Press.

———. 1954. *History of Economic Analysis*. New York: Oxford University Press.

Sheehy, Paul. 2002. "A Duty Not to Vote." *Ratio*, n.s., 15: 46–57.

Singer, Peter. 1974. "All Animals Are Equal." In *Environmental Ethics: What Really Matters, What Really Works*, ed. David Schmidtz and Elizabeth Willott, 17–26. New York: Oxford University Press.

Smith, Adam. 1776. *An Inquiry into the Nature and Causes of the Wealth of Nations*. Vol. 1. Indianapolis: Liberty Fund.

Smith, George. 1982a. "The Ethics of Voting, Part I." *Voluntaryist* 1.1: 1–5.

———. 1982b. "The Ethics of Voting, Part II." *Voluntaryist* 1.2: 3–6.

———. 1983. "The Ethics of Voting, Part III." *Voluntaryist* 1.4: 3–7.

Sokal, Alan, and Jean Bricmont. 1999. *Fashionable Nonsense*. New York: Picador Books.

Somin, Ilya. 2004. "When Ignorance Isn't Bliss: How Political Ignorance Threatens Democracy." *Cato Policy Analysis*, no. 525. September 22.

———. 2006. "Knowledge about Ignorance: New Directions in the Study of Political Information." *Critical Review* 18: 255–78.

Sunstein, Cass. 1997. *Free Markets and Social Justice*. New York: Oxford University Press.

Surowiecki, James. 2005. *The Wisdom of Crowds*. New York: Anchor Books.

Taylor, James Stacy. 2005. *Stakes and Kidneys: Why Markets in Human Body Parts Are Morally Imperative*. Surrey: Ashgate.

Tetlock, Philip. 2000. "Coping with Trade-Offs: Psychological Constraints and Political Implications." In *Elements of Reason: Cognition, Choice, and the*

Bounds of Rationality, ed. Arthur Lupia, Matthew D. McCubbins, and Samuel L. Popkin, 239–63. New York: Cambridge University Press.

———. 2007. "Diversity Paradoxes." *Science* 316: 984.

Timmons, Mark. 2002. *Moral Theory*. Lanham: Rowman and Littlefield.

Titmuss, Richard. 1997. *The Gift Relationship*. New York: New Press.

Tomasi, John. Forthcoming. *Market Democracy: Economic Freedom and Social Justice*. Princeton: Princeton University Press.

Tuck, Richard. 2008. *Free Riding*. Cambridge, MA: Harvard University Press.

Van Parijs, Philippe. 1993. "The Disenfranchisement of the Elderly, and Other Attempts to Secure Intergenerational Justice." *Philosophy and Public Affairs* 27: 292–333.

Waldron, Jeremy. 1981. "A Right to Do Wrong." *Ethics* 92: 21–39.

———. 2003. "Participation: The Right of Rights." *Proceedings of the Aristotelian Society* 98: 307–37.

Walzer, Michael. 1984. *Spheres of Justice*. New York: Basic Books.

———. 1989. "Citizenship." In *Political Innovation and Conceptual Change*, ed. Terrence Ball, James Farr, and Russell L. Hanson, 211–19. New York: Cambridge University Press.

Weiss, Jeffrey H. 1988. "Is Vote Selling Desirable?" *Public Choice* 59: 177–94.

Wellman, Christopher Heath, and A. John Simmons. 2006. *Is There a Duty to Obey the Law? For and Against*. New York: Cambridge University Press.

Westen, Drew. 2008. *The Political Brain: How We Make Up Our Minds without Using Our Heads*. New York: Perseus Books.

Westen, Drew, Pavel S. Blagov, Keith Harenski, Clint Kilts, and Stephan Hamann. 2007. "The Neural Basis of Motivated Reasoning: An fMRI Study of Emotional Constraints on Political Judgment during the U.S. Presidential Election of 2004." *Journal of Cognitive Neuroscience* 18: 1947–58.

White, Stuart. 2003. *The Civic Minimum*. New York: Cambridge University Press.

Index